INSIGHT INTO ADLERIAN ART THERAPY

INSIGHT INTO ADLERIAN ART THERAPY

Through the Lens of Individual Psychology

Judy Sutherland PhD
Adler University, Publisher
17 North Dearborn
Chicago, Illinois 60602

Dedication

This book is dedicated in loving memory
to my husband
Edmond (Ted) R. Sutherland, Jr.,
to Sadie "Tee" Dreikurs,
my friend and Adlerian art therapy mentor
and to Evadne McNeil,
my art therapy instructor.

To Joanna
wishing you
success on your
journey to becoming
an art therapist
Judy Sutherland
6/1/16

Contents

Foreword · ix
Preface· xi
Acknowledgments· ·xvii

Chapter 1   The Creation of an Adlerian Art Therapy Program · · · · · · ·1
Chapter 2   Portraits in Reflection ·15
Chapter 3   The Use of Art in Group Counseling · · · · · · · · · · · · · · · ·20
Chapter 4   Historical, Theoretical, and Postmodern
             Perspectives of Art Therapy ·35
Chapter 5   Art in Culture and Time: Socio-Cultural
             and Systemic Perspectives ·53
Chapter 6   Ethical Considerations for the Art Therapist· · · · · · · · · · ·72
Chapter 7   Child and Adolescent Adlerian Art Therapy · · · · · · · · · · ·84
Chapter 8   An Adlerian Approach to Couple and Family Art
             Therapy· ·103
Chapter 9   Art Therapy with Older Adults · · · · · · · · · · · · · · · · · ·115
Chapter 10   Art Therapy Studio: Professional Development· · · · · · ·121
Chapter 11   Art Therapy and Psychodynamics Surrounding Life
             Challenges· ·132
Chapter 12   Loss/Grieving: Art Therapy and Psychodrama · · · · · · · ·149
Chapter 13   Addictive Behavior and the Use of Art in Recovery · · · ·159
Chapter 14   Group Dream Work Using Art and Psychodrama · · · · · ·170
Chapter 15   Group Art Therapy Supervision · · · · · · · · · · · · · · · · ·180

Chapter 16   Thoughts about Research ·184
Chapter 17   Conclusion – No Easy Answers · · · · · · · · · · · · · · · · · · ·200

              Glossary· ·203
              References · 217
              Index ·239

Foreword

I am writing this Foreword mainly from the perspective of being a student in the M.A. in Counseling Psychology: Art Therapy program, directed by Judy Sutherland. However, now that I am an art therapy educator myself, I am doubly grateful for all I have learned from her teaching and ongoing mentorship. Judy writes in her introductory remarks about how she and other students felt when Sadie "Tee" Dreikurs book, Cows Can Be Purple, was published. She says, "I remember how thrilled we all were that now we could have a book which describes Tee's method." Speaking for myself and all Judy's students over the years, we are thrilled to now have a book that describes Judy's method.

This book also documents Tee Dreikurs' important contribution to the field of art therapy. Unfortunately, she is unknown to most art therapists and her perspective is absent from the dominant discourse and historical narrative of our profession. Yet, the therapeutic art approach she first developed while working with delinquent youth at Jane Addams' Hull House in the mid-1930s, likely constitutes the beginnings of group art therapy. Tee began working with Rudolf Dreikurs in 1938. In 1962, Tee was invited to work as an art therapist with psychiatric patients at St. Joseph's Hospital in Chicago. Over the following decade, she created a truly Adlerian approach to art therapy by combining her group art process with her extensive knowledge of Adlerian psychology. A few years later, art therapy was incorporated into the curriculum of what was then called the Alfred Adler Institute as an elective, titled "The Use of Art in Group Counseling."

Nearly all contemporary art therapists work with groups at some point in their career. This book will give them a helpful philosophy and successful techniques to guide their practice. It will also appeal to anyone interested in democratic, practical, and socially-embedded methods for working with many populations of people using psychology and the creative process.

Too few people know the importance that Alfred Adler placed on creativity and his high regard for artists. Adler stated, "If we apply the social measure to artists and poets, we note that they serve a social function more than anyone else. It is they who have taught us how to see, how to think, and how to feel. We owe to them the greatest good of mankind." (Adler, p. 153). Judy incorporated Adler's philosophy on creativity and his timeless construct of social interest into every class. She modeled for us how to encourage ourselves as well as the people with whom we work through the art process. Upon reflection, I recognize that the art experientials we did in class were intended to teach us what we needed to know about ourselves in order to effectively work with our clients. To help them, and ourselves, find place of belonging with others in a socially useful way and face life's challenges with courage and creativity rather than retreat into thoughts and behavior that disconnect us from others.

When reading this book I feel as if Judy is exploring with fresh eyes a lifetime of learning about Adlerian psychology, philosophy, art, and teaching with the simultaneous understanding that she has only scratched the surface. Her choice to write using the present tense and first person is similar to how she asked us to speak in class, gently guiding us to say "I" and take responsibility for our words. Her voice is authentic, experienced, welcoming, and humble. Just as I first experienced it in her classroom many years ago. I have been privileged to watch this book come to life from idea to this final form. To hold it in my hands is a great joy.

— Heather Leigh, ATR-BC, LCPC

Preface

Sadie "Tee" Dreikurs, Judy Sutherland

This non-fiction book describes the theoretical constructs and practical techniques of Individual Psychology as it coalesces with the creative process of group art therapy. It indirectly suggests ways to build a curriculum for an Adlerian Art Therapy program that can be combined with Counseling Psychology for a Master's degree.

Sadie "Tee" Dreikurs was my first instructor in art therapy, and it was in her course, "The Use of Art in Group Counseling," that I was able to study her unique approach. Later I was her assistant and friend. I cannot improve upon Tee's method, but can only offer my contribution and some expansion in terms of my observations and understanding of her theoretical approach to art therapy and how it has worked for me in my life, in the classroom and in my practice. After graduating from the Alfred Adler Institute in 1985, I studied in depth the theories of other art therapists in order to become a board-certified art therapist (ATR-BC). I subsequently earned a PhD in Art Therapy while developing the M.A. in Counseling Psychology: Art Therapy program for what is now the Adler University.

This is a collection of personal curricular essays that are also invitations to use your own art as a mirror to your life and a way to create community with others. This interdisciplinary approach to art therapy integrates thoughts on philosophy, education, art, ethics, socio-cultural issues, dreams, addiction, research, professional development, and supervision, all of which informed the Art Therapy part of the M.A. degree. My wish is that those who read this book will find a common ground with their own thoughts, beliefs and values and will welcome this kind of synergy.

THOUGHTS LEADING TO AN UNDERSTANDING OF INDIVIDUAL PSYCHOLOGY

Thanks to Darwin's (1859) breakthrough regarding evolution by natural selection, and current neurological evidence, today we know that our minds are adaptive, not rational, and have evolved to help us survive in our environment. On one hand, I agree with Jean-Paul Sartre that human life has no ultimate purpose, that survival is not a moral problem. And I agree with Darwin that species disappear when their habitat dwindles and they are unable to adapt to a new one (Weiner, 1994). It is the very nature of evolution on Earth, although we have yet to prove it (ibid, p 81). Our fate will likely be no different. On the other hand, we are endowed with an adaptive mind, only 1%, maybe 2%, different than the DNA of all other life forms. We do try to create order out of chaos, to make sense of life and our place in it. We are biological creatures and evolution for humans involves the activity of the brain and consciousness and the ability to talk with one another in ways that lead to new ideas. The evolution of consciousness is the key to our future and our health (Ornstein, 1991).

With the above references in mind, I offer you thoughts about Individual Psychology. Because there is no such thing as universal peace, we can at least work toward helping each other in the spirit of social interest to prevent more trouble before it arises (Dreikurs, R., 1967). Alfred Adler believed that social problems evolve out of feelings of inferiority which lead to discouragement and a lack of compassion for others. To encourage cooperation with the social order of life we need to focus less on feelings of inferiority and more on social equality and continue to learn how to actively contribute and work toward the benefit of all. We create our own purpose for living based on how we understand our place in the world.

Adler's humanistic and holistic theory offers an optimistic and positive method to meet what he considered the three main tasks of living: getting along at work, getting along with friends, and getting along in an intimate relationship. Implicit in these three tasks is what Rudolf Dreikurs and Harold Mosak called the "self task; the ability to get along with oneself" (Dreikurs & Mosak, 1967, pp. 51-56). This task calls for an "evolution of consciousness" or self-awareness (Ornstein, 1991). It is an ongoing task that takes place over our lifetime and changes as we experience life situations and learn to adapt to our surroundings. It includes understanding the meaning we give to life, our attitude toward self and others, and the purpose of our goals.

Adler's theory provides a foundation for social equality and learning that challenges us to take responsibility for ourselves as we strive toward perfection, wholeness and commonly useful goals. This theoretical foundation used in our relationships with others is what can help us to have "the courage to be imperfect" and the feeling of belonging (security) as we go into life caring for ourselves, for each other, and for the earth (Dreikurs, R., 1957).

USING ART THERAPY TO ENCOURAGE SELF-AWARENESS

My art reflects the intuitive creative form of the myth I tell myself about my life (my private logic) and over time I am provided with no end of surprises in the way I come to understand myself and can choose to make changes in my relationship to others. Becoming self-aware is a life-long process and continues to evolve as I learn to take others on their personal journey, knowing that I can walk with them only as far as I have been willing to go myself.

When I look back on my life, with its successes and failures (especially the failures), I find that very little of it has been within my control, and took place in a world that is mostly indifferent to my existence. Still I know that in my attitude and actions I can find happiness, and this, in response to the absurdity of fate, to the chaos of life, is the search for self-understanding and the freedom to be myself.

SOCIAL ETHICS

We all can be successful by working together, to adapt in ways that will help us survive in our environment, not by some working for the benefit of others. Without this synergy of collective consciousness there will be no collective wisdom and we put ourselves at risk of extinction. Provided that some natural disaster doesn't claim us all first, life will go on – we just may not be a part of it. However, I believe in the words of William Faulkner, who said upon receiving the Nobel Prize for literature in 1950, that we will prevail, because each of us "has a spirit capable of compassion and sacrifice and endurance." Alfred Adler called this "Gemeinschaftsgefühl": giving to and receiving from others in the spirit of social equality. It is the single most important task in life "to merge self-interest with the interest of humankind" (from a letter written by Kurt Adler, Alfred Adler's son, to his daughter Margot, in 1965, read aloud at the 2011 Adler graduation ceremonies.)

This is what we learn how to do based on the art experiences we have in the group art coursework as first designed by Tee Dreikurs in "The Use of Art in Group Counseling." It is her theory, based on her understanding of Adlerian theory as she learned it from Rudolf Dreikurs, I use in creating the M.A. in Counseling: Art Therapy.

Acknowledgments

A deeply heartfelt thank you goes to Kerry Cochrane who, from the beginning, enthusiastically supported the writing and completion of this book and has been my faithful, patient and gentle editor; to those who offered encouragement: Eva Dreikurs Ferguson, Jon Carlson, and Heather Leigh; to my professors who believe in and live the philosophy integrated into Adlerian theory, especially Harold Mosak, Bernard Shulman, and Leo Lobl; to Randall Thompson and Mark Stone, the leaders at what was then the Adler School of Professional Psychology, who invited me to create the art therapy program; to many of those who taught art therapy with me: Dora Castro Ahillen, Nancy Chickerneo, Renee Dobkin Dushman, Mary Farrell, Barbara Fish, Carmen Ulberg Haley, Wendy Lauter, Russell Leander, Linnet Miller, Erin Mooney, Kathryn Patterson McCarthy, Mary Pulscher, Suellen Semekoski, Eric Spruth, Terri Sweig, Suzanne Peroutka Tretina; and to friends: Mary Anne Powers, who put me in touch with art therapy training; to Carol McConnell and Helen Dunbeck Zimmermann, who knew, even before I knew, exactly what information I needed most and sent it to me; to Gwenn Waldman and Carolyn Collins who co-founded Art Therapy Connection with me; to my family, who gave me the reason for going back to school and the space and time to develop the art therapy program, especially to my sister, Sally Hall, who holds the light for me; to my students who shared their lives with me and gave me valuable tips for improving the art therapy course work; and to my clients, who courageously faced times of discouragement and were willing to "trust the process" of Adlerian art therapy and life. There are so many others... thank you.

1

The Creation of an Adlerian
Art Therapy Program

This book is written from an Adlerian group art therapy perspective as I understand it. This means that it is based on the theoretical constructs found in Individual Psychology, a system conceptualized by Alfred Adler more than one hundred years ago, and art therapy, a therapeutic discipline that has grown out of the benefit of self-expression and self-awareness through involvement in the creative process founded over 50 years ago. Adlerian theory is based on a growth model that recognizes that we, as individuals, are always actively, but not always consciously, creating our own reality based on how we perceive our interactions with others. Group art therapy as designed by Tee Dreikurs encourages spontaneity, creativity, and reflection in response to life situations and can help to make us more conscious of those interactions.

OVERVIEW OF INDIVIDUAL PSYCHOLOGY

Alfred Adler (1870 – 1937) was a Viennese physician and clinician who stressed the need to understand individuals within their social field, believing that we are each unique human beings, endowed with free will and the ability to make conscious decisions with a private sense of reasoning that he called "private logic" (Ellenberger, 1970). As children we unconsciously create our own social goals for our lives based on how we subjectively understand our early social experiences and our place in the world. We act within this framework throughout our lives. It is our self-chosen lifestyle pattern.

All behavior has a social purpose and can be thought of as on a continuum from negative to positive, useless to useful. As we grow older and have more experience we can come to a more conscious awareness of our own private logic and begin to take responsibility for the purpose for our behavior.

Adler believed that social problems evolve out of feelings of inferiority which lead to a lack of a feeling of belonging and compassion for others. Adler preferred to call this "discouragement" rather than personal pathology. When we are discouraged, we tend to unconsciously create fictional ways to relieve, rather than overcome, our feelings of inferiority.

To encourage cooperation with what Adler called the "iron-clad logic of social living," we need to focus less on feelings of inferiority and more on social equality and continue to learn how to actively contribute and work toward the benefit of all. His theory provides a foundation for social equality and learning that challenges us to take responsibility for ourselves as we strive toward perfection, wholeness and commonly useful goals. Each of us has the innate potential to strive to contribute to the welfare of our communities. Adler called this "*Gemeinschaftsgefühl*," social interest or social feeling, and it is an important component of human development, maybe the most important one. It is vital for bringing peace and health to our lives and for living in a democracy at its best.

In Tee Dreikurs' course, "The Use of Art in Group Counseling" we learn that each of us has a spirit capable of contributing to the work we are doing in class – social interest – and that by doing so we create a place where we feel a sense of belonging and social equality.

SADIE "TEE" DREIKURS, MY MENTOR AND FRIEND

Jacob Ellis and his wife emigrated from Lithuania to Chicago in the 1880's. After his first wife died, Jacob married Lena, who bore him three children, the middle one being Sadie born in 1900. Sadie Ellis had a friend named Blanche Maggioli and when they were around 11 years old they started art lessons at Hull House and met Jane Addams. Addams found a way to grant the two friends scholarships to the School of the Art Institute – Chicago. For financial reasons, Sadie dropped out after about a year but went back to Hull House to take weekend painting and drawing classes. It was here that Sadie began to study with Leon Garland, who volunteered his services as an instructor of batik at Hull House and later became a resident. Both studied painting together and often went out into the surrounding neighborhood to paint the people and the buildings. In 1927, Leon and Sadie were married at Hull House, where they lived earning their room and board and saving to study modernist painting in Europe. In Paris, one instructor in particular, Andre L'Hote, impressed Sadie with his style of giving instructions. L'Hote encouraged students to learn and understand the history of art and his style, but then "to paint as they liked." One art directive was to "make a spontaneous sketch from your immediate emotional response to the subject." It was this approach that Sadie later used as a model for art therapy sessions.

The Garlands next traveled to Berlin, where Leon studied commercial art, but here both faced discrimination and hostility due to differences in ethnicity, heritage, and religion and they soon came back to Paris. They continued to paint under the guidance of L'Hote, each finding success, until the 1929 stock market crash. They returned to Chicago and the studio apartment that Jane Addams had promised them upon their return. Both continued painting, Leon mostly in oils and Sadie, in watercolors. Soon Sadie Garland turned more to teaching art to children at Hull House and eventually began counseling clients under the guidance of Jane Addams. Sadie earned a social work position with United Charities in Chicago. Back at Hull House, the police placed some delinquent boys in her art class. Sadie quickly realized that the way to get the boys involved was to ask the leaders to take charge and they, in turn, were able to persuade the rest of the boys to work together in teams. These group art projects were later carried over into her work in art therapy with psychiatric patients at St. Joseph's Hospital.

As Jane Addams's health began to fail, Sadie Garland took over much of the administrative work. At the same time, Leon's health was worsening as a result of permanent damage to his heart which he suffered when they were still in Europe. Sadie put aside her art, not wanting to be in competition with Leon and also not finding the time or energy due to her caretaking role of both people. Art then became, for her, a way to relax on a Sunday afternoon. There was an exhibit of the work they both had done in Europe, but sales were few due to the hard financial times. Leon had a massive heart attack in 1934. For the next seven years he was able to work a few hours each day staying close to their home in Hull House. He was interested in portraying the Depression's impact on the unemployed. Jane Addams died in 1935 and both Sadie and Leon Garland served on the Hull House Board until a new head resident was elected. Hull House continued to be known for its settlement work and world-wide efforts for peace. Sadie "was among a powerful group of women who championed reform measures for social welfare, including strong labor and compulsory education laws" (Dreikurs S., 1986, p. xii).

The Garlands did not have children of their own, but there were many children in their lives. Sadie's older sister had a daughter who had trouble pronouncing "sister" and the word came out as "tee taw." From that time on family and many others knew Sadie as "Tee." The Garlands became good friends with Rudolf Dreikurs after he moved to Chicago with his family from Austria in 1938. Dreikurs was a close associate of Alfred Adler and took the theoretical concepts of Individual Psychology with him to America. Tee began to study with Rudolf since she found the Adlerian theory useful in her work with children and clients. Leon continued his painting, primarily of men at work and people in the surrounding environment, but then he had a fatal heart attack in 1941 in the Hull House apartment. His art was later displayed at the Art Institute of Chicago and was the first one-person exhibit ever held there. Tee also exhibited her work there between the years of 1928 and 1941.

Two years after Leon died, Tee married Rudolf Dreikurs and they continued to collaborate: he would talk or lecture, she would write down his words and later type them into book form. Tee never returned to her art even though Dreikurs encouraged her to do so, but instead she began her career as an art therapist.

I owe much of the above information to David Sokol's essay in Garland, L, Garland, S., and Koehnline (2013), and Dreikurs, S., (1986).

In 1952, Rudolf Dreikurs, with the help of Dr. Bernard Shulman and Dr. Harold Mosak, founded the Alfred Adler Institute in Chicago. Tee was their companion and hostess for many of their planning days together. Later Dr. Shulman, chair of the psychiatric department at St. Joseph's Hospital in Chicago, knew and understood Tee's talent using art based on Adlerian theory in group work. In 1962, he invited Tee to come and do group art therapy with the patients there. When Rudolf Dreikurs died in 1972 at age 75, Tee was already working with patients. Soon after that, Tee was asked if she would be willing to teach her group art therapy approach to students at the Adler Institute.

Over the course of several years, two Adlerian therapists, Nancy Catlin and James W. Croake, interviewed, taped and edited Tee's responses to their questions about her life, art, art therapy, and group work. In 1986 Tee published her book, *Cows can be purple,* now in its 5th printing (2009). The book begins with an autobiographical chapter and moves on to describing the methods and art experientials that Tee developed based on the tenets of Individual Psychology, using quotes to denote Rudolf Dreikurs' interpretation of Adler's theory. The book conveys Tee's creative approach to art therapy based on her life experiences and her understanding of Adlerian psychology. I remember how thrilled we all were that now we could have a book which describes Tee's method. Tee suggests three prerequisites for becoming an art therapist, "spontaneity, creativity, and the courage to be imperfect."

The art experientials that Tee designed for her course have been taught all over the world, and continue today to be taught by those she trained. The wisdom in Tee's method comes from being an artist, teaching art and using art with children and also with patients in psychiatric treatment. Watching Tee lead a group of patients at St. Joseph's Hospital in Chicago provided another chance to see Adlerian art therapy in action. Tee writes in her book that art done in a group has the "goal of mental health based on social interest" (Dreikurs, S., 1986).

Adler was the first clinician to propose and recognize the value of work that can be done in groups. "In 1928, Rudolf Dreikurs introduced group psychotherapy into his private practice, becoming probably the first psychiatrist ever to do so" (Terner & Pew, 1978, p, 78). Rudolf and Tee Dreikurs continued this democratic approach in the classroom and in their work with clients.

BECOMING AN ART THERAPIST

At least eighteen hours of formal art training is required in order to be accepted into a Master's-level art therapy program. Knowledge of the art materials and how to use them is imperative. A student new to the art therapy program needs to integrate creating art, personal and professional development, and the theories of Individual Psychology. This is a challenging task both cognitively and emotionally. The Art Directives put the focus on the student, making it difficult to resist self-awareness. Because the process demands openness and self-confrontation, the student's sense of privacy and control is threatened (Robbins, 1994, p. 19). The art therapy instructor needs to respect the individual student's sense of timing in terms of comfort level in revealing lifestyle goals and beliefs, just as a therapist would. Students need to learn how they each negotiate life so that they will better understand the experience of their clients and learn not to so quickly label dysfunctional or inappropriate behavior as a disorder, but rather as signs of deep discouragement.

We all can experience discouragement at those times when we are in a place where we feel inadequate to handle life situations and we each find different ways to compensate for our feelings of inferiority. Adler called this "moving from a minus to a plus." Inferiority feelings are normal throughout life, beginning when we are children and experience being small and dependent on others to care for us. At that time inferiority feelings usually serve as an incentive for growing and developing ways to find our place in the social world. As adults we can experience a feeling of inferiority or inadequacy sometimes as a result of having adopted unrealistically high compensatory goals, such as one of perfection or being the best in some field. Compensation is normal, from birth until death, as we grow and strive for recognition, but can take a negative turn toward striving for superiority and power over others. Overcompensation might reflect a useful direction toward exceptional achievement beyond the normal range or under-compensation when one gives up and expects others to care for them. Adler coined the term "inferiority complex" to describe the extreme expectation of failure in the tasks of life.

"Moving from a minus to a plus" involves understanding our thinking, feeling, and the emotion we unconsciously create when we experience a provocative social interaction. "We often feel driven by our emotions in response, when actually we create them" (Terner & Pew, 1978, p 249). Anger, sadness, or depression are useless ways to compensate for our immediate feelings of inferiority and keep us on the minus side. Becoming more aware of our thoughts, feelings, and goals, however, helps us find more useful ways to bring ourselves back into well-being.

In our lives we find that it is almost impossible to attain neutrality or to escape bias. The words we speak and the language we use shape our thoughts, feelings, attitudes, and behavior. Memory, too, in the stories we tell, often has a way of warping the way we remember things as we struggle to give coherent meaning to our lives. The truth will be in the art rather than in the words. Words can distort the truth, even hide it and become self-serving. However, when I look at my art and talk about it in the group setting, the truth about my attitude, thoughts, and behavior becomes visual. I can ignore it, I can misunderstand it, I can keep it to myself, but I cannot falsify it, and that is what makes the group art therapy process useful.

The student learns that art-making is a nonverbal form of communication in which both the process and the product are important. Both express one's subjective experience in the "here and now" moment.

The art reflects and gives form to and is privately symbolic of immediate thoughts and feelings.

MY IN-CLASS EXPERIENCE

There are two main ways to respond to stress, no matter what the source, although they are understood on a continuum: coping in a useful or a mature way (positive) or defending ourselves in a regressive style (negative). Learning and accepting others in the spirit of "social interest" helped me move toward greater self-acceptance. I began to trust the healing dimension of the creative process; to take life on life's terms; to learn that opportunity springs from obstacles; that disappointment can lead to awakening; that it's okay, even necessary, to let go, change directions, to have "the courage to be imperfect" (Dreikurs, R., 1957). The art process and product make it possible to see, to experience, and to remember these life lessons.

To summarize Tee's words taken from her book (Dreikurs, S., 1986): The central goal of Adlerian group art therapy is to promote social interest and a feeling of belonging, through self-understanding and encouragement; to learn to come together as a group and to develop cooperation without sacrificing individual uniqueness; and to have concern and take action for the welfare of others. To me, this last statement means to first recognize injustice and then to work toward giving others the chance to gain power over their own lives without either taking responsibility for the choices they make or doing the work for them.

MY TEACHING PHILOSOPHY

I design the art therapy curriculum to involve students in their own process so that what they are learning will be personally relevant to them and to the work they will be doing as therapists. I find that teaching and learning are inseparable: that teaching, like being a therapist, is an art form and that we learn together. I also know from being a student that it is not so much what I am teaching, but it is who I am as a person that plays a role in my relationship with them. Students begin to understand that each of them has a piece of the Truth, that they are responsible for their own learning, that they learn from contributing to the group process, that learning needs to happen in a safe environment, and that part of that safe environment includes feeling connected to each other. I cannot tell students what to do, nor can I interpret their art for them. I do know that I have to hold them to a level of professionalism expected in an advanced degree program, to model, and encourage them to develop professional conduct specific to the ethics of art therapy and the helping professions. This includes being able to display values, beliefs, and attitudes that put the needs of the client above those of the therapist.

Giving students new ideas to think about helps them become aware that learning evolves rather than is goal-oriented. Truth is based on personal experience: we decide what is true for us. Art helps to encourage creativity and integration of new ideas into our lives. Art invites a journey to a deeper level of understanding self in community with others, our "truth made visible" (Rodin & Gsell, 1984). Art can also be a catharsis enhancing self-esteem. The common language of art can help us solve individual problems, but also can unite people in support groups, in the community, in the work place, in times of crisis and disaster, in the world.

In some of the following essays I have put forth my current thinking about group art therapy work in the areas of addiction, loss and grief, dreams, trauma, and psychodynamics surrounding life's challenges. Other essays include working with children and adolescents, couples and families, and older adults. Necessarily there will be repetition of Adlerian theory since each essay is written to stand alone with a particular course in mind.

Art Directives are included in this book as well as the rationale for them when needed. As much as possible, following the Art Directive will lead students into the process of understanding the value of art therapy as well as coming to a better understanding of their own private beliefs and behavior. I trust that students will take what they learn about themselves and the art therapy process, whether insight-oriented or art as therapy and use it in creative ways with clients no matter what the population.

There is no one right way to do art therapy. What the client needs most is someone who can understand them, not through interpretation which is invasive, but just by being present. In fact, it is always satisfying for clients or students to do the work themselves and come to their own conclusions. In the classroom, we share observations and may offer ideas to the student who is willing to receive comments. This helps prepare the student for their own practice and helps them become aware that everything observed, including behavior, facial expressions, and body language, is useful in understanding the client (Dreikurs, S., 1986, p. 67).

THE ROLE OF MUSIC

Music is integral to the atmosphere of each class, which, in turn, gives the student an idea of the possibilities for using music in the therapeutic setting. The effects of music have long been recognized. Plato regarded music as the "medicine of the soul." Music, softly played during the art activity, can help focus attention more on the task of doing and less on feelings of inferiority and isolation. It was Tee's belief that if one is encouraged to paint to the rhythm of the music the creative spirit takes over and one paints more for the joy of doing it "without regard for approval or success" (Dreikurs, S.,1986, p. 63).

The effects of music on the individual will depend on the meaning he or she brings to it. Memory and emotion are very similar phenomena. Music, through rhythm, moods, and harmony, exerts its own influence. Rhythm is culture-bound and can be a strong social force which unites people. Music implies order which we feel intuitively, and may provide the bridge to move from misbehavior and alienation to cooperative behavior especially when used with children or with those who cannot be reached with words. Music is like nature with its own repeated refrains: the assurance dawn follows night, spring follows winter, and wave follows wave.

Music therapy involves not just listening to music, but talking about what happens while listening, asking ourselves what images appear, what memories and emotions are invoked or reawakened. The goal is to have a conversation about the music, as one would do with the art in art therapy. The conversations is what maintains the connection, which has been scientifically proven to keep people (especially those with dementia) socially involved. The neurologist Oliver Sacks (2008) explains that the part of the mind that manages music is the last to fall victim to dementia.

The first ever collaboration or the Illinois Art Therapy Association (IATA) and the Illinois Association for Music Therapy (IAMT) was held at the Lurie Children's Hospital of Chicago on September 22, 2013 and provided an opportunity to learn about the benefits of each modality and how both therapies can be used in conjunction with each other to benefit clients. We found that many of our beliefs about expressive therapies share common ground.

BEYOND TEACHING AT ADLER UNIVERSITY

I still look for the "inward significance" (Aristotle) in the art I create to have as self-knowledge, and I encourage my students and clients to do the same. I believe the validation for art therapy comes from having them tell me how, through the creative process of their own art-making, they have improved the quality of their lives by coming to a deeper understanding of the unconscious attitude (their "private logic"), that they bring to social situations. I trust this self-reporting process more than the rigidity of scientific research, although I know both are important to the profession of art therapy, counseling, and the field of mental health.

Today, in post-graduate supervision I work with students and interns toward registration as art therapists (ATR) as well as licensing by the state of IL (LCPC). I find that there are many innovative approaches being practiced with many different populations. In fact, I am stunned by the creative use of art in working with clients, whether in schools, hospitals, disaster areas, programs for older adults or the developmentally delayed, clinics, foster children, adoption, shelters, open studios, addiction centers, prisons, anywhere or with anyone. When art therapy was just in its infant stages, there was neither the chance nor the inclination to work in many of these facilities. Some did not even exist. I applaud the art therapists who have had the courage and the ability to extend art therapy into many areas of treatment going beyond the resistance of both the hierarchy found in facilities and the hesitancy of individuals, making art an appreciated value where before it was not even recognized. This is not to say that it is always easy to establish such a working arrangement or relationship. Rapport in the form of trust and respect has to happen before there can be acceptance of any kind of treatment, art or any other kind of therapy.

Younger art therapists are bringing their own unique definitions of art therapy to the field. There is room for all of us: we have a mission statement that is inclusive to what we are doing in the field, training that is appropriate to the needs of the field yesterday, today, and tomorrow, and the knowledge that we still need to tailor art therapy to whatever the therapeutic situation of the individual or the group demands at the moment. Only in the richness of our diversity can we achieve unity and survive as art therapists. Taking Tee's work to create an Adlerian art therapy program for students at what is now Adler University, and watching it expand from the classroom into the therapeutic world in Chicago and other places in the world is exciting.

The Art Therapy program at the Adler University means experimentation: taking what we learn and using it to create meaning for ourselves and to cooperatively engage with others in the spirit of social equality "without losing our uniqueness as individuals" (Dreikurs, S., 1986). I offer my book to link what I learned from Tee and her approach to art therapy, to and through the years while I served as the creator of and program director (1993-2006), and now into the capable hands of those teaching and leading the program into the future. In a way, you could say this is a work in progress: telling the history of art therapy at Adler University, beginning with Tee Dreikurs and continuing her legacy into the future.

I encourage students to join the following organizations:

The **American Art Therapy Association (AATA):** was founded in 1969 and "advances the research and understanding of how art therapy functions in the treatment, education, development, and life enrichment of people." Membership includes the *Journal of AATA*. Annual conventions are held in the United States.

The **Illinois Art Therapy Association (IATA)** is the state version of AATA. IATA holds an annual convention and sponsors programs of art therapy interest throughout the year.

The **North American Society of Adlerian Psychology (NASAP)** was founded in 1952 under the leadership of Rudolf Dreikurs and is designed to promote research, training, and application of Adlerian theory. Alfred Adler's concepts include "social equality, mutual respect, encouragement, holism, and an optimistic view of the human creative potential." A convention is held in a different location in North America annually. Membership includes the *Journal of Individual Psychology*, published quarterly as well as the NASAP Newsletter published six times a year.

ICASSI (the **International Committee for Adlerian Summer Schools and Institutes**) was founded in 1962 by Rudolf Dreikurs who was dedicated to the task of spreading the teachings of Alfred Adler, not only as a psychological method of treatment, but as a philosophy of life. Rudolf Dreikurs began practicing psychiatry in Vienna, and from there spread his work into the community, to the nation, and then internationally, first to Brazil in 1937, again in 1946. Dreikurs moved from Vienna to the United States in 1937. He was convinced that if children could learn in a democratic atmosphere, at home, in school, and in community, that they would be able to handle the responsibility of citizenship in a free world. Dreikurs felt that prevention was more important than the treatment. He believed that once people accepted the vision of "Social Interest" and experienced living in social equality, life would be more peaceful. The hope for ICASSI was that it could be held in a different country each year especially wherever a new group was forming and in need of encouragement from others dedicated to teaching the theories of Individual Psychology (Dreikurs, S., 1991).

In 1987, I attended my first ICASSI. There I met others from around the world, some of whom were trained by Tee and all who were invested in spreading the concepts of Adlerian theory. In most all the years I have attended and sometimes taught at ICASSI, Rudolf Dreikurs' daughter, Eva Dreikurs Ferguson, has been the Chairperson continuing the ICASSI experience and its spirit. The Summer Institute provides an intensive two-week educational and multi-cultural experience for participants. Always there is so much to be learned from the amazing selection of courses taught by instructors very experienced in teaching Adlerian-Dreikursian theory and practice, some in English, some in German. Even children and youth attending ICASSI found themselves in an encouraging atmosphere where they could learn about themselves, play games, and have the opportunity to make friends with young people from other cultures and nations around the world. Going to ICASSI is an experience I wish for everyone!

At the end of each chapter I have included a haiku or a short poem. These poems sometimes suggest a beginning to thoughts that can open a path to personal involvement and meaning for us. The Japanese form of poetry called haiku is constructed of seventeen syllables in three lines. These poems are meant to crystallize, in a very few words, a feeling, a memory, an experience. They can even lead to enlightenment. As students, we practice writing haiku to encourage our experience of the here and now, both for ourselves and as a gift to others. Just as we – without conscious awareness – sometimes change the meaning we give to early recollections as we grow over time, so we also might change the meaning we give to these poems to fit our current experience in life.

In a land, not my own,
A stranger takes my hand
And I follow the path set forth

2

Portraits in Reflection

The M.A.in Counseling Psychology: Art Therapy at Adler University began with a two-day event on October 8 and 9, 1993. Bryna Gamson, the Public Relations Director for Adler, took the initiative by contacting the artist Jeanette Pasin Sloan and advertising the "Portraits in Reflection," an Open House and one-day workshop for anyone interested in learning more about the field of art therapy. Over thirty people arrived, and out of that group we had enough students who wanted to matriculate into the newly forming courses of the art therapy program.

Jeanette Pasin Sloan and I co-presented at both the Open House and the one-day workshop. Jeanette started the Friday evening program by describing how, after she was divorced, she taught herself to paint by using highly polished silver pieces from wedding gifts and their reflections as subjects. The silver, able to hold reflections, became for her a symbol of everlasting promises, something to be valued, also a metaphor for enduring strength in face of loss and grief.

She showed many slides of her work, and told us that art critics called her art "hyper-realistic domestic still life painting brought to the thin edge of abstraction with canny depictions of reflection and distortion." In the beginning Jeanette was unaware of the distortions but as time went on she realized that she was creating metaphors for how she saw herself reflected in the silver. She began to include her own reflection explicitly along with fabric and other objects, and eventually her paintings became self-portraits. Thus came about the title for our work-shop, "Portraits in Reflection."

Jeanette explained to us how she used art to first heal herself and then to reconnect to others. She talked about how her divorce was the catalyst that led her to risk trying something new. As it is for all of us, the source of Jeanette's creativity is conflict, pain, and suffering. In her art work she found happiness and success, and was able to share that with others. She demonstrated the connection between the autonomous world of the art-ist and the world of relationships: first with members of her family, then in the world of art galleries, and with us that night. Her courage to share this journey was a gift to us.

Jeanette's words about her art led us to begin forming our own words, not to explain or judge, but just to create meaning based on our own life experiences. We found ourselves going beyond the almost photo-graphic realism of her work to the deeper reality of the soul, the thoughts that might be filling her mind and our own. In my part of the program I said that imagery, not words is the language of the mind, as it is also the language of children. Art reconnects us with childhood experiences. We unconsciously bring some of those childhood experiences which have most impressed us into our adult world to guide us in our lives. We think in images, we dream in images, and we unconsciously create art with our personal imagery. Our art is the way in which we make sense of what we experience in our world and how we connect to the world of others. Simply said, I believe with Carl Jung that making art puts our inner experi-ences into images (McNiff, 2011).

In the beginning, for Jeanette, the language of art is autonomous. Autonomy disregards relationships. The goal of painting for her was to discover, to invent forms, a different viewpoint, not for us, but for herself. It expresses her style, her attitude, and her unique vision; and yet, each painting taps into feelings that are universal. These feelings help us to bond to Jeanette even though we may never have met her before. What appeals to us in Jeanette's work? What does it touch in each of us?

All art, we learn, expresses emotion. Emotion is what gives meaning to art whether we are talking about paintings, stories, poetry, music, or songs. We as human beings uniquely express how the world appears to us, how we feel about it, delight in it, are stunned by it, disappointed by it, and strive to give it validation. Maybe it is an unconscious hope that giving testimony to life through the images we create, for ourselves and for others, may bring us a "felt sense" of belonging (Gendlin, 1981): "A felt sense doesn't come to you in the form of thoughts or words or other separate units, but as a single (though often puzzling and very complex) bodily feeling."

Art, in whatever form, leads away from feelings of failure. Jeanette knows the power of art in her own process of healing. As an art therapist and in my own life, I have witnessed many occasions when the power of one's own creation enables that person to see how he or she functions in life and, with awareness, to choose to transform some mistaken ideas about self and others into thoughts that are more life-giving.

In the workshop the next day, we give importance to our own self-portraits as we explore the meaning and therapeutic significance of this art form. With each other's permission, we make observations about what we see and make guesses about the meaning in our own art work. What we say reflects who we are. Getting to know each other through our art helps to create a safe environment where we can trust and re-spect each other.

We watch for the themes that emerge, the themes that form a uni-fied, holistic pattern for what Adler calls our lifestyle: the basic concepts of self, others, and the unconsciously chosen life goal. The unity of the personality, a fundamental principle of Individual Psychology, means that one's art work, like all one's actions, thoughts, and attitudes, fits with the individual's holistic lifestyle pattern. The art cannot be seen as separate from the artist: the one gives shape and meaning to the other. Art cre-ates a bridge between the physical and spiritual, between inner and outer world, between unconsciousness (that which we have yet to understand about ourselves) and consciousness, between "private logic and common sense" (Dreikurs, R., 1967).

Adler believed that that all life is movement, and called expression which has been given static form "frozen movement," helping us understand that all art serves as the artist's inner vision mirrored out to self and others. What is real? What is reflected? Can reflections be deceiving or do we deceive ourselves? Think of the fairy tale Snow White, where the queen asks: "Mirror, mirror, on the wall, who is fairest of them all?" We realize that the way we see the world is the way the world will be for us, that one is a reflection of the other.

Creative expression is not a structured language. If paintings were structured, we would be able to translate them. Interpretations are invalid and also invasive, because everything we think and say when observing the creative work of another is a projection or reflection of what is currently going on in our own lives. The art creates the bridge to cover the distance between ourselves and the life of the artist and allows us to give meaning to our own lives and connect to each other.

In the Workshop, we take the time to create our own portraits. We are open to what others have to say, knowing that it can lead to personal growth and satisfaction. Being open to the process does not mean we have to tell our darkest secrets, it just means listening and describing what is going on for us in the moment.

THE ART DIRECTIVES:

1. Draw how you see yourself on one sheet of paper and the way you think others see you on another sheet of paper.
2. Draw yourself based on how you understood the expectations your mother had for you, and one for those your father had for you.
3. Create a self-portrait using found objects in the room: branches, yarn, colored wire, shells, and or seeds. Walk around the room and pick up objects, hold them, observe them, and respond to

them from a "felt sense" without trying to match a preconceived image of what you want to portray.

4. Draw yourself at work, with friends, and with a significant other.

We process all the art work, attending to the thoughts that emerge, our biased apperception (that we see ourselves and life as we think we are), and how thought elicits emotions and how emotions breathe life into our portraits. All of our art is a self-portrait in that it reveals the truth of what we think and believe (McNiff, 1992). Our art work provides for the process of self-reflection and continues throughout the program in all the coursework.

Still point, still life,
Absence of wind or breath
Self-portrait, a reminder of death
The meaning I give to life
Captured in a moment of light and perfection
Reveals itself in reflection.

[Sutherland, 2006]

3

The Use of Art in Group Counseling

I t is in this course, designed by Tee Dreikurs, that students first experience Adlerian group art therapy by being involved in art-making tasks and processing applicable to group counseling. This course provides the guiding philosophy, theory, and format for all of the other classroom art experientials in the art therapy program. Tee's book, *Cows Can Be Purple* (1986) gives a complete explanation of her art therapy experientials. Her writing makes clear the purpose of each of her art directives, her theory and practice. I briefly describe her art experientials and process in this chapter.

With each new group of students I follow Tee's example of meeting the students at the door. The greeting is simple: I introduce myself and welcome the student. When asked later how students feel about this greeting, most felt comfortable and agreed that it was a good way to put clients or patients at ease when meeting a new therapist and participating in an unfamiliar approach to therapy. Class members then introduce themselves to each other. The tables are set with brushes, water and paint, pastels and other drawing media to welcome them. (Dreikurs, S., p. 63). We talk about the materials, and that colored paper and music softly playing during times of art making are used to counteract the fear of failure (ibid., p. 62, 63). As Tee did, I ask the group's permission before beginning any new project. Students learn they will always have a choice about what they will do.

RATIONALE FOR ART DIRECTIVES:

To take risks by entering into the art-making process; to take responsibility for the choices we make; to be aware of selective listening and how it impacts our lives; to gain understanding of the Family Constellation and Early Recollections, how they can help in understanding the lifestyle pattern; and to observe the way "a client approaches and completes the drawing task which can also reveal factors such as perfectionism, insecurity, humor, courage, dependency, control, rebellion and others" (McAbee & McAbee, 1979, p. 143).

We learn that art makes objective that which is subjective, that images can be understood as messages from the psyche and can help us become more aware of our own myths and symbols, and that art helps us to expand our boundaries outward in perspective and inward in depth. We appreciate and show deep respect for the integrity of each individual. We develop optimistic conviction about the healing dimension of the creative art process both for ourselves and for others.

The Art Directives are not rule-bound dictates to be precisely followed, but are designed to initiate students into a spontaneous process of art-making and then begin to recognize, accept and understand the subjective meaning reflected in their process and in what they have created. We do the art activity first, and then later discuss the way our experience enriches our understanding of ourselves, and how it relates to Adlerian theory.

THE ART DIRECTIVE: Carousel (Dreikurs, S., 1986, p. 68).

Process: Each of you chooses a large sheet of colored paper and puts it on the table in front of you. Listen to the music and, when you feel ready, begin painting on your paper. After a few minutes I will stop you and ask you to move to your right and continue to work on the painting that was started there. All the paintings stay in their original positions. You move around the table to each one until you come back to your own. Take the painting you started and tape it on one area of the wall, leaving some of the wall free. Then take another sheet of paper and paint your own picture. Tape this one on the wall as well.

One person volunteers to choose three paintings which he or she then tapes in the space on the wall that was left empty for this purpose. Students are asked to offer non-judgmental guesses as to what the volunteer is telling us about him or herself through his or her choice of paintings, keeping in mind that everything we say reflects our own bias. Very quickly the group is able to pick up and identify characteristics and attitudes seen in the chosen art work, and, in turn, the volunteer finds him or herself agreeing with most of what is said. The student is then asked to tell us what he or she liked about each of the selections as well as those thoughts and guesses which best fit with the way she or he understands him or herself.

Students learn that we choose paintings that reflect how we feel about ourselves and our life as it is for us in the here and now. A tentative personality emerges as one that can be intuitively "read" by the other group members. Students are surprised they can do this with very little practice. Other questions might include: "Did you like it better when you worked by yourself or with the group? How did you feel when others painted on your picture? How did you feel when you painted on someone else's painting? Did you learn anything new about yourself in this process?" (ibid, p.69).

Objective: To see what happens when we move around the table and paint on each other's work.

Rationale: To experience Adlerian art therapy theory in action; to encourage cooperation, a feeling of belonging, and social interest.

The "Carousel" experiential seems to be a non-threatening way for students to get to know one another, and can be especially encouraging when students feel understood by the others. The movement around the table provides the opportunity to become sensitive to what others are doing, to align goals in a manner of being equal and respectful, and to minimize feelings of inadequacy and isolation. The shared responsibility of the task might alleviate personal feelings about success or failure and help them to think about their personal style of interacting with others.

Very quickly a sense of unity and group cohesiveness begins to evolve (ibid, p.72).

We talk about what happens when someone is not willing to cooperate and may try to destroy the art work by painting over it in black. However when others come along and add new colors, the purpose of rebellion is lost and the person begins to feel the benefit of cooperation without any words being said.

WHAT DOES THE ART IMAGE EXPRESS
AND HOW DO WE MAKE SENSE OF IT?

Images transmit a "life-giving energy" (Arnheim, 1974, p. 460), and we can impart meaning to them by letting the words come spontaneously. A certain image might keep appearing in the art work. What meaning or message can be attached to it?

The sentence beginning: "I see...," "I feel...," I am..." offers a starting place for integrating the truth of who we are by using our senses, intuition, and reason. It is with the cooperation of these three measures that we can more fully comprehend the meaning we give to our art work. Add to this another sentence, "In order to have a place in life, I need to...." and we have the basic outline of the lifestyle pattern.

THE ART DIRECTIVE: Paint on the same piece of paper (Dreikurs, S., 1986).

For this experiential I am going to give the directions only once. I will not answer any questions after we start. You will see why when we process our finished paintings.

Process: I want you to look around the room and choose someone that you don't know very well, but someone with whom you would like to work. Together choose one large sheet of colored paper and two small sheets and art supplies. From that time on there is to be no communication of any kind between the two of you. Go back to your place and the two of you paint on the same large piece of paper. When you feel you have gone as far as you want, then each of you take a smaller piece of paper and immediately paint your response to this project. Put the large painting on the wall and put the two smaller ones directly underneath it.

How did you choose each other? How did you hear the directions? What did you learn about each other? What did you learn about yourself? Where are you in your Family Constellation? What can you "read" in your partner's drawing response?

Objective: To see how two people who hardly know each other hear and understand the directions for doing the art experiential, and how they apply that information to the drawing task, to learn about Family Constellation and how the relationships you have with your siblings influence and contribute to how you live your life: your lifestyle pattern.

Rationale: To remember that we are selective in what we hear and that what we hear fits with our lifestyles. We hear and remember only what is useful to us. To learn about each other by listening to how others heard the directions and how that influenced the manner in which they adapted to the art task. Some might hear, "Work together on the same piece of paper." Others might hear, "Work on your own side of the paper." Another might hear, "Make a drawing together." There is no right or wrong in how we understand the directions. It just helps us to understand how we prefer to work in life and the consequences of our choices.

THE ART DIRECTIVE: Hand Painting (Dreikurs, S., 1986).

Process: Take a piece of paper, choose any color you wish, and begin by positioning your hand on the paper and drawing around it. Use this outline as a starting place for the rest of your drawing. Ask yourself the following questions: Where do my hands lead me? What do my hands say about who I am right now? If you are willing, choose some drawings that you like and tell a story about them, or, simply give each one a title.

Objective: To observe the way we create movement in life; to learn that we are each unique and follow our own patterns for interacting with each other.

Rationale: To have awareness of the creative movement in life and the uniqueness of the individual.

THE CREATIVE PROCESS

Art done in art therapy is done spontaneously. It is an intuitive and subjective expression of how we experience life. Art happens without any art experience. The art is what guides us to a better understanding of our inner thoughts and feelings, while at the same time, processing in the group connects us to others. We begin to learn from each other and from there to understand how life is for them and what is true for each of us. Both are necessary for survival.

Hearing what others have to say can be useful, but we have to work out our own meaning for life if we are to grow and learn, to live independently yet in harmony with others. No matter what others say, we still have to cope with our own fears and create our own order out of the chaos of life. We can do this best with encouragement and connection to each other. There is no end point in this journey; striving for perfection is an up-and-down, back–and-forth ongoing experiment, a continuum.

THE ART DIRECTIVE: Frustration/Fulfillment Drawings (Dreikurs, S., 1986)
Process: Take two pieces of paper, any color, and paint in any way that works for you – symbolically, abstractly, or realistically – that which fulfills you on one piece of paper and that which frustrates you on the other. You will get a chance to describe what you have drawn. When taping your pictures on the wall, put the fulfillment painting on top and the frustration painting under it.
Objective: To recognize common themes of frustration: betrayal, prejudice, violence, not finding a job, not having enough money, broken promises, lies, failure, illness or sickness; and common themes of fulfillment: mutual trust and respect, being playful, pets, a job, traveling, playing sports, being in nature, music, learning new things, a sense of

order. To find out what is more important in our lives at the moment, that which frustrates us or that which fulfills us, by noting the positions of our papers on the wall.

Rationale: To find that what fulfills us can also frustrate us, and that which frustrates us can encourage us to make life better for ourselves – they are two sides of the same coin. We might choose to blame others when things don't go the way we want them to, or decide that we won't be happy unless we have a certain amount of money, the right job, the perfect house, or the best grades. Thinking that we can be fulfilled by objects, money, living in a certain place, other people doing what we want them to do, we tell ourselves that "Life would be perfect if only..." (Dreikurs, S., 1986).

We forget that we would not know fulfillment if we did not have frustration, that frustration can be an incentive to make our lives better, and that we are in charge of making that happen for ourselves.

THE CREATIVE SELF

Adlerian therapists believe in the creative power of the individual and in the healing power of the creative process, whether it is art, music, dance, or just creating a new way to think about life and our place in it. The goal of courage (which the ancient Greeks considered the essence of soul) implies a confidence in the ability of each individual to cope with and to meet the social challenges of life. "Art is caring for the soul" (McNiff, 1992). The link between soul, imagination and life experiences can be strengthened through the creative process.

Symbols, like our images, evoke emotion which can help us understand how we subjectively feel about a situation. The issues in life are universal, but the symbols and inner messages are not. Art can help to shift us from inner messages that might be self-deceptive and discouraging toward an attitude and behaviors that are more life-sustaining.

THE ART DIRECTIVE: Magic Wand Painting (Dreikurs, S., 1986)

Pretend that I have a magic wand that will take you wherever you want to be. Paint a picture of the place you have chosen for yourself.

Process: Where are you? What would be different in your life if you were in that place?

Objective: to possibly find out against what or whom you are protesting.

Rationale: In these last two experientials (four and five), we can identify a commonality of themes: to learn to take responsibility for our own lives, to learn that there is no one way to justify or prove that what we are learning about ourselves will solve our problems in life, or even improve our ability to get along with each other, but it might encourage us to change whatever is unpleasant in our lives into something more satisfying.

THE CONTINUUM

As we go through life we become more consciously aware that some of our thoughts, attitudes and behavior are helpful in getting us what we want. Or, moving toward the other end of the continuum, we develop feelings of inferiority leading to useless behaviors and emotional problems, a normal response which we all suffer at one time or another in our striving for perfection (wholeness). Sometimes our ideals hold mistaken ideas such as the conviction that "unless I can please (others) I am nothing" (Dreikurs, R., 1972, quoted in Dreikurs, S., 1986, p. 110). The last two art experientials explore the question: "What would be different in your life if you didn't have "this symptom," or "this problem?" Drawing (sometimes symbolically) what frustrates us on one piece of paper and what fulfills us on another piece, or "draw wherever it is you want to be" can bring to light experiences "that are related to control and avoidance of responsibility" (ibid., p. 100).

THE ART DIRECTIVE: Painting Blind (Dreikurs, S., 1986)

Process: Take two pieces of the same size paper. Arrange your materials so that you know where they are and are easily accessible. On one piece of paper, paint with your eyes closed. When you have finished with the first one put it under the table. Next, paint on the other sheet of paper with your eyes open. When you are finished with both, tape them to the wall, with the one you did "blind" on top and the other one underneath it.

Do you see anything special about the two paintings? Which painting do you like best? What do you think is the purpose of this experiment? What is remarkable about your paintings? How is this experiential useful to you?

Objective: To have a better understanding of how you cope with and find the courage to solve problems when you are experiencing something that happens to you over which you have no control.

Rationale: To see if this experiential can be linked to social problems in your life right now. To better understand your creative process in solving problems, and to give you courage in looking for ways to improve troubling situations; to see that the overall pattern in both paintings has the same rhythm or pattern.

MOVEMENT

As in the continuum above, there is always movement between two principles, light/dark, inner/outer, past/future, beginning/end, and perfection/imperfection. The same is true for us as we attempt to understand the question "Who am I?" by separating and moving between inferiority feelings and guiding self-ideals. I might present one side of myself without the other as I identify with what I like about myself and reject the rest. This starts to feel false. What works therapeutically toward resolution of the unconscious dialectic between inferiority feelings and the guiding self-ideal may begin with the experience of suffering. Suffering is a sign of our deep discouragement and it is an important catalyst to the evolution of consciousness. The stress or dissatisfaction that I experience can serve as a wake-up call to explore some misconceptions about myself or others and/or a mistaken goal, possibly wanting attention, power, revenge, or to prove inadequacy.

Unwillingness to look at and accept a painful situation can be a safeguarding technique I might use to maintain a sense of self-worth. I first need to want life to be different in order to move away from suffering and toward the goal of social interest. Personal consciousness is a continual process of deconstruction and construction necessary for survival, both physically and psychologically. We are always in the process of forming a new self whether we are aware of it or not (Mosak, 1977).

The path then is progress toward a deeper understanding of self in community with others. The light of social logic and insight guides us away from fear, doubt, and judgment toward working with others in the spirit of social equality.

THE ART DIRECTIVE: Paint As If You Are a Young Child (Dreikurs, S., 1986)

Process: Think back to the kinds of paintings or drawings you made when you were young, then choose a piece of paper and proceed to paint a picture that will look just like the ones you painted when you were a child. Tell us about your painting. How old were you when you painted this picture?

Objective: To evoke feelings that you had as a young child, to bring back memories and possibly an Early Recollection.

Rationale: To see the relationship between what you just now painted as a child and what you remember as a child; to see the connection between feelings you experienced as a child and the feelings you have today; to recognize common themes between past and present; possibly to learn something new about yourself.

THE ART DIRECTIVE: Paint an Early Recollection (Dreikurs, S., 1986)

Process: One person volunteers to tell an Early Recollection (ER): "Think back to when you were a young child and tell us about a one-time event that you remember. How old were you when you had this Early Recollection? What were your feelings? What was the most significant moment in your ER?"

The rest of us listen to the student's ER and then respond by painting the ER as if it were our own. After posting our paintings on the wall we are each asked, in turn, to tell the story of the ER in first person, present tense. The student who volunteered the ER is the last to tell the story of his or her ER and then is asked to choose what he or she liked from all the other paintings and stories, including what was learned or what was helpful. Sometimes the volunteer may choose a different version, liking it better than his or her own.

Objective: To bring an ER to the group; to understand that what happens in an ER is often an experience common to others in the group.

Rationale: to recognize how easy it is for us to see ourselves in another person's ER; that what was important to the volunteer also has meaning for us, but may reflect a different attitude or feeling; that there is more than one way to give meaning to an ER; that what might be true for one is not necessarily true for someone else.

> **Example:** One person told an ER: he and his sister were across the street from their house in the park. They had taken off their shoes and socks to play in the sandbox. An older boy came along and tied their shoes together. When mother called them to come home, they couldn't get their shoes apart and were afraid that mother would be angry with them for being barefoot.
>
> **Most Vivid Moment:** seeing their shoes tied together
>
> **Feelings:** frustrated and scared

Another group member painted the ER, but in her drawing she drew an imaginary pair of scissors to cut the shoelaces apart. Years later I saw this student and he remembered the drawing of the other student. He told me that whenever he is feeling stuck in his life, he thinks of that drawing and is able to find a way to "cut through the crap." Encouragement from another student helped him put this ER to good use and he was able to move from being helpless to being in control of the situation.

THE VALUE OF USING EARLY RECOLLECTIONS IN THERAPY

"The interpretation of ERs is, for the Adlerian therapist, a *sine qua non* of their process, for herein lies the expression of the basic beliefs that underlie the individual's current style of life" (Beames, 1992).

ERs are useful to us and reflect something of how we unconsciously look at life, who we are, and what we want. We retain at a level of consciousness only those few experiences which express our approach to life. They reflect our perceptual framework within which we interpret life's experiences. They help us understand our thoughts, feelings, and attitudes about ourselves and life as well as the purpose or goal of our behavior. We look beyond the conscious actual experience to find hidden wishes and defenses. We might even be able to recognize old feelings which originated early in life and are carried as part of the lifestyle pattern into current life situations. When we accept responsibility for creating the feelings and goal, we can also change them to something more useful.

We pay attention to the people who are mentioned (or not mentioned) in the ERs. They reflect a role model, such as a mother, or a prototype, i.e., an authority figure, in our lives. We observe whether or not the individual in the ER is active or passive. What common situations or themes appear in the ER? What method is used for dealing with a certain social challenge, is it hesitancy, avoidance, withdrawal, or a socially useful method? We might recognize some mistaken ideas we have about ourselves, other people, or the world. "Basic mistakes are irrational, impossible, intolerant and can be egocentric, vindictive, compulsive, or insatiable" (Shulman, 1973, quoted in Dreikurs, S., 1986, p. 110).

During the course of therapy the ER can change in meaning. The attitude might change, or the behavior, or the situation. Different people might be involved, or the ER itself might be forgotten. The original ER stays with us as long as it still reflects a way we want our lives to be.

CASE EXAMPLE WITH A CLIENT'S EARLY RECOLLECTION

I quote Tee Dreikurs who said: "People might express something different in their painting than what they have already verbally reported." The visual ER will have a different impact on understanding than either the verbal or written ER (1984).

An elderly client volunteers an ER from a time when she was five years old. "I am playing in my sandbox and make a sandcastle with my pail and sand toys. I am so pleased with it." Seeing her completed sandcastle was her most vivid moment. A stockade fence took up most of the space in her drawing of this ER, and behind the fence all that could be seen of the child was the red ribbon in her hair. Others in the group drew variations of her sandcastle and faces with proud smiles and even showing the sandcastle to a mother. One or two of the drawings showed other children playing together in the sandbox. This pleased the elderly woman. Later, when looking at this woman's drawing, a group member asks about the fence. The woman replies with hesitation and to her surprise, "I guess the fence keeps me safe — and, ummm, maybe from getting too close to people."

Even though the fence was not part of the verbal memory in the original telling of the ER, it seems that it was the most cogent symbol in pinpointing what this woman was experiencing in her life at the moment: distance from others and a negative attitude toward social life. The size of the fence in the drawing gave meaning for what was true for her.

By visually focusing on the symbol of the fence, this woman was able to become aware of and understand her hidden intention (the goal to avoid or withdraw from others). She could then understand why it was important for her to have the fence in her drawing: that the fence kept her from being hurt by others, but also that she was giving nothing to others just as she accused them of doing to her. Once the client saw this for herself, her attitude began to change from one of discouragement to one of hope. She began to interact with the other group members in just the same way as they were inviting her to do with them.

The symbol of the fence still showed up in her drawings, but sometimes there was a gate, and once she was on the other side of the fence walking to school with a friend. The size of the fence in the original drawing no longer served the purpose it once did, and her later drawings reflected a positive change in her attitude and behavior toward others, choosing connection rather than avoidance.

HOLISM

Adler found in the holistic philosophy of Jan Smuts a confirmation of his own ideas and a philosophical basis for Individual Psychology (Ellenberger, 1970). In *Holism and Evolution* (1926), Smuts developed the view that evolution is a sequence of ever more comprehensive integrations. Holistic theory postulates that "the whole is greater than its parts, it influences its parts, the parts influence the whole, they influence one another and the whole influences the environment." Smuts saw in the universe an impulse towards wholeness in every living thing; to achieve completion of an ideal pattern. Just as every plant or animal has such an impulse to realize an ideal, so too, does a human being strive for perfection (Adler, 1964), completion (Adler, 1958), wholeness, self-realization (Horney, 1951), self-actualization (Goldstein, 1939; Maslow, 1954).

Perfection is a concept, an ideal, and to some degree we are free to create our own "ideal" pattern, something that is virtually impossible to achieve and may even bring us into conflict with others; the good part of ourselves exaggerated, i.e., helping others when they are capable of helping themselves. At any rate, ideals are sure to be prevented by circumstance. At some point Tee Dreikurs would want us to tell ourselves, "We are good enough as we are."

CONCLUSION

The combining of the senses – auditory, visual, working with shapes and colors; and tactile, using brushes and paint, invites one to enter into the creative process with others. The feeling that one is in charge of what he or she will do, cooperation through shared responsibility, encouragement of self and others, builds unity and a sense of belonging in the classroom and later in the practice of art therapy.

Students eventually find out that the art they create is no different from the art of clients. This information helps remove concern with perfection or with failure as well as to create a feeling of social equality. Art for the Adlerian art therapist is not a test of some kind – it will not be used to diagnose, assess or label behavior nor is it busy work. When the art work is displayed, others tend to say encouraging and appreciative remarks about it, a sign of social interest which brings people closer together in the group.

Odd, that in a class
Full of strangers, I find new
Meaning for my life

4

Historical, Theoretical, and Postmodern Perspectives of Art Therapy

Art therapy can be done with any client population and with any theoretical orientation. Art therapy works well on an individual basis, privately, with a therapist, or in a group setting. The three main theories in psychology are psychoanalytic, (Freud, Jung), behavioral (Skinner), and humanistic. Adlerian theory can be considered humanistic and uses a bio-psychosocial model for understanding human behavior (Sperry, Carlson, & Maniacci, 1993).

The art itself – the drawing, painting, or sculpture – becomes a visual extension of the individual and can serve a therapeutic purpose: sometimes as an assessment to help plan treatment, sometimes to make visual or objective that which is subjective, e.g., to bring unconscious thoughts into the open, sometimes to help emotionally disturbed children modify their behavior, to encourage cooperation and the feeling of belonging (Dreikurs, S., 1986), and often just for catharsis and enhancement of self-esteem.

Art reflects and gives form to our creative and intuitive life process. "Art is the creation of forms (privately) symbolic of (our immediate) human feelings" (Langer, 1953, p. 40). The metaphor in art can be considered a form of symbolization uniquely suited to bridge what we know and that which we do not yet understand about ourselves. It embodies and can evoke emotions congruent with how we perceive and experience our lives. Art therapy might encourage creativity, or help when words are not available. It might lead to taking responsibility for one's own behavior since the art expression is of the artist's own making, and it may lead to insight and change of behavior through understanding one's metaphors and symbols in the art work. Self-disclosure begins and proceeds at the student's or client's own tempo.

Since the beginning of time there have been two approaches to healing. One uses rational means and is scientific, logical: the medical model which includes assessment and diagnosis, medication, and sometimes surgery. The other approach is humanistic or spiritual, involving intuition, prayer, art-making, god(s), objects, and/or rituals. Both approaches illustrate the swinging back and forth between two attitudes, something that happens in the history of culture as we work to come to an agreement about what method or law (and maybe both) works best in any given situation.

With certification and licensing required to practice as art therapists in different states and countries, we have had to bridge the gap between the healing potential of creativity and the medical model (art as a diagnostic tool), the spiritual and the scientific, and find ways "to integrate our practice with other psychological disciplines in a holistic way" (Baker, 1994).

PSYCHODYNAMIC PSYCHOANALYTIC THEORY
AND THE ORIGIN OF ART THERAPY

Freud's contributions to the field of psychology are ground-breaking, extensive, and well known. He broke with rational materialism and postulated an unconscious level of awareness, he recognized that we think in images by exploring dreams (1932), and he realized that feelings and thoughts are uniquely expressed. Freud originally saw psychoanalysis as a research tool, not as a treatment, and he based his theory on observing psychiatric problems in asylums in the early part of the 20th century. Instinctual drives are seen as prime motivators for behavior, especially libido or sexual energy. His theory operates on the premise that most mental processes occur on an unconscious level and that unconscious sexual conflicts can bring about disorders. Freud organized the personality into three parts: Id (instinctual drives seeking expression); Superego (internal parental restrictions and demands which lead to conscience and guilt feelings); and Ego (the self which mediates between the demands of the id and the restriction of the superego, called the executive function). There are also stages of libidinal development; oral, anal, and phallic. The belief was that each stage needed to be resolved before the child can pass to the next stage.

Freud understood that unconscious conflicts produce neurotic symptoms. Certain behaviors which ward off anxiety but may cause problems of their own – phobias, compulsions, addictions – are symptoms unconsciously disguised as attempts to gratify drives, or can be thought of as developmental delays. Strict Freudians believe that developmental disruptions in childhood are the basis of adult psychiatric disorders ("deterministic" model in contrast to "free will"). Freud later came to believe that neurosis results from the unsatisfactory resolution of the child's conflicted drives, not usually from the parent's failure. Resolving conflicts requires understanding the past and unconscious thoughts, feelings, and attitudes that are carried into the present.

Freud's work formed the groundwork for later development of a formulation of a psychology of creativity. Ernst Kris (1952) considered art to be "regression in the service of the ego," the specific means whereby unconscious material can be made conscious. Free art productions were used to make ego defenses visible and to uncover conflicts. Freud considered not the painting itself but the message behind it, the latent content, as the pathology, and this became the foundation behind early art therapy. At the time those interested in the art of the insane began to wonder if art reveals the mental state of the artist, and began to look for diagnostic clues. We spend time exploring this possibility in the course, "Art Therapy and Psychodynamics Surrounding Life Challenges."

FOUNDERS AND EARLY LEADERS OF ART THERAPY
Two books edited by Judith Rubin, *Approaches to Art Therapy: Theory and Technique (1987)* and *Introduction to Art Therapy Sources and Resources* (2010) are both required reading for this course, and were the source of much of the information in this chapter. Key figures in the theories of

psychology and personality development are presented along with the contributions of some therapists who adapted art therapy to these theories. What is presented here, at best, is a minimum amount of theoretical information; just enough, perhaps, to allow us to follow the art therapy connection to each theory made by the pioneers of art therapy, and to experiment with it in the classroom.

Margaret Naumburg studied with Freud and became the founder of Art Therapy. Her book, published in 1966, is titled, *Dynamically Oriented Art Therapy: Its Principles and Practices.* She saw the patient's art as a form of "symbolic speech." She put emphasis on integrating Freudian insights about behavior, personality, and pathology with the art. Using what she learned from Freud, she agreed that art comes from the unconscious, makes visual the unconscious, and therefore "makes the unconscious conscious," clarified through verbal communication. She called this the process of uncovering and gaining insight, and realized that art therapy could encourage a change in behavior. She also valued spontaneous art activity and saw releasing the repressed (unconscious) through imagery as cathartic as well as a way to communicate to others.

THE ART DIRECTIVE: Self Box

Process: Choose an empty box and pictures from magazines. On the outside of the box, paste those pictures that could be used to describe how you think others see you. On the inside of the box paste those pictures that describe how you understand yourself. Whatever you feel comfortable sharing is processed in the group.

Objective/Rationale: To explore that part of ourselves that is not visible to the world and contrast that with what we believe others see when they meet or know us. Naumburg: "to make the unconscious conscious."

Art products used as assessment or diagnostic tools are called projective tests. One is "House-Tree-Person" (H-T-P) where the "house" is seen as a connection to one's emotional "home," "tree" is viewed as the psychological representation of self, and the drawing of a "person" might indicate certain strengths or weaknesses (Buck, 1948). In the

"Kinetic-Family Drawing" where the direction is "Draw a picture of your family doing something together," therapists look for who is there and who is absent and what that might mean (Burns & Kaufman, 1970, 1972). These projective drawings are administered for the purpose of obtaining symbolic information which can be translated into theoretical meaning for use in interpretation during the clinical art therapy process. They can also be a guide to planning treatment.

THE ART DIRECTIVE: Draw a House, a Tree, and a Person

House-Tree-Person (Buck, 1948) is a projective drawing technique originally designed to assess for brain damage or limited ability to communicate.

Process: Take a pencil and three sheets of white 8½" by 11" paper. Draw a house on one sheet, a tree on another, and a person on the third.

Objective: For this assessment, the role of the clinician is 1) to develop skills in assessing the symbolic meaning of the art work in order to provide diagnosis and treatment; 2) to build alliance with the client by being supportive; 3) to be an unbiased and attentive listener; 4) to be able to create meaning (possibly to interpret meaning) from the art work; 5) to understand the client's imagery. Attention is also paid to the process of sublimation – using art as a means to divert unwanted behavior into something more useful.

Rationale: To become familiar with your own symbols and what they mean to you, and begin to recognize patterns in your own art work; to put yourself in the client's position when you would be asking them to follow these art directives.

Margaret Naumburg's older sister Florence Cane was an art educator who worked with children. In her book, *The Artist in Each of Us* (1951), Cane writes of her experiences bridging art education with art therapy, both the psychological and developmental aspects of learning with personality growth. Cane understood that the art and the artist were one, and that the creative expression of the child's art could give form to emotions and thoughts. She recognized the inherent creative ability and therapeutic value of art in the work of her students, and recognized that it revealed something unique about each child.

THE ART DIRECTIVE: Free Drawing

Process: Take paper and art supplies and create a free drawing.

Objective/Rationale: to experience creating art without a set of directions and process what happens for you when you do this.

Hanna Kwiatkowska was interested in working with families to minimize child delinquency. She introduced a process starting with a family "Scribble" drawing to elicit unconscious material, described in *Family Therapy and Evaluation through Art* (Kwiatkowska, 1978). For her, the primary task of the therapist was to be in touch with the family's dynamics, the experience and need of each member, and how they interact with one another.

In 1958 Edith Kramer first published *Art Therapy in a Children's Community.* She recognized art as therapy and she also emphasized the notion of sublimation, art as an acceptable outlet to express forbidden impulses. Her focus was on creating a holding environment for the child. She introduced the concept of the "third hand," assisting children during the creative process without being overly intrusive or imposing ideas which are alien to the child. She adapted this method of working within the child's metaphor from Theodor Reik (1948). Rudolf and Tee Dreikurs used the term "listening for the gold mine" to understand the hidden purpose of the behavior (Dreikurs, S., 1986, p. 112).

Kramer recognized transference in that art sometimes mirrors what is going on in the client-therapist relationship. She stressed the unity of the process and product, recognizing that teaching art is concerned with a product while art therapy is interested in the process. The process reflects inner experience as well as inner consistency.

THE ART DIRECTIVE: Portrait drawings

Process: Choose a partner and take turns drawing each other's portrait.

Objective/Rationale: To recognize yourself in the drawing you made of the other person – projection – but also to pick up on possible transference or how we relate to one another based on past relationships.

Elinor Ulman shared with the others a belief in the transcendent value of expressive art; that art can be both psychotherapy and art education; that art is the meeting ground of the inner and outer world and expresses the client's experience; that therapy aims at a favorable change in personality; that the basic task for the art therapist is to help people begin to understand themselves through the art form and process. She felt that the quality most needed by the art therapist is "the courage to trust the process without attempting in advance to chart the voyage."

Janie Rhyne (1984) is part of the Third Force in humanistic psychology, belonging with those who call themselves existentialists, phenomenologists, mystics, and Eastern philosophers. These are theorists who believe that we seek self-actualization, and that the human self is by nature endowed with a patterning that guides us toward healthy growth. In this group are Jungian art therapists ("active imagination"); Tibetan Buddhists who use art as a discipline, and those who use art for centering, and Gestalt art therapists who focus on increasing awareness of individuals in a here and now environment, Existential art therapists who simultaneously dialogue with the art and dream imagery of their clients and explore their subjective experience, and Adlerian art therapists, who focus on the value of group work and connection with others as well as the phenomenological experience of their clients.

Mildred Lachman-Chapin (Object Relations Theory) saw the value of group art therapy, and warned to avoid activities aimed primarily at keeping the patients busy. Visual imagery was the most important, because "art symbolizes what the ego suppresses." She used movement to encourage art work, believing that movement is personality made visible. Groups work well when the power of the leader(s) is minimized and when others are invited by the artist to contribute their thoughts.

THE ART DIRECTIVE: Draw where you are right now.

Process: choose any art supplies and then draw where you right now.

Objective/Rationale: We ask the questions, "How does your drawing help you to understand what is going on in your life right now?" "How is this drawing different from the free drawing?" to demonstrate that it is possible for you to understand what is going on in your life in the moment when you explain your drawing to others. Using dialogue with the images helps to bring the unconscious into consciousness.

CONTRIBUTIONS OF C.J. JUNG TO ART THERAPY

Carl Jung (1865-1961) founded analytical psychology and extended the role of therapist as researcher-observer-listener to that of active participant while centering on the patient. The technique of "active imagination" encourages the patient to fantasize (invent) the continuation of possible endings to dreams. Dreams and fantasies are related to cultural myth and symbol. Jung believed that the deepest levels of the unconscious are already pre-structured at birth by the archetypes that psychologically parallel the biological instincts, and thus his theory is called "depth" psychology. Like all instincts, archetypes can remain dormant in an individual until activated by events in that person's life (e.g., a mother "mothering," a soldier "soldiering"). Archetypes unconsciously structure universal happenings in life such as the symbiotic attachment to and eventual separation from the mother.

Images and symbols are seen as communication from the psyche, a belief that "the unconscious does not lie" (Jung), and so images can be a metaphor for inner need. "What is deeply felt but only dimly perceived can only emerge as a symbol" (Jung). Successful interpretations of images can only be made through mutual understanding and insight between the patient and therapist. Jung's early impact on art therapy was more inspirational than conceptual, but he did recognize the human spiritual need for self-understanding, and hypothesized that "madness" is not sickness but an attempt at self-cure, something he felt he himself had experienced in his own life recovering from what he called a psychotic break (Jung, 2009).

Jung believed "the healing force comes from the life force of the patient" and that the therapeutic aim is to encourage the process of individuation, self-discovery, and attainment of wisdom. Individuation is the process of becoming aware of oneself through the life stages toward becoming a person separate from others. We enter into a relationship with an image which prompts the question, "What is your art work telling you about how you live your life?" The idea is to understand the symbolic image and to transcend the meaning the ego might give it knowing that the ego sometimes needs to defend itself against the truth. Jung called for an integration of opposites: that of which we are unaware, "the shadow," with that of which we are aware. Jung also acknowledged that the "Self" can compensate for any imbalance that can arise.

"Self" is understood as "Inner wisdom" or "inner guide" and also what Edith Wallace (1990) calls the "creative source" and recognized that "if we do not live our potential, we become sick." Living our potential means health and wholeness. Clients take different colors of tissue paper (the only art supply besides glue and paper that Wallace provides) and tear them into pieces, something that is done playfully. They then glue down the pieces to form a collage. Attaching meaning to their art work is part of the process. Wallace felt that art therapy accelerates both healing (self-understanding) and a chance to be creative – the two are seen as synonymous.

THE ART DIRECTIVE: Tissue Paper Collage
Process: Tear up tissue paper into pieces and use those pieces to create a work of art. If you are willing, discuss your art work with others.
Objective/Rationale: We process with each other to discover how our art has relevance to our current life situation.

CONTRIBUTIONS BY OTHER THEORISTS
Neo-Freudians include Henry Stack Sullivan, Karen Horney, Erich Fromm, and Donald Winnicott. Each made their own contributions along with developmental theorists Jean Piaget and Erik Erikson. For these theorists,

the interpersonal relationship becomes more important than intrapsychic operations. Winnicott believed in the value of play and used art extensively in his work with children. He did "squiggle" drawings where he and the child would take turns adding to the "squiggle" and then talk about what they saw in their work together. We practice doing "squiggle" or "scribble" drawings with each other.

OBJECT RELATIONS THEORY AND SELF PSYCHOLOGY

Object relations theory is a psychodynamic construct based on psychoanalytic psychology. Heinz Kohut (2009) postulates that how we subjectively relate to the world is based on deterministic principles; the behavior is "determined" by how we experienced and related to our mothers ("objects") when we were infants. The primary motivation of the child is object-seeking, finding satisfaction in relationship to others. The child's reactions to the repeated, but perhaps not intended, empathic failure of the mother can become a threat to self-esteem and make it difficult for the child to separate and become an individual. The child might not be able to achieve an identity and object constancy, a term used to describe knowing the mother is there even though the child cannot see her. Children are usually able to substitute with a transitional object, e.g., a small blanket or stuffed animal that represents mother's comfort (Baker & Baker, 1987).

The difficulty, according to this theory, is that self-esteem, self-control and self-confidence are lacking due to failure of parental empathy to meet the developmental needs and transferences of "mirroring, idealizing, and alter ego" during childhood, leaving the child overly dependent on those in the environment to provide these functions (Kohut, 2009). These internal needs are called self-object needs and are different from object needs. Objects are valued for who they are, independent and autonomous. Self-objects are valued for the emotional stability they provide. Meeting the needs of the self-object is more important than who meets it. The way in which the child resolves this serious failure (lack of acceptance, trust, respect, and encouragement) is reflected in the adult personality. The "self" in self-psychology is the center of the individual's psychological universe.

The dual nature of self is underscored, not the unity of the personality: the "I" that experiences itself and the "I" that takes action.

In infancy self-object needs are intense and must be externally met. During adolescence, the peer group is a crucial self-object; in adulthood, the spouse, friends, and even career may be self-objects. The individual whose needs have been adequately met is able to develop reliable, consistent, internal ways of meeting self-object needs and also broaden who or what may serve as self-objects (Baker & Baker, 1987). Failure in integration and self-cohesion possibly result in borderline and narcissistic personality disorders. Both disorders are a retreat from autonomy and an attempt to return to the perfection of an early state of oneness with the mother.

The narcissistic personality suffers from feelings of inner emptiness (which may lead to addictions), a deep lack of self-esteem (which is played out in grandiose behavior), and perfectionism. Three basic personality types that result from consistent shortcomings in mirroring self-object relationships are 1) merger-hungry personalities, which must continuously attach themselves to self-objects in such a way as to be unable to "discriminate their own thoughts, wishes, intentions from those of the self-object;" 2) contact-shunning personalities, which avoid social interaction and become isolated; and 3) mirror-hungry personalities, which are compelled to display themselves in such a way as to obtain continuous confirming and admiring responses, without which they feel worthless (ibid, p. 30). These personalities will alternate between depressed, hopeless withdrawal and outbursts of enraged acting-out. They want you to admire them and keep busy with them. Most symptomatic behavior is viewed as an (emergency) attempt to maintain and/or restore internal cohesion and harmony.

Donald Winnicott, a pediatrician turned psychoanalyst, believed that therapy necessitated a "careful understanding of the early failures" and "provision for a safe environment in which the intra-psychic structures can develop and the potential for creative living can be regenerated" (Winnicott, 1971). The art process can illuminate the above symptomatic behaviors, and the art product encourages creativity and the client's progress to individuate. Progress is made when the client becomes more invested in his or her own art work which can become a self-object, relieve tension, build ego strength, and make the inner imaginative world more congruent with outer reality. In object relations theory, insight or cognitive awareness is not as important as having a healthy relationship ("a transitional space") with the therapist as a way for change and cohesion to take place (Winnicott, 1971). "The significance of the transitional object in establishing trust has become an invaluable concept, especially when we encounter narcissistic (and borderline) disorders" (Robbins & Sibley, 1976, p. 5).

BEHAVIOR THEORY AND BEHAVIOR THERAPY TECHNIQUES

B.F. Skinner (1904 – 1990) believed that awareness is of social origin: we learn the consequences of our behavior from others through punishment or reward. Skinner studied nature and believed that positive reinforcement creates a world from which people are not likely to defect and which they are likely to defend, promote, and improve. In behavior therapy, art therapists encourage the art process with their clients from the belief that creating beautiful things increases the chances for living in harmony with self, others, and the world around them. Operant conditioning is a form of learning in which an individual's voluntary behavior (the action) is modified by its consequences either by reinforcement or punishment, and sometimes extinction (Wolpe, 1990).

Other techniques to modify maladaptive stimulus-response patterns used to increase useful functioning in life and to encourage more social responsibility include aversion conditioning – designed to modify antisocial habits or harmful addictions by creating a strong association with a disagreeable stimulus; and systematic desensitization – designed to help the individual learn relaxation techniques to help with extinguishing fear and anxiety responses to specific phobias (ibid.). Aversion conditioning can be thought of as a form of punishment, and can bring about revenge. Positive reinforcement is almost always more effective.

The behavior therapist is not looking for conformity (which can be interpreted as a threat to individuality), and is not concerned with the unconscious (dreams, fantasies or the meaning of an art product). Art making is used especially to help children shape their experiences, their reality (truth), with an increased awareness of abstraction. Using art therapy with autistic, emotionally disturbed, and mentally challenged children can be "helpful with sensory regulation and integration, self-expression, cognitive and physical development and visual-spatial skills" (International Art Therapy Organization). Art materials provide sensory stimulation – texture, color, shape – to implement self-expression and conditioning techniques, replacing old or undesirable behaviors with ones that can reduce dysfunction and improve the quality of life. Art can also encourage movement from an outer locus of control to inner locus of control by offering choices and ways to create symbols and signs when language does not work.

THE ART DIRECTIVE: Create form and "something beautiful" by using colored shapes in different sizes.
Process: Cut colored paper into shapes of different sizes, working individually or in collaboration. Select shapes and create an art piece.
Rationale: That something beautiful can be made by using simple forms; children whose disorders range from low functioning to high functioning can find success with this art project.
Objective: To invite the children to choose and create something with the pieces that they have chosen.

HUMANISTIC THEORY: THIRD FORCE
MOVEMENT (MASLOW – 1908 - 1970)
Some useful philosophical and psychological contributions to humanistic theory include an optimistic view of human nature and of the human condition, a hopeful sense for the future, and holism, the view that the whole

is greater than the sum of its parts (Smuts, 1926). Our disposition toward the positive has its origins in genetics and in the chemistry of our brain and in our own creative process. People are exceptionally prone to the influence of suggestion as researched by Jerome Frank (1961) who developed the Expectancy Theory: "What I think is what I get." The use of a placebo shows an improvement rate of 35%. We usually move in the direction of making our anticipations come true. Julian Rotter (1966) called this the "self-fulfilling prophecy." The term "resistance" is used when the client is not ready or able to move in the direction of health, and discounts anything that is emotionally unbearable at the time.

The art therapist coming from a humanistic point of view believes that we all have the potential to grow and develop, that we can be creative and take responsibility for our own lives, and that interpersonal relationships are of primary importance when working with others to solve problems and improve performance. The primary source of well-being is the conviction that our lives have meaning and direction; that to change our lives we must first change interfering beliefs and/or behavior that is creating conflicts in our relationships with others; that art reveals more than words can say.

Phenomenology is the study of the development of human consciousness and self-awareness, understanding how we subjectively experience life. Carl Rogers (1902-1987) believed that the client has the capacity to find solutions to his or her problems, given a sympathetic listener. Martin Heidegger (1889-1976) was a German existentialist who noted that how we perceive says something about who we are. He believed that art can reveal the hidden aspects of our being by making them accessible to consciousness and to conscious investigation. He also held that we need to intuit the information from the art piece because there is no standardized meaning. We subjectively give meaning to the art work, which represents our inner reality.

William James (1842-1910) brought us the idea of "a stream of consciousness," the creative process of life that can be made visible through art. Wolfgang Kohler (1887-1967) introduced us to Gestalt psychology:

that our lives (reflected in art) present a unified pattern; no part can be separated from the whole. Kurt Lewin (1890 – 1947) a German-American psychologist, also a Gestalt thinker, contributed to social psychology: "Behavior is a function of person and environment."

Bruce L. Moon is an art therapist who wrote, among other books, one called *Existential Art Therapy: The Canvas Mirror* (1990), which looks at understanding the client's inner conflict due to confrontation with death, freedom, responsibility, choice, and the possible meaninglessness of life.

Shaun McNiff (1992) is an Expressive arts therapist using the framework of depth psychology: "attending to the soul." He promotes the classical form of the dialogue with the image as an ongoing process. There are no fixed meanings or objective labels.

Natalie Rogers (daughter of Carl Rogers) wrote *The Creative Connection: Expressive Arts as Healing* (1993). She believes that using the expressive arts can enhance and deepen verbal psychotherapy; that it is a natural evolution of the philosophy that integrates mind, body, emotion, and spirit. Her training program is dedicated to personal and planetary healing through re-awakening the creative process.

Adler, his disciple Rudolf Dreikurs, and other Adlerian therapists theorize a biopsychosocial understanding of human beings: We know more than we understand; we make choices; the life of the human soul is not a "being" but a "becoming." We move toward self-chosen goals that we feel will give us a place of belonging in the world, provide us with security, and will preserve our self-esteem. We strive for significance, completion; perfection; self-mastery; and inner equilibrium. Sometimes we find out that the real cause of discomfort in our lives reveals itself in a hidden belief. It can be a deeply rooted fear (or doubt) about ourselves that began in childhood long before we could make sense of it. Sometimes the situation in the family, the school, the community, or the environment needs to improve.

When making art, feelings of inferiority leading to tension and anxiety can be replaced with a sense of peace. Feeling at ease encourages personal insight. Insight frees us to create new possibilities for understanding and resolving conflict in our lives. From these possibilities we can then choose new behaviors and attitudes which might help us meet the challenges of life in more useful ways. Reflections on individual issues can also be reflections on universal issues.

THE ART DIRECTIVE: Torn Paper Collage, (Dreikurs, S., 1986)

Process: Take old paintings that no one wants anymore and energetically tear them into scraps. Roll out large pieces of brown paper onto the tables, take the torn pieces and create one or more collages. If there is more than one collage, move around the room and add whatever you want to each one. Feel free to use paint on the collages. Tee thought this was a good way to express anger, and sometimes this worked. I usually told students to tear up the pieces in whatever way feels right to them.

Then, using more of the torn-up pieces, create your own collage.

Tape the large collage to the wall and also the smaller individual ones. We talk about the process and the art work and what it means for us in our lives right now.

Objective/Rationale: to encourage cooperation and a feeling of belonging; to learn that no matter how much is destroyed, together we can build something new and beautiful; that we can create beauty out of chaos (Dreikurs, S., 1986. p.85); a metaphor; that by letting go of irrational thoughts or useless ways of behaving leading to conflict and unhappiness can open the way to transforming them into new thoughts, attitudes and behaviors.

A POSTMODERN PERSPECTIVE ON
ADLERIAN ART THERAPY

The followers of Modernism, a philosophical movement beginning in the late nineteenth century, rejected the empirical deterministic world as found in the beliefs of the Enlightenment and opened the way for acknowledgment of self-consciousness through art, poetry, and literature. People began to realize they had the power to create and to improve their environment by experimenting with new ideas using scientific knowledge and technology. Knowledge or truth produced by the rational objective knowing self was thought to always lead toward progress and perfection and the universal truths about the world.

Postmodernism rejects the certainties of Modernism. Postmodernism is a world view that denies the existence of universal truths, or the possibility of using reason to establish objective fact. Truth and justice are considered abstract notions. The Postmodern view suggests we not set ourselves up for failure with an idealistic humanist tradition that no longer works in the eyes of the world. From a postmodern perspective there is no universal ethical principle guiding our moral acts, and absolute truth about reality does not exist.

How does this philosophical approach fit with the practice of art therapy? We understand that the creative process in whatever form it takes is as intrinsic to us as speech as a way to express ourselves. The art done in art therapy is understood as an expression of how we experience the world around us and documents our process of "becoming;" that we each have a piece of the "truth" (Dreikurs, S., 1986) and so the "truth" takes on many different meanings. We create the "truth" to confirm what we already think, or as others have said: "We create the world we live in by the way we think." Twenty-four centuries ago, Democritus wrote that, "There is nothing true, or if truth exists, we do not know it. We have no means of ascertaining the truth on anything. Truth is at the bottom of an abyss" (Lefèvre, 1879, p. 89).

THE ART DIRECTIVE: Chasm drawing (Evadne McNeil, 1987, Atira art therapy program).

Process: Take a sheet of paper, any size and any color, and art supplies with which you want to work. On your paper draw or create a chasm, an abyss. Include where you are in the drawing and how you would get from one side to the other of the abyss. Journal about your art, and if you are willing, share what you have written with the class.

Objective/Rationale: To see how you find ways to solve problems, how your movement to seek the truth fits with your lifestyle pattern; confront, avoid, take the long way around, fly over, build a bridge, or any number of other ways.

CONCLUSION

Ironically, it is only in the process of becoming individuals, breaking the bonds of dependency from childhood, that we learn to function more usefully in our social relationships. In adapting to our environment, both social and physical, common sense as Adler conceptualized it becomes the means for finding balance and connection served by social interest and made more acceptable by evidence provided by scientific research.

Art in all forms helps to illuminate this growth process as we "compete" to find our way, not to be better than, but to improve our lives. Adler believed that artists and poets are the "leaders of mankind" (Ansbacher & Ansbacher, 1956, p. 153). The essence of art and Adlerian art therapy is human connection. Art therapy helps us understand, question, and challenge ourselves as well as those social and cultural conditions which are responsible for the abuse of power and control; domestic and community violence, educational choices, employment practices, immigration issues, health and welfare benefits.

Adlerian art therapy is a pragmatic approach to difficult situations, both personal and global. We learn to deal with problems that exist in specific situations in a reasonable and logical way. Together, we can work to foster a just and sustainable world. The truth reveals itself in art therapy, and can be measured by its practical consequences.

Our minds are shaped by
The continuous tension between
Wilderness and civilization, chaos and order,
Just as surely as by the genes we inherit.

Inspired by Barry Lopez, (1998). *Crossing Open Ground*

5

Art in Culture and Time: Socio-Cultural and Systemic Perspectives

Slides of Stone Age art give visual image to one of the ways we understand art therapy in today's world. From the development of specialized tools for different tasks, to cave paintings, rock art, and burial rituals, we have come to believe that art was used to convey what was important to the survival of early tribes. Some art objects and rituals from later cultures are still used today, e.g., Navajo sand paintings to treat both social disorders and physical illness, or as a focus for meditation and to direct creative energy. For many cultures around the world, such as the Sacred Dreamtime in Aboriginal Australia, art is considered a means to survival and can be considered just as important in our own lives.

Giving our own meaning to the symbols and emotions evoked in ancient art provides the background for discussing cultural issues. The purpose is to heighten awareness and sensitivity to possible cultural beliefs inherent in our lives through the language of art.

Evolution implies continuity as well as differentiation. The ability to make symbols and to create meaning arose in the complex interplay of social interaction. The confronting questions then and now are: "Who am I?" "Why am I here?" "What is the value of my life?" Art provides the ever-present, ongoing reflection of our experiences in answer to these questions, as well as a visible connection to others. Culture is the visual symbolization of the meaning given to events in our lives. Every culture throughout history searches for meaning and makes its beliefs manifest in their art (Arnheim, 1966).

Art records the changing belief patterns common to every culture and imparts those patterns to us as guides to living our own lives. For instance, religious art connects us to stories of forgiveness, redemption, and transcendence. Depending on how we experience life and how we understand the myth, these stories captured in symbol can still influence what we believe.

When we look at art, whether indigenous, classic, or modern, Eastern or Western, we are encouraged to experience its meaning emotionally and intellectually. The images, symbols, and myths that are represented all speak to us about our own experiences. We begin to realize that only the surface situations have changed over millennia. The emotional experiences of lives and relationships have changed very little; they are, in fact, universal. Myth and art, religion and history give us a window into our humanity and help to keep us connected to ourselves and to the social world around us.

We make art that demonstrates our spiritual connection to a particular culture: an African mask, an ancient rock painting, a Tibetan mandala, a Navajo sand painting, a crest or shield. In this sense, the word "spiritual" means to awaken or reveal to me something about myself, of learning not only who I am, but who I want to be – a personal journey – and it is the art which deeply connects me to the spiritual journey of others. We discuss the development of personality, the evolution of consciousness and spirituality, and learn once again that our experience shapes our lives according to how we understand, give meaning to, and remember it (Campbell, 1988). With art, we can make visible our invisible, intuitive world (Arnheim, 1966).

MOVEMENT IN LIFE

The creative process is the life process. As Adler said, "As artists we create our personality and lifestyle. Our movement (behavior) is directed by the goals we create" (Adler, p. 66). These goals often come out of the culture in which we live and are reflected back in the art we produce. From an Adlerian perspective, there is one central personality dynamic and that is what directs our forward movement in life. As children we learn to compensate for feelings of inferiority and look for a way which seems to promise security and success. The final fictive goal unconsciously directs our behavior as we attempt to move toward significance and success. It can be a goal of socially useful behavior or, in mental disorders, it becomes an unrealistic goal of exaggerated superiority over others due to an exaggerated feeling of inferiority thereby creating distance in relationships. The unconsciously chosen goal becomes the "final cause" of the behavior pattern and it is this pattern that we seek to understand in our art work. It takes courage to replace a socially useless goal for behavior with ones that lead to cooperation with others in a useful way.

Early art serves as a powerful reminder of the tribe's symbiotic relationship with the natural environment and how it served them, and still today serves us, as inspiration for awakening inner knowing, creativity and imagination and survival. Early stone sculptures of fertility goddesses had similar shared meanings to the cultures that made them. These goddesses were symbols of birth, life, animals, and the hope of an abundant harvest. These tangible figures symbolized concepts that were basic to the survival of the culture. Elaborate ritual objects made for burial sites connote the importance of the never-ending search for the meaning of death. Art became the bridge for coping with loss and for more abstract concepts such as what happens in the afterlife.

Several of the following art directives work especially well with children and adolescents, and also with families.

THE ART DIRECTIVE: Making a Mask

Process: Using whatever materials you want (paint, feathers, yarn, shells, sequins) create a mask using a paper bag. The front is to express what you want people to know about you; the back is designed to keep what you want hidden from others. What happens for you when you reveal the story of your mask?

Objective/Rationale: To understand that what we think we keep secret about ourselves reveals itself in our creation of the mask. My art therapy instructor liked the back side of my mask more than the front side. Surprise, I did, too.

THE ART DIRECTIVE: Stone Painting

Process: Choose a stone (or let a stone choose you) and paint on it or decorate it. Later you tell the story of your stone. This can include questioning current beliefs; remembering that some things last a long time, but nothing is forever. Sometimes a loving message is put on the stone and given as a gift in remembrance of a relationship. Or, once I remember a client took his painted stone and threw it into the lake. It was to symbolize letting go of a thought and behavior he was now willing to give up.

Objective/Rationale: We recognize that "Perception develops in the service of needs," (Arnheim, 1966, p. 187). All of life functions with the goal of survival in mind. Coping behavior (we change direction when meeting an obstacle) is distinguished from expressive behavior (refers to who we are through the use of symbolic imagery) (Maslow, 1954). "We see not with the eye, but with the soul," (Samuels & Samuels, 1975). Inner reality structures outer reality and will be in accord with the goals we unconsciously create for living.

ART AS LANGUAGE AND REFLECTION OF CULTURAL INFLUENCE

Art conveys the soul of a culture and provides the framework for the written word used to describe it. Ancient alphabets were based on drawings and symbols and have evolved into their present form. In visual art, the vocabulary is shape, line, color, volume, area, texture and composition which functions to convey individual and cultural meaning. A drawing is a visual metaphor – a symbolic interpretation of the images creatively imagined. Art is preverbal and can be understood by even very young children who recognize that drawings represent objects. Art is a "universal language" which is understood by people of every nation and culture.

Susanne Langer (1953) refers to art as "the creation of forms symbolic of human feeling" (p. 40). Language is not a substitute for images, but can add meaning to them.

Emotion is expressed in a work of art and relates to the soul. In Adlerian theory we speak of creating emotion based on what we unconsciously tell ourselves (private logic), and then use it to support our attitudes and behavior. Looking at the art of a client we would need to first understand the uniqueness of the meaning one attaches to the form or object in order to understand the feeling or emotion, and then still be careful to bypass the intrusion of our own projections.

With mass communication to explain what is important in the world and modern technology to keep us constantly connected to one another, we tend not to value our individual intuitive, creative selves as much nor do we spend much time alone. This leads to an imbalance, one that can put us at risk for discouragement and physical illnesses.

SYMBOLS

There is no direct transformation of experience into form and so symbols take on metaphorical meaning based on the intuitive meaning one brings to the form. Arnheim (1966) reminded us that "in a work of art every element is symbolic, that is, represents something beyond its particular self" (p. 219). Anthropological and art history along with the help of neurological research indicates that basic visual patterns appear in the art of every culture. These include the circle, cross, square, triangle, and spiral as well as dualities such as light/dark; chaos/order; above/below; left/right. There is no consensual or right way to understand symbols; they can have many meanings. "Dark" and "light" represent perceptual qualities. "Darkness" can evoke a mental response such as fear (evil and death), but also safety. Similarly, "light" can represent fear as with glaring light, but also airiness, lightness, playfulness, goodness, and knowledge. These are just thoughts meant to convey ambiguity since life is too complex for simple answers.

Other perceptual concepts that move beyond the form of light and dark would include familiar objects. A house can be conceived as a symbol of shelter and also a metaphor of the self. Likewise, a tree can be thought of as a growing thing which provides us with shelter and sustenance, but also can be a metaphor of the innermost self. It is no surprise then that early art therapists designed the house-tree-person projective test to assess aspects of a personality, brain damage, or intellectual functioning (Buck, 1948).

The Taoist yin-yang symbol or Taijitu is an ancient emblem symbolizing the principle in Chinese philosophy that everything is composed of two forces that are opposing yet complementary. This symbol represents the constant change as found in nature, but also constancy; that we can count on change in predictable ways: night and day, seasons for planting, growing and harvesting, and a time for rest. The polarity of the yin and yang can be understood as two principles seeking balance within the unity of the circle. The yin is the female principle and represents darkness, cold, moisture. The yang is the male principle and stands for light, warmth and dryness. Both symbols represent self and reveal mutual interdependence.

Harmony is not a given as "self" swings back and forth seeking balance with chaos. The two shapes might represent responsibility and freedom, or conformity and rebellion; introversion, extroversion; or even something as common as optimism and pessimism. These two sides carry over into society, influencing beliefs and values (culture) which might evolve into liberalism and conservatism; authoritarian and democratic; fighting and peace-making; kindness and violence. Two sides are not only inevitable – they are an intractable part of human nature and essential to a healthy society. This is no different than thinking about the symmetry of the human body and how externally and internally our bodies seek balance. Nature, too, seeks harmony or perfection in balance. Both sides are needed to bring balance.

THE ART DIRECTIVE: Yin-Yang Symbol

Process: Draw a circle. Using the yin-yang symbol, take disparate aspects of your life such as happiness and despair, and make each shape fit what you are experiencing in life right now.

Objective/Rationale: To express how you feel which will determine the size of each shape.

The circle is an ancient symbol used for understanding the self and is called a mandala. The eye perceives the sun in the form of a circle. Early human beings identified with the sun. Today we know that the sun is the center of our solar system, but our unconscious goals and feelings sometimes make us think we are the center of the universe. In moments of conflict and transition we need to take the time to center ourselves internally so that we can re-acclimate to the external world. The mandala acts as a gestalt for introspective reflection and consciousness, much like a diary. It can be thought of as an archetypal symbol representing the womb, the center of the universe, a chalice, regression, a temporary stopping place, or simply life, death, and rebirth.

The circle or mandala can be divided into four sections (combining the circle and cross) which are united into one. Jungians recognize four aspects of human behavior as thinking, feeling, intuition, and sensation. The Adlerian describes the holistic pattern of behavior using the terms perceiving, thinking, feeling and acting. A personal mandala is always in transition or transformation. This is the process of individuation for which the mandala is a symbol and can contain number formulations. For instance, the number four is the number of the cardinal directions, north, south, east and west; the four elements are earth, air, fire, water, and the four races of humankind, red, yellow, black and white (considered a subjective classification since we all share 99.99% of the same genetic material belonging to the same species, *Homo sapiens*).

The circle is a way to connect to the greater universe as well as to one's inner being. A ritual mandala is idealized and illustrates all aspects in total harmony that human beings strive for but are not able to attain. In Christian mandalas, Christ appears in the center, sometimes on a cross. The cross symbolizes the concept of the crossroads; letting go of the old, giving birth to the new. It also symbolizes the tree of life signifying the seed, life, death, resurrection.

THE ART DIRECTIVE: The Mandala Drawing

Process: Draw a large circle on your paper. Divide the circle into sections as you see fit: one section represents work; another friendship; another intimacy; and the fourth, spirituality. Inside each section draw your symbol for each task and for spirituality, a symbol to represent yourself. (A workshop presented by Norma Lou McAbee at the 1988 North American Society of Adlerian Psychology Annual Convention.)

Objective/Rationale: To heal the duality between the ideal self and the real self and to follow the innate impulse toward wholeness. There are no "good" or "bad" aspects to the situations expressed in the mandala. All experiences are thought to be equal and the task is to accept, understand the lesson they hold for us, and to integrate them in a useful way into our lives. Mandalas in Tibetan Buddhism are used as an aid to meditation and serve as models for "active imagination" (Jung, 1971). If one has stress, conflict, or a serious personal problem, one can construct a mandala and work towards a solution. This usually involves integrating one's own power rather than putting the power outside of self (giving power to others).

The circle represents connectedness to unconscious forces. Black Elk, the Oglala Sioux chief, speaks of the power in circles. All power comes from the sacred hoop of the nation. "Everything the Power of the World does is done in a circle. The wind, in its greatest power, whirls. Birds make their nests in a circle, our tepees were round and were always set in a circle" (Argüelles & Argüelles, 1985, p. 60). Time is thought of as circular. Indigenous people realize that in every moment and in every act there is an inseparable relationship and interdependence with every other creature and thing on earth and in the universe. Their lives and their art reflect this simple, yet dynamic ordering principle of the universe.

One of my students created a mandala for each day of the year after her mother died. It helped her deal with loss and to remember the gift of her mother's life and her life as well. She shared this book of mandalas in class with us, describing the meaning she gave those that caught our attention.

THE ART DIRECTIVE: Family Crest

Process: Take a piece of cardboard and create a family crest using symbols that mean something to you. Create the shape you want it to be.

Objective/Rationale: A family crest, sometimes called a "coat of arms," contains symbols to honor the family history and is an important piece of art usually associated with European cultures. This works well as a family project.

ART, SPIRITUALITY AND HEALING

There is a close association between art-making, spirituality and healing which has survived to the present day in many cultures. A primary purpose of making art is to explore the discipline of creating as a spiritual practice, as a way of awakening to our true nature and connecting to the beauty and mystery of life. It is in this connecting process that art-making has healing capabilities. Words tend to separate and create distance between who we are and what we experience. The art process and product serve to create and preserve this unity.

Early people saw themselves as part of a unity encompassing the physical and the spiritual, the visible and the invisible, and art was an everyday part of their lives. Native Americans and other indigenous people do not set out to create art for its own sake; weaving, pottery, or making jewelry is part of their life process.

Anna Walters (1989) writes, "In traditional Indian thinking, there is no separation between art and life or between what is beautiful and what is functional. Art, beauty, and spirituality are so firmly intertwined in the routine of living that no words are needed, or allowed, to separate them" (p. 17).

The Native American shaman describes disease or illness as disharmony or a loss of soul. In the process of sand painting, the Great Spirit is contacted, made manifest in the art and therefore available for healing. With the help of the Spirit, the soul can reconnect. The art object becomes embodied with the Spirit and thus becomes available on a physical plane for healing use by humans.

THE ART DIRECTIVE: Sand painting

Process: Take a flat box and tubes of differently-colored sand. Create a sand painting in your box with the option of adding sand tray figures. Write a story or a journal entry about what you see in your tray.

Objective/Rationale: to explore the meaning of your sand painting.

CONNECTING TO A GREATER POWER

Connecting with a greater power through art is a theme repeated many times in religious or indigenous art. For example, in the Catholic faith, healing energies are thought to be extracted from the many statues or small charms that people use to symbolize their relationship to God. The image of Jesus Christ and the cross are used also in many Christian churches to symbolize Christ's healing power. By focusing on these symbols with prayer, one is able to bring the energy to a personal level. Similarly, Tibetans create mandalas as a focus for meditation and to direct their spiritual energy toward self-awareness and expansion of consciousness.

For the Zuni people who live in New Mexico, fetishes are used for healing imbalance as well as celebrating new beginnings. Like the icons of the Christian faith, these small figurines "have a symbolic intent and are used to remind a person of the values that might help him or her live a more harmonious life" (Bennett, 1992, p. 3). Fetishes and the stories associated with them provide the Zuni with reminders of the natural forces around them and help them to access ancient wisdom in solving problems. They are used as tools for exploring one's own inner world and creative forces as well as asking for spiritual help. All creatures are thought to have spiritual power. Because of this, animal fetishes can act as a bridge to communicate with the natural forces of the world.

THE ART DIRECTIVE: Fetish or animal

Process: Take some clay or Model Magic and create a fetish or an animal for yourself. Give it meaning based on what you value in life.

Objective/Rationale: To use art to bring the unconscious, our private logic, into awareness so that we can have a better understanding of ourselves.

When the souls of animals are captured in stone, the animals continue to live on a spiritual level according to Zuni myth. Each animal also possesses unique qualities that are admired by humans. For instance, the Black Bear is associated with introspection, healing, solitude, change, inner strength in the face of adversity, and the color blue. The White Wolf is associated with loyalty, insight, revelation, social and familial values, clarity, inner guidance, expression of personal truths, new choices and the color white. A Zuni would consult the animal fetish that is believed to be the most helpful for solving difficult problems.

Without an art object people can still visualize by simply remembering an object or an experience. This is what Samuels and Samuels (1975) call "seeing with the mind's eye" (p. 39). These are called memory images. The person who holds an image in his mind can still experience the effects produced by the specific energy of the image. It seems to me that memory images are no different than what the Adlerian therapist calls early recollections (ERs), those early childhood memories which give direction to our lives, and that we can change the ER either consciously or unconsciously based on our experiences in life.

It is probably safe to say that since the beginning of time as we know it, people have received benefit from meditating on or visualizing an art object, whether it is in a cave or sand painting, a mandala, the figure of Mary, a family crest, an animal, or an Early Recollection. A person's own art speaks directly to that person about his or her own truth of self. Thomas Moore (1992) said that "the point of art is not simply to express ourselves, but to create an external, concrete form in which the soul or inner spirit can be evoked and contained – it is about arresting life and making it available for contemplation" (p. 303). Art constantly builds on the past and is constantly changing to reflect new ideas. Just as the artistic style changes with a change in the culture, personal style also changes to reflect this evolution in consciousness.

Healing then is about wholeness, completion, the unity of inner/outer, and the process of self-understanding. It means to understand and to integrate the gift of the symptom (i.e., depression, addiction). By accepting and understanding the symptom and its possible etiology we then have the power to change our attitudes, beliefs, and goals and possibly bring ourselves back to wellness. Neuro-scientists, doctors and psychologists have come to the agreement that the mind can improve the healing process in ways that traditional medicine cannot (Kotulak, 2006). Art and healing come together; art opens the mind and healing can begin. I believe we are beginning to know more about the complex interactions of the brain and can now target, chart and possibly modify areas to bring about certain kinds of healing, especially healing from trauma. The creative value of using art for bringing our private logic into awareness is so that we can have a better understanding of ourselves. The art also can be used to change those ERs which have only served to keep us trapped in feelings of fear and despair.

SOCIO-CULTURAL AND SYSTEMIC PERSPECTIVES AND THE USE OF ART SOME CONSIDERATIONS ON SOCIAL ACTION

Socio-Cultural and Systemic Perspectives and the Use of Art offers the opportunity to discuss the value of art and art-making as it relates to responsible social action. This opens us to current social issues as well as toward understanding our own cultural bias. We read theory and learn about research done on the role of community psychology in treating problems related to a range of pervasive social justice issues such as foster care, adoption, child custody, gender equality, transgender, youth delinquency, gay rights, gun control, health care, racism, immigration, re-migration, and environmental issues, all of which can impact the mental health of individuals.

Students spend a minimum of five hours a week involved in supervised community service engaged in activities such as youth tutoring, neighborhood development, and advocacy work. Child or adult, we are all the same in terms of vulnerability and creative potential. Separating us are life circumstances and certain policies, and these affect all of us in one way or another.

Many graduate schools and organizations design vision statements with the goal of promoting social justice and educating socially responsible practitioners. It requires critical thinking and informed inquiry. Social action begins first with becoming aware of where there is injustice and then understanding how this impacts and shapes our experiences as human beings. The goal then is to engage the community and use the power of the people to create new policies to attain health and well-being as well as caring for the natural world; the ideal of social justice or democracy.

SOCIO-CULTURAL DEVELOPMENT

Socialization is the process by which an individual becomes a member of a particular culture and takes on its values, morals, beliefs, and other customary behaviors in order to function in it. Culture shapes the brain just as does the land we live on, the families we live with, and the genes we inherit. Today there is greater focus on cultivating an awareness of the interconnectivity of life. In order to be culturally sensitive art therapists we need to be involved in learning about our own bias and then learn to recognize the cultural bias in the art of our clients so that we don't' misinterpret, or worse yet, "pathologize" the expressive art of our clients (Hocoy, 2007).

RESPONSIBLE SOCIAL ACTION

All life forms have very complex inherited behavior patterns for survival, including the ability to cooperate and compete with one another. In addition, humans have the ability to talk, agree, disagree, and come to new decisions. All human life means finding ourselves in the "circumstances" of the social and natural world around us. Ideally, social responsibility requires trust and respect for each individual and an understanding that each individual needs to act in the best interest of all others. When ethno-centric or self-centric interests are served at the expense of the common good, prejudice and pathology take over. "The three main components common to all psychopathology (maladaptive behavior) are discouragement, faulty conceptions, and lifestyle beliefs" (Sperry & Carlson, 1996, p. 5).

Adler was concerned about the unjust power of some over others and, like so many others throughout history, recognized the need to develop policies to care for all life forms. Without caring for one, the other will not survive (Adler, 1931, p. 241). Adler began with understanding oppressive policies in the workplace. He met with groups and encouraged cooperative effort to reform unjust existing situations. The members of the group shared a common effort and found success in working together toward creating social equality (Dreikurs, R., 1950, p. 6).

ART THERAPISTS AND COMMUNITY LEADERS AS CHANGE AGENTS

In class we discus social issues, how they constitute a reality for us and affect our behavior in both negative and positive ways. Art therapy is one way to bring into awareness, question, and challenge those social and cultural conditions which are responsible for the abuse of power and control, hatred, social isolation, guilt, and shame.

We need to think critically about those policies, including their underlying moral and ethical values that marginalize people or lead to personal suffering (Hocoy, 2005, p. 8). Art therapists rely on the image to bring to conscious awareness the reality of a current social problem as well as an individual's personal account of suffering. It is the image which awakens the conscience and leads us to a continuous process of social action (Hocoy, 2005), knowing that there will be no ultimate or certain truth.

There will always be a need for counseling, but equally important is the task to develop policies that bring about peace and social equality. As therapists we need to be culturally sensitive to the needs of the individual or group when we engage with them to solve their problems. We need to understand that no matter how oppressed a group might be, they still have the capacity to look critically at their reality and collectively solve their problems (Doherty, 2004). It is not helpful for one group to take control of another group no matter what the good intentions are for "fixing" unfair situations.

Taking responsibility for another group rather than encouraging their independence and autonomy invites entitlement, apathy, and resistance. Apathy discourages an interest in shaping one's own destiny (Allport, 1961). Learning and change happen faster when there is active participation in the process. Resistance may sometimes be a sign of strength that will help us know when power is being misused. These are complex tasks for complex times, but the challenge is not new.

EXPANDING THE USE OF ART THERAPY

One of the ways to encourage dialogue is through the art therapy process. As art therapists we have had to explain our process wherever we have worked: in hospitals, schools, prisons, treatment centers, living centers for older adults, and community-based studio programs. We will need to work just as hard to bring a broader narrative of art therapy into the lives of those with whom we work to empower them to create quality-of-life changes. We can do this through making art together, step-by-step, first by developing self-esteem and a sense of empowerment, and then by challenging social perceptions and attitudes. Ideally, we will be able to encourage social interest and a more global ethic that benefits not just the individual but also the community.

We as human beings, citizens, and therapists have much to offer to one another. We understand quite well the social etiology of many mental disorders and physical illnesses, and know that some of these can best be addressed through changes in social policy. This fits with Adler's concept of shared social responsibility. The whole point for us as teachers or therapists is to become gradually expendable, to begin to recede to the sidelines as community members grow in expertise and confidence. The fight against poverty, neighborhood violence, a lack of health care and educational opportunities can be done by ordinary people helping and supporting one another toward healthy, creative changes in their lives. This takes time and the road is not smooth.

TWO EXAMPLES OF SOCIAL ACTION: USING ART TO ENCOURAGE STUDENTS TO STAY IN SCHOOL

Many inner city schools lack support services for students who are at risk of failure. These students live in impoverished neighborhoods and experience constant threats on a daily basis. Many students with emotional, behavioral, or social interaction problems drop out of school before graduation. Art Therapy Connection was established as an inner city year-long school art therapy program utilizing an Adlerian approach to help with group identity, group cohesion, and cooperation. In turn, a feeling of belonging and trust was established in the school system. Research revealed that a higher percentage of students who attended this program felt encouraged to stay in school and graduate (78%) as opposed to those who were not part of Art Therapy Connection (56%). (Sutherland et al., 2010).

"PUT AWAY YOUR GUNS, PICK UP YOUR PAINTBRUSHES"

This program was developed by Gail Roy, an art therapy instructor at Adler University, in response to a group of community leaders wanting help in addressing crime and gun violence in the troubled neighborhood where they lived. Those who came together, children, adolescents, adults, used art-making as a way to express the constant fears, loss of life and overwhelming grief in response to violence on their streets, chronic crime, domestic abuse, and murder. It helped people become aware of what it means to work together to not only protest the use of guns, but to do something proactive to counteract the frightening circumstances of their lives.

GROUP ART THERAPY WITH INMATES

Some students find practicum or work placement in the prison system either with juvenile delinquents or with adult men or women. To prepare students for this kind of work, we approach the subject as we do with any therapy, in this case, with an Adlerian approach to understanding criminal attitude and behavior. Our job as art therapists in the prison system is to provide mental health services in the form of group art therapy for the purpose of inviting healthy social interaction.

We meet with the prisoners and give them opportunities to do art and tell their stories. We use the same art directives as practiced in the course work. We are not the ones to determine guilt or innocence, nor do we make any kind of diagnosis. We are not there to correct the behavior, but just to provide space so that they can use art as a catharsis, and possibly be open to new learning in their social interactions.

ADLER'S PERSPECTIVE ON CRIMINAL BEHAVIOR

Adler would say that most criminals are able to act in accordance with the law; that most are not psychotic or "legally insane," but are lacking social interest and are not concerned with the well-being of others. Like all of us, they are struggling "to rise from an inferior position to a superior position" (Adler, 1976, p.131). In 2013 Kathleen Sebelius, former head of the Department of Health and Human Services, stated that "the vast majority of Americans with a mental health condition are not violent. In fact, just 3% to 5% of violent crimes are committed by individuals who suffer from a serious mental illness."

In the summer of 2008, The Chicago Cultural Center mounted an exhibition of approximately 100 art works by prisoners in some of Illinois' most restrictive prisons. Members of the Art Committee of the John Howard Association of Illinois, the state's only prison reform group, worked with the Illinois Department of Corrections to gather the art work and bring it to Chicago. The show, "Light from Inside: Art from Illinois Prisons," was meant to focus society's attention on the need for prison reform. Most of the artists were long-term prisoners or "lifers" who were self-taught because there are no art education programs in Illinois prisons. The art is inventive since the inmates use only what they have available: food wrappers of foil or plastic, candy or gelatin desserts, pencils, paper, and envelopes.

Participant George Goodman wrote: "When I'm painting, my mind and spirit are in the piece I'm working on and free from the confines and adversities of life in prison" (2008). The hope behind the exhibit was "to give insight into how justice programs are delivered and how programs using art can help prisoners" (John Howard Association of Illinois, 2008).

GENDER ISSUES FROM AN ADLERIAN PERSPECTIVE

Gender issues are discussed from a universal perspective and as the subject fits with Adlerian theory; recognizing that it was not until the 1970's that homosexuality was declassified as a psychiatric disorder in the *DSM*. Homosexuality occurs naturally across cultures and across species (Bagemihl, 1999). Sexual orientation is now believed to be genetically determined, and for the most part fixed, apart from any explicit choice, by early adolescence if not by early childhood.

Since 1983 Adler's theory for homosexuality has been publicly challenged and affirmation has been given to lesbian, gay, bisexual, and transgender (LGBT) individuals. In 2008, Dr. Erik Mansager wrote, "I would like to acknowledge without equivocation that many, many LGBT individuals do indeed 'meet the life tasks with courage, commitment, caring, confidence and in the direction of social interest'" (Mansager, p. 229). Since social interest was Adler's criterion for mental health, these two men publicly acknowledge that nothing else matters, and other Adlerian educators and clinicians agree.

The difficulties suffered by this group of individuals can be understood as a social injustice along with those which Adler has already championed (fair treatment and wages for laborers, social equality for women, democratic treatment of children in families and schools). Now we are at last beginning to understand the conditions the LGBT population has had to endure and against which they have had to protest, but there is still much work to do.

Today Adlerian therapists understand the conceptualization of Adler's challenge to work, friendship, and intimacy and want to make efforts to contribute to that purpose by reducing unwarranted prejudice. We need to move away from inhuman and abusive treatment and toward encouraging social inclusion. This becomes our unequivocal responsibility wherever and whenever we see discrimination and prejudice.

The feeling of belonging keeps us deeply rooted in life around us and holds the key to understanding ourselves and to developing social interest. We know about the effects of social isolation in different life situations. We find that by using art therapy with older adults, the home bound, those who are ill, especially children confined to the hospital, and in-school and after school programs, with troubled neighborhoods, we can find success in helping to cope with feelings of loneliness, fear, and anxiety.

Art therapists in this country have held art exhibits, symposiums, and conferences to spark discussion of different social issues. Part of our calling as art therapists is to understand and to look for ways to infuse responsible social action into our practice and advocate for basic human rights; an example of Adlerian theory in action.

THE ART DIRECTIVE: Draw your response to the work you are doing in the community.

Process: Keep a journal of your responses to your in-class art as well as in your community psychology course and community service practicum to be reviewed with your advisor and program director.

Objective/Rationale: to keep a record of your experiences in the community.

A unique self
Shaped by our social experiences
Emerges in our thoughts and behavior

6

Ethical Considerations for the Art Therapist

There is a code of ethics for every form of therapy and profession which students need to learn and practitioners need to follow. Ethics is defined as the study and evaluation of human conduct in the light of moral principles which may be standards of conduct designed by and required of the individual or group. All moral laws are simply statements that certain kinds of actions will respect all life. Morality is a social practice first learned as young children living in families. Moral concepts change as life changes. The idea of movement and change comes from the work of Heraclitus (535-475 BCE) that taught there is no permanent reality except the reality of change; that we are all in the process of becoming. All living things strive for perfection (wholeness) and survival, and ethical codes are designed and changed as needed, to protect and defend that right.

The moral imperative of most religions can be thought of as "love thy neighbor as thyself" and is understood as a logical outcome of consciousness that recognizes the interconnectedness and shared interdependence of all things. Religions evolve gradually from more ancient truths and continue to influence the cultures in which we live. Religious morals represent values which reflect what is subjectively considered essential for sustaining life. Self-awareness and knowledge of others influence how we experience and respond to the social and moral dilemmas of our lives.

THE ART DIRECTIVE: Responsibility and Freedom

Process: Draw two poles on either side of your paper with a line between them. Label one pole "responsibility" and the other pole "freedom." Draw where you are on the line between these two poles. Look at the drawings and give them meaning. Talk about what it means to be free and what it means to be responsible and what happens when there is too much or too little of either one.

Objective/Rationale: to remember that there can be no freedom without responsibility.

Some students felt imprisoned by their responsibilities: a job to pay their bills, school to finish, an unpaid practicum where they had to spend time with clients and report to supervisors, and also friendships to maintain. On the other hand, the knowledge that they were working toward social change and to make a difference in the world around them brought them satisfaction. Freedom, by comparison, felt empty, void of fulfillment, lacking connection to others, maybe even selfish, but important to have in our lives as a balance, but still to live responsibly (Patterson, 2004, personal communication).

"THE CATEGORICAL IMPERATIVE"

Immanuel Kant (1724-1804), a German philosopher, proposed The Categorical Imperative (1785) which is based on moral reason and not empirical experience: "Act only according to that maxim whereby you can at the same time will that it should become a universal Law." With this imperative you are not allowed to opt out of it or claim that it does not apply to you. For instance, Kant wanted to ban certain types of actions including murder, theft, and lying in every kind of situation. The rightness or wrongness of these actions depend on fulfilling our duty and not on their consequences, and is an example of deontological or duty-based ethics. The basic requirement in Kant's theory is the belief in the existence of God, a Higher Power, because without that existence there can be no morality. Kant believed a person was good or bad depending only on the motivation or intent of one's actions, and not on the consequences of those actions. By ignoring the possible outcomes of one's actions, this imperative was certainly subject to the whims of the individual for either altruistic or egotistical purposes.

Georg Wilhelm Friedrich Hegel (1730-1831), a post-Kantian philosopher, was educated in theology. His absolute idealism envisaged a world-soul that develops out of, and is known through, a dialectical logic. In this dialectic, one concept (thesis) inevitably generates its opposite (antithesis), and the interaction of these leads to a new concept (synthesis). This is the process of creativity, and it can be done alone or with others. This evolving process speaks to both the interdependence and the freedom of individuals interacting to create harmony. Freedom of choice and democracy do not exist when monarchy rules, inviting rebellion; moving toward anarchy, or dependency; allowing us to blame others or find excuses for our behavior.

Søren Kierkegaard (1813-1855) influenced the philosophic movement known as Existentialism. He taught that our moral standards are, and only can be, chosen but that it is our duty to live the Christian doctrine; "Do unto others as you would have them do unto you." Moral precepts are chosen based on our "subjective (intuitive) truth." We intuitively "know" right from wrong.

Social Darwinism is a sociological theory that applies evolutionary theory to social and economic relations. It holds that competition among individuals, groups, or nations ensures sociocultural advances, but Darwin himself thought the ideas of "hereditary improvement" were impractical and made no sense. Darwin's theory is based more on changes in the environment that eventually influence the collective sense of individuals. Darwin's theory does not equate evolution with progress, except in the sense that evolving species will be better suited to their changing environment. Darwin did believe that the cooperative effort of human beings could be understood as an evolutionary success. That would include learning to cooperate to improve the social and natural environment since survival is important for all living things. Some of us would believe that it takes a war to make improvements in social living; abolishment of slavery, for one. But even though slavery is banned, racial prejudice is still with us, and there are still many other inequalities which put distance in relationships.

FRIEDRICH NIETZSCHE (1844 - 1900)

According to Nietzsche, power over our own lives brings happiness and satisfaction that is the fundamental human goal. He saw ideal power in those lives where the limitations of self-love have been put into perspective. In such cases one is interested in and concerned about a situation, responding to it with respect for those involved and for the purpose of finding a useful solution, but not by either submitting to authority, or by putting oneself in power over others.

Nietzsche believed that, if the "will to power" is not allowed expression, if we don't feel we are in power or in control over our own lives, then we turn against others in outrage and even war. When others are in power over us and' try to control us, we sometimes respond by becoming discouraged. We demonstrate this feeling of powerlessness by being defiant, breaking the law, wanting revenge, or acting as if we are incapable of taking responsibility for ourselves by withdrawing. It could be said that the fundamental conflict in human life is between those who hold power and use it to oppress others, and those who are oppressed by power and seek to free themselves of it.

Alfred Adler's hypothetical construct of *Gemeinschaftsgefühl* or social interest is an ideal. It does not offer a do-it-yourself prescription and offers no easy solutions to finding harmony in social relations, but refers to an innate potential based on emotions that can be learned beginning in early childhood. We train ourselves to look inward to follow the natural inclination of our emotions as well as outward towards conscious awareness and service in the spirit of being socially equal with others. It is in our connection with others that we feel a sense of belonging, so necessary to living our lives on earth and survival. For Adler, social interest is the meaning of life; for Dreikurs, it is "contribution."

Social Interest has three components, the cognitive, the emotional, and the behavioral:

Cognitive: The ability to understand others and the human connection to all of life;

Emotional: The ability to feel attachment, empathy and compassion;

Behavioral: The willingness to cooperate with the social order of life.

The confusion arises when we seek not to be selfish, but also to keep our own advantage in mind. If we act according to what is best for us as individuals we will also be acting for the greatest advantage of others. An attitude of love toward our selves leads us to loving others. Genuine love is an expression of productiveness and implies care, trust, respect, responsibility and knowledge both for ourselves and others.

John Dewey (1934) wrote that human behavior is chosen by human beings to solve both individual and social problems (Instrumentalism) and that since life is constantly changing and bringing about conflict, the methods for dealing with problems must also change. Dewey conceived of democracy as a primary ethical value and considered education a tool which would enable the citizen to integrate culture effectively and usefully. All learning is a continuous process of reconstructing our beliefs and attitudes in life, and this leads to changing and keeping only those values that are useful in bringing about a democratic resolution to social problems.

Reinhold Niebuhr reminds us that the perennial tragedy throughout history is that we project the highest ideals but they are ideals we can never realize in social and collective terms. Most of us report having a moral compass and that we make ethical decisions intuitively without conscious reasoning. I can think of many examples where lives were saved because someone or some group of people spontaneously and courageously responded to a life-threatening situation involving others without giving any thought to their own safety.

In *Man for Himself*, Erich Fromm (1947) cautioned that problems of ethics cannot be omitted from the study of personality, either theoretically or therapeutically. The value judgments we make determine our actions, and their validity influences our mental health and happiness. Fromm believed that neurosis itself is, in the last analysis, a symptom of moral failure. In many instances a neurotic symptom is the specific expression of moral conflict, and the success of the therapeutic effort depends on the understanding and solution of the person's moral problem; movement from useless safeguards to what can be considered "common sense." That is, we have the capacity to move along a moral continuum from revenge to forgiveness, from cruelty to compassion, from selfishness to altruism.

SITUATION ETHICS IN ACTION

Circumstances bring the occasion to choose the appropriate behavior. Situation ethics calls for us to decide how to do good for whom in the moment of the circumstance (Fletcher, 1966). It focuses upon pragma (doing), not upon dogma (rules).

Ecology is the study of the relation between an organism and its environment. Ecological ethics takes as full account as possible of the environment for every moral decision. To be truly ethical, we have to decide and take responsibility for what we think best fits the situation and then be willing to learn from the consequences of our behavior. Situation ethics calls us to be sensitive to the here and now situation in all its complexity. It is not simplistic nor will it be perfect. One knows the rules but one is not afraid to break or change them. We are the ones to decide if we make the most fitting decision or not. It calls for a continuous effort to serve others in a responsible way without asking for anything in return.

ON DIALOGUE AND CREATIVITY

Theoretical physicist David Bohm (1992) took dialogue to an ideal by suggesting that people learn to listen to one another, to hear each other's ideas without judgment. His theory fits with the Adlerian goal of social interest. In true dialogue there is **no** attempt to make one's particular view prevail. It is more a common participation, in which people are working together to solve life's problems. Dialogue, Bohm proposed, can lead to a transformation of consciousness, both individually and collectively. It is only when we make decisions for ourselves that we can build unity and cooperation with one another. This involves first a deeper understanding of our own perceptions and then a conscious decision to make those changes (social action) that we think can enhance wellbeing.

Social emotions, such as compassion, shame, guilt, contempt, and gratitude, serve and can inform moral values. Each emotion includes a specific behavior to move us toward, away from, or against others. Some emotions bring personal rewards; others invite self-punishing thoughts (Damasio, 2010, p. 47).

From a postmodern perspective, art and social action can be thought of as interdependent. Focusing on social justice in the world outside of school, students find themselves to be key players in promoting community based projects with community members to intervene and reduce some of the disadvantages interfering with safety and well-being. For instance, Northeastern Illinois University Nan Giblin, Professor Emerita, helped to develop the International Conference on Art in Response to Violence (2010) to encourage understanding toward the role art plays in facilitating education about violence as well as healing from acts of violence.

HUMAN CARING AND CARE OF THE NATURAL ENVIRONMENT

Altruism – acting with the goal of benefiting another – even at risk to self, is a part of human nature (Piliavin & Charng, 1990). Human caring and the memory of being cared for become the foundation of our ethical and moral response to the social and natural world around us. Studies show that caring relationships are encoded in our genetic make-up and can improve the health of the helper as well as those being helped. The key seems to be in that mutual moment of feeling *connected* to others and/or the environment, rather than the outcome. It is in the process of changing oppressive or unfair situations that can help bring about mutual health and wellbeing.

To continue to help clients increase their influence over the outside factors that are limiting them or contributing to their problems takes co-operation among community members, businesses, volunteers, schools, churches, shelters, health clinics, governing organizations, and police with the therapists providing encouragement. We know that we all need to participate in our own destinies. We can learn to help those who are suffering due to unjust social situations, but we cannot do it for them. This is *Gemeinschaftsgefühl* or social interest: a sense of oneness with the community and cooperative action for the welfare of all. We need to act without losing the uniqueness of who we are and without giving up the power we have over our lives as individuals, free to make choices, but also to take social action when needed.

THE SOCIAL PURPOSE OF ADLERIAN ART THERAPY

Adlerian art therapy calls for us to constantly move toward an ideal that integrates the practice of therapy with the work of social action. Essentially Adlerian art therapy can be thought of as a living, growing system while maintaining structure and continuity. Like any system, it is incomplete and needs to remain flexible in order to make new choices in an increasingly complex environment. Conflict and diversity are necessary for growth. Learning from and taking responsibility for the consequences of our behavior is an ongoing process and calls for self-awareness.

The immediate goal of art therapy is to enhance cooperation and the feeling of belonging. Through the art-making process feelings of in-feriority leading to tension and anxiety can be reduced. Feeling at ease encourages personal insight. Insight frees us to create new possibilities for understanding and resolving conflict in our lives. From these possi-bilities we can change our attitudes and behaviors into ones which might help us to meet the challenges of life in more useful ways (Dreikurs, S., 1986).

THE ART DIRECTIVE: Come to an Agreement (Dreikurs, S., 1986)

Process: In small groups of 4 – 6 students take a large piece of paper and create a mural without talking or communicating in any way.

Then, staying in your group, take another large piece of paper and come to an agreement about what you will paint. No work is to begin until the group has come to an agreement about what you will do either as a group or individually toward what you will be creating.

When finished, the group is asked "Which of the two murals do you like best? Why?" "What transpired for each participant?" " In what ways does this process remind you of your Family Constellation?" "What was that experience like?" "What did you learn from your parents and from your interactions with your siblings?" "Was there a group leader?" "If so, what was the group's response to the leader?" "Is there a difference between the way you thought, felt, and acted as a child and the way you think, feel, and act today?"

Objective/Rationale: The democratic process takes time to evolve; that for an idea to work, everyone has to agree; that coming to an agreement takes time; that everyone can contribute something, that division of labor can bring satisfying results; that by cooperating and contributing, we find our place of belonging; that some people don't want to participate, and notice how the group responds when that happens; to look at the role of leadership, our expectations, the role of emotions, learning from interactive experiences, and the process of self-reflection.

FOSTERING PROFESSIONAL ATTITUDES AND BEHAVIOR

Positive professional attitudes and behavior are first modeled by the instructor in the classroom as students learn to effectively interact with one another while discussing various issues and the self-created art that they voluntarily share. Students learn to respect each other and maintain appropriate boundaries of privacy as they integrate the Code of Ethics for art therapists as well as for counselors. Learning to express empathy and to respect autonomy is a sign of encouragement to clients, as is taking social conditions into consideration while maintaining professional competence.

The skills that are learned in the classroom can be carried over into the workplace, both with other professionals and with clients. Professional development includes self-directed learning, self-assessment, and taking responsibility for professional and personal choices. Students enrolled in the Art Therapy program today are required to take a Professional Development Seminar. This might be an appropriate time for students to create their own "class pledge of professionalism" to include agreements about desirable attitudes and behaviors, teamwork, community service, and participation in professional organizations.

Even though I don't believe that ethics can truly be "taught," it is necessary to integrate this topic throughout the art therapy curriculum to encourage self-reflection, personal values, shared stories, and a collective method of inquiry. If I were teaching this course now, I would include the following experiential designed by Duanita Eleniak, Director of the Adler University Vancouver Campus Art Therapy program, called "Image of Ethics." She asks her students to "create a personal 'Image of Ethics' to take into their offices after graduation – as physical reminder to always practice at the highest level of integrity."

THE ART DIRECTIVE: Image of Ethics

Process: Create a piece of art, using any materials you wish, to express the meaning you give to the term "ethical practice." This work can be done individually or in a group.

Objective/Rationale: To discuss the feelings that came up when working individually or in a group. To explore the meaning behind the visual image and the following words:

- goodness
- beauty
- integrity

- trust
- cooperation
- communication
- connection
- belonging
- creativity
- democracy

To integrate the meaning of ethical behavior and to have a visual reminder as you begin your practice in the world where there is poverty, homelessness, prejudice, fear, isolation, violence always on a continuum with beauty, kindness, grace, wealth, generosity, harmony, good will, and friendship.

CONCLUSION

I remember working with my colleagues to create the following vision statement for the Adler School:

"Socially responsible graduates are those who embrace a diversity of perspectives; work to build and maintain bridges across social, economic, cultural, racial and political systems; empower others to identify and address shared problems; and foster the development of social equality, justice and respect through compassionate action throughout the global community" (ASPP, 2006).

Well-being begins with the individual, which in turn, can influence the well-being of the family, which leads to being contingent on the conditions of the community, and so forth. It is a mistake to think that therapy can focus only on individual interventions; it must take into consideration all the other socioeconomic determinants of health, values, policies, and resources for the well-being of all. Cooperative participation in change is necessary so that we can all have power over the decisions that directly affect our lives. Social action and art therapy can bring about confrontation of the injustice of social problems and environmental issues, as we look for ethical and sustainable solutions.

In class, we read and discuss the current *Ethical Principles for Art Therapists* as written by the American Art Therapy Association (2011).

Art calls for a compassionate
Response to the needs of the world
And to each other

7

Child and Adolescent
Adlerian Art Therapy

We are all social beings with the need to belong and to be accepted. We do this by striving for significance. According to Adler, it is our basic human motivation. Security, or the lack of it, depends upon our feeling of belonging. The absence of a connection with others has an adverse effect on our thinking, feeling, and behavior, as well as on our physical and mental health. The art therapist's task is to understand the purpose of the child's or the adolescent's maladaptive behavior as well as the source; whether it is biological, familial, environmental and/or socio-cultural. Art therapy can act as an intervention to improve emotional and social well-being by encouraging cooperative behavior and social interest leading to the feeling of belonging (Dreikurs, S., 1986).

AN APPROACH TO UNDERSTANDING CHILD DEVELOPMENT
Emotional closeness and communication greatly depend on the early relationship between the child and mother or caregiver. A pattern of intimacy is shaped when the mother's and infant's needs are mutually satisfied. Separation from the symbiotic bond begins when infants learn they have some control and can influence the relationship to mother and others by the response they get to crying, smiling, babbling, and making eye contact. This, in turn, can influence how secure the child might feel, how verbal he or she might be, being able to separate and function independently, and even the kind of adult relationships the child might have.

As young children grow in awareness of others, they learn to fear in response to what they innately experience as a very real threat to survival and also a perceived state of helplessness and abandonment especially when there is no response to their cries for help. Children lack the experience needed to interpret life situations and to make their needs known in ways that others can understand. Fear and helplessness can shut down communication and the ability to learn, bringing about discouragement.

Discouragement can also lead to misbehavior, which can continue until steps can be taken to address the mistaken goals of misbehavior – whether it is to get undue attention, power, revenge, or to withdraw from others – so that the child can reorient toward more useful behavior (Dreikurs & Stoltz, 1990; Dinkmeyer & McKay, 1976). Healthy relationships depend on others being able to understand the child's needs and respond to them appropriately. But none of this *determines* the behavior of the child. Children are creative and make their own choices based on how they grow and understand their experiences in life.

PARENTING

Growing up in a family has a profound impact on how we choose to be parents to our own children. Even though parenting styles have changed over the years, we mostly parent as we were parented until we find it doesn't work and then we try something else. I learned along the way that handing out punishment or rewards puts responsibility for the child's behavior on me. Punishment invites resistance, power struggles, and retaliation; rewards communicate that it is more important to meet the demands of other people than to become inner-directed. Encouragement implies cooperation and is not the same as praise or reward. Encouragement allows for the happiness of success as well as the pain and frustration of failure, and lets the child take responsibility for both. Acknowledging the effort and improvement fits with the concept of encouragement and has proven to be successful through the benefit of research (Dinkmeyer & McKay, 1976).

Watching a child play or draw can usually communicate to a therapist the extreme fear and feelings of inadequacy that a child can experience when his or her needs are not being met. The therapist can then communicate this understanding to the child, and the attentive response affirms the child's experience. The social connection is made: trust in self (I can do something for myself) and trust in another (others can understand and appreciate me) is maintained or restored.

Creative and mental growth is the ability to be sensitive to problems, to attitudes and feelings of other people, and to the experiences of life. Inhibitors to the creative process include pressure to conform, undue competition, rewards, and even grades (Kohn, 1999). We can begin to understand a child's growth or an adolescent's experience of fear and inadequacy by observing their art. Watching a child create is the most reliable measurement of his or her understanding of the world. The attitude and behavior of the child give deeper meaning to the way the child experiences life. In contrast, the important part of an adolescent's drawing is more the content than the process, although both are important. I remember a boy of 12 who was given the choice to live with his mother or his father long after his parents divorced. I invited him to draw two pictures: one of what it would be like to live with his mother, and another showing what it would be like to live with his father. In the one with his father, he was happily reading to his step-sister, while in the other he was hiding outside of the apartment building where he lived with his mother. When he saw and understood the meaning in his two drawings, he knew he would be happier with his father. His mother and I were both surprised, because the mother had insisted that the boy wanted to live with her.

DEVELOPMENTAL STAGES IN ART

It is important to be familiar with the developmental stages in both the creative art and the child's behavior when making a connection between the creative expression and what the child might be experiencing emotionally.

In class we look at samples of children's art showing a cognitive and affective developmental sequence as proposed by Lowenfeld and Brittain (1987) so that we have a better understanding of a child's ability to "communicate" through art. Art challenges the child to create expression for feelings and thoughts, and because there is no right or wrong in an art production, the art becomes a source for success. We pay attention to the following:

1. Random Marks – evident in the child's experimentation with waving hands in the air or using fingers in finger paints.
2. Uncontrolled Scribbling – continued experimentation of kinesthetic experience
3. Controlled Scribbling (ages 2-4) – the child conceptually recognizes a connection between a mark on paper and him- or herself. Lines and color take on meaning.
4. Pre-schematic Drawing (ages 4-7) – The child makes representational attempts and is aware of him- or herself as the center of his or her world. Begins to draw human figures, houses, trees and discovers the relationship between drawing, thinking, and reality.
5. Schematic Drawing (ages 7-9) – The child's art work is highly individualized and signifies his ordered world of spatial relationships, baseline, skyline, and realistic use of color. Child moves from egocentric behavior to social interaction.
6. Dawning Realism (ages 9-11) – Peer influences now evident. More attention to details, realistic interpretation, more colors, decoration for art projects, disappearance of skyline.
7. Pseudo-Realistic drawing (ages 11-13) – there is heightened concern for natural surroundings. Greater interest is shown in proportion, perspective, color variation, detail, and sexual characteristics.

ART THERAPY WITH HOSPITALIZED CHILDREN
Using art with children in a hospital setting can provide opportunities for the child to reveal mistaken ideas about what is or will be happening

to them. By using the child's drawings, the art therapist can retell the story in a way that corrects misperceptions and minimizes fear and fantasy. Children will adapt their art making processes to their own needs. The art therapist is there to guide the child to understand his or her situation in a way that can be more comforting. Hospitalized children can regain access to their knowing, intuitive selves when the art therapist accepts and responds to their art work. This helps children move from fear of others to trusting others.

Thick layering of colors might indicate anxiety; certain body parts with which the child is experiencing difficulty might be omitted; heavy clouds might represent congestion; weather paintings could relate to the way they are feeling. I remember one painting of "rain," but done in a wash of beautiful rainbow colors as if looking through a prism. There are other findings that could be related to the feelings and psychological states of these children: selecting the same color paper and crayon might indicate a desire to blend in with their surroundings; smoothing over their work might be an attempt to "smooth" away their pain. Drawing a picture and then verbally describing all sorts of hidden surprises could be understood to mean they are looking to the future with the hope that it will be happy (McNeil, 1986).

The hospitalized child needs an art therapist who will not overprotect, feel sorry for, or create a dependency. The task is one of helping the child move toward acceptance or recognition of the situation and the concept that possibly he or she will need more help than other children. Often children "know" that everything that can be done is being done for them. Children are willing to cooperate and to adjust to difficult situations if they are treated with respect.

GENETIC DISEASE AND ART THERAPY

Children who are suffering from a life-threatening disease experience overwhelming feelings of impotence, alienation and isolation especially when they become aware of the seriousness of their condition. It is useful to find ways to help these children acquire some sense of power and control over their circumstances. Art therapy can be one of those ways which can help children work through conflicts of dependency, self-esteem, anger, body image and control over both body and environment (Dosamantes-Beaudrey, 2000). Art therapy with the families of the child who has a genetic disorder can help to alleviate the issues that follow diagnosis and to bring the family back into balance again.

One example of an inherited genetic disease is cystic fibrosis, a disease that affects the lungs and digestion system. "It is the most common genetic disease in the United States today and claims more lives than any other genetic disorder" (Fenton, 2000, p. 15.) The disease is noncontagious and is common to both males and females. It affects 1 in every 2,500 babies. Life expectancy has increased due to early diagnosis and improved treatment, but still there is no cure (ibid). Without denying the possibility of death, somehow a balance must be established that helps the child image hope and health. Art can provide a cathartic effect as well as empowering the child to face existential problems.

USING ART WITH SOCIALLY DISADVANTAGED CHILDREN

Children diagnosed as having ADD (Attention Deficit Disorder), learning disabilities, organic disorders such as Asperger's syndrome or autism, or any other developmental or emotional challenge, are socially disadvantaged children. Some of these children are on medication. According to the Centers for Disease Control and Prevention (2014), autism spectrum disorders affect one in 68 children from all walks of life (1 in 42 boys and 1 in 189 girls). One of the most complicated neurological disorders, with no known cause, it presents challenges facing families every single day. Today scientists believe that genetic and environmental factors both play a role. The art therapist's goal is to use art to build a trusting relationship with the child. A caring relationship with the child can help to counter feelings of detachment and even lead to an increased ability to trust and connect to others.

A nine-year old boy with autism came to see me once a week for several months. He liked to draw and could put on paper an exact replica of a certain ship, one that had many portholes, a unique feature of this particularly observant child. Over time he and I could have a short conversation about what he was drawing, but it was a long time before he could even look at me. He did allow me to sit next to him, and one of the things he liked to tell me was that he was not interested in playing with his brother or sisters or sharing his possessions with them; in fact, he would get angry if they even came into his room. Mostly he and I had a working agreement: I would furnish the paper and art supplies, and he would draw. I think that was as close as I could get to being able to establish a social connection with him. I always told him how happy I was to see him, but only once could I tell him how happy I was and hoped he was happy, too, when he mentioned that he had given some of his drawings away to others in his family.

This boy could experience fear or rage, and take pleasure in his drawings, but seemed to lack empathy for other people or to experience joy. One theory is that the mirror neurons in autistic children have been found to be dormant and inactive rather than missing. Stanley Greenspan and others have found that positive social interactive floor-time play appears to activate these mirror neurons and the child begins to develop emotionally by being able to include joy and compassion in his or her relationships with others (Greenspan & Wieder, 2009). I wonder what would have happened if this nine-year old boy had been in a group and we all did art and played together. Would he have been able to learn and join in with other children having fun and laughing and be able to do the same? Could it have helped to change the inner workings of his brain so that being with others would bring him the feeling of pleasure rather than pain? Maybe someday neuroscience will have the answer to this question.

USING ART TO COUNTER FEELINGS OF ABANDONMENT

Art therapy can also help to counter feelings of abandonment a child might have experienced at an early age possibly due to premature separation from a caregiver, possibly a divorce or a death. There are heartbreaking situations with children whose parent(s) is in prison or who are in the foster care system. Art offers a way for the child to express the rage, fear, pain, hopelessness and confusion which he or she might be feeling in response to the loss of attachment, or to other situations in which the child feels unfairly treated. Angry feelings usually come from a feeling of helplessness or powerlessness, sometimes fear.

FOSTER CHILDREN

Foster children present a challenge of their own that covers every single area of child and adolescent development besides the need to adapt to foster parents. Many of the art therapy students find work with DCFS and need to have a basic understanding of what this work entails so they can be helpful to both the children and the foster families. Helping the child feel a part of the family when many of these children have endured some of the worst abuse life has to offer presents a tough therapeutic practice where it is difficult to succeed. Most foster parents want to provide a safe home and to offer love, but sometimes discouragement takes over and both the children and the foster parents need therapeutic direction. This work, not unlike other therapeutic work, calls for flexibility and patience, hope and optimism, respect for and connection with the family. Working together as a family on an art project can help bridge the distance created among the foster child, other children in the family, and foster parents when there are misunderstandings and feelings of abandonment.

USING ART WITH SEVERELY AND PROFOUNDLY IMPAIRED CHILDREN

Intellectual impairment limits language development, problem solving ability, imaginary play, the ability to abstract, while physical and emotional development is slow and uneven (Wilson, 1997, p. 87). Still, there is the need for encouragement as art materials are used to expand the child's sensory, perceptual, and motor experiences and ability to connect with others. The ability to reach out and touch may come slowly. Appropriate materials can include water: soapy or colored, warm or icy; sand: wet or dry with sand toys as an option; crayons, chalk, washable markers, and paint to be used with brushes or fingers and white or colored paper; clay or Model Magic; items from nature; buttons, yarn, beads, and fabrics.

Care must be taken with these children so that the materials are used in a safe way. Sometimes equipment needs to be adapted for the child's use. Small steps can sometimes be made toward greater independence, more coherence, and flexibility as observed through the making of art. It can only happen if the child finds satisfaction and pleasure in the creative process along with a connection to someone who is gentle and caring, but not overprotective or interfering with the child's art (Lowenfeld & Brittain, 1987).

CHILDREN AND DEATH

Before the age of five the child experiences death as separation anxiety. The concept of death can usually be understood by the time the child reaches adolescence. Drawing can provide a "safe" place to be in times of confusion and uncertainty and allow for the expression and communication of unspoken fears in visual images. There are therapeutic groups for children who have experienced the death of someone close in their family. Art and creating a connection with others is important to reducing the feelings of isolation and loneliness.

WORKING WITH CHILDREN WHO HAVE EXPERIENCED TRAUMA

A traumatic event can be understood as a crisis for which one is never prepared. It can happen to anyone. Sexual abuse, as experienced by a child, is a traumatic experience that can have negative effects on the child's ability to socialize, and can affect long-term cognitive, behavioral, emotional, and physiological aspects of the child's life. Sexual abuse is understood as any type of sexual activity inflicted on a child by someone with whom the child is acquainted or is in a dependent relationship.

Sexual abuse may be done in a threatening or forceful way or it may be pampering where the child is made to feel special or enticed (Slavik, Carlson, & Sperry, 1995, p. 361). Family values for sexual behavior may fall on a continuum from comfort and affection to power and control leaving the child wondering what to accept and believe. "In sum, abused children...are frequently trained or self-trained to think of themselves as worthless or special" (Slavik et al., p. 361).

Trauma can also be experienced by children who have been physically abused, neglected in terms of basic needs and left without protection. Being a witness to violence toward a loved one or losing a parent or caregiver to death creates trauma in the form of stress, pain, and suffering, especially if that person is the source of security. Trauma experienced by children or adolescents can leave memories of unspeakable terror. Trusting others is difficult especially when pain is forced upon the child by a loved one.

In my art therapy training class Mary told us of her childhood sexual abuse by her stepfather and her older brother. Her mother was not protective, possibly due to her own history of abuse as a child. At age 13 Mary gave birth to a child.

In class as an adult, Mary continued to create art with us as a way to integrate newly emerging fragmented thoughts and frightening images from her years of abuse. She taught us that the early trauma experiences are too overwhelming for a young child to assimilate and therefore become dissociated. Dissociation is not the same as repression, and it was only in her twenties and early thirties that she could reflect on the symbolic meaning the unbidden trauma images and intrusive thoughts held for her life. I invited Mary to join me as co-instructor for this course. Mary shared with us the value of making art: that only by drawing the images and feelings that were now coming to her in her adult life could she move beyond the unending pain of abuse, isolation, terror, and dissociation to integration and relationships. She found trusting connection first with a therapist, then with us in the training program, and now with the students in our class. It was a gift for her to share her drawings of integration with us. In response, some of us drew our own moments of terror that came up for us and others drew the moment of resilience, showing how we were able to cope with terror-filled moments in our own lives.

Traumatic events also include terrorist attacks, mass violence, killings in public settings, domestic-violence including homicide and suicide, physical abuse, and neglect. The trauma may be ongoing, or it may be a significant single traumatic experience which might include a near fatal accident, or a natural catastrophe such as a flood, a hurricane, or a fire.

There is no definition for a traumatic experience that allows us to infer that it will cause certain emotions or behaviors. It is that individual's unique response to a subjectively experienced traumatic event that the therapist seeks to understand.

PERCEPTION OF TRAUMA

It is within the social context of the trauma that an individual's unique perceptions, phenomenology (how one experiences life), and the goals for behavior can be understood (Manaster & Corsini, 1982). This statement holds true for any of us and for any age and for any event in life. The child who is abused, however, seems to be at greater risk for loss of trust, power, control, and self-esteem.

Emotions in response to the trauma of sexual abuse can include sadness, horror, anger, fear, and anxiety; in relationships there might be fear of more abuse and betrayal coming from others, along with feelings of helplessness and inferiority, lack of autonomy and healthy development of social functioning (Herman, 1997). In the United States, the number of children at risk for post-traumatic stress disorder (PTSD) exceeds 15 million according to Dr. Bruce Perry (Szalavitz & Perry, 2010), a disorder that can carry over into adulthood. Besides emotional problems such as depression, dissociation, and anxiety, the experience of abuse can sometimes lead to substance dependence or abuse, self-injury, suicide attempts, eating disorders, personality disorders, and perpetrating violence towards others.

We know that interpersonal trauma does not discriminate and can include any race, age, class, gender, religion, and nationality. The development of social feeling and social interest can be severely limited, delayed, or negatively impacted by the event(s) of sexual abuse and assault (Cash & Snow, 2001).

For any of us, child, adult, and survivor alike, we can feel vulnerable and live in fear, possibly thinking we are always at risk of being in danger. We can suffer from PTSD and might unconsciously try to compensate for our feelings of inferiority with self-serving and self-centered beliefs and goals, arranged to preserve self-esteem and self-confidence. We put distance between ourselves and others when we find useless ways to compensate by abusing alcohol and drugs, developing an eating disorder, or resorting to self-injury.

The terror of the sexual abuse trauma often keeps the survivor from talking about what happened to them (Herman, 1997). We explore ways through art therapy to "break the silence" (Malchiodi, 1997) and to assist survivors as they learn to integrate their feelings especially as they relate to the unconscious safe-guarding patterns of behavior; depression, anxiety, and poor self-esteem (Slavik et al., 1995). The goal is first to offer comfort and support and, eventually, to provide a safe place where feelings of fear, rage, shame and doubt can be expressed. The creative process of art-making keeps one "in the moment" and can be a means of reconciling emotions, providing a safe catharsis of intense affect, and of restoring self-esteem.

For many children, group art therapy can be the place for a child to establish a trusting relationship first to one and then to others, to enjoy the connections made in the group, and then to extend this ability to create trusting relationships to the outside world. Self-reporting and observation of the child's attitudes, beliefs, and behavior help in understanding when the child has been able to make transitions that demonstrate cooperation, social interest and the feeling of belonging.

ADOLESCENCE

A task in adolescent years is the development of a sense of identity with which to meet the world. This calls for a greater awareness of self and others, especially in times of deep emotional disappointments and ambiguities about life. Most of what adolescents know about themselves they learn experientially in relationships with their peers. It is just this phenomenological aspect of life that is made visible through the images that emerge in their art work. In group art therapy, adolescents can focus on their strengths and what works for them in social situations as they learn to compensate for feelings of inferiority and inadequacy. Art-making encourages taking responsibility for behavior, and letting go of feelings of rage, helplessness, or inadequacy, which can be understood as unproductive attempts to be in power and to demand services from others.

In adolescent development, the familiar concepts of trust and respect continue to be equally important as in child development. Adolescents have the additional challenges of ongoing autonomy, initiative, sex differences, and individuation. The timing for development differs for boys and girls (Blos, 1979). Adolescents begin to find support more among their peers as they learn to separate from being dependent on parents. They begin to find a place of belonging by surrounding themselves (or not) with a new group. Although the personality is somewhat formed by this time, it can change based on peer relationships. Whereas the child had once modeled him- or herself on a parent, the adolescent now experiments with conforming to, and depending on, peer group standards for acceptance and belonging. This can work on a continuum both ways: one where the adolescent is rewarded with loyalty, empathy, and understanding, or risks rejection, ridicule, and ostracism if he or she does not conform. In response, again on a continuum from socially useful to socially useless, the adolescent will behave in ways that fit with his or her unconsciously chosen goal. Many adolescents choose to cooperate in a socially equal way with concern for others while other adolescents might exhibit an increase in being self-centered and striving for personal superiority over others.

I worked with a group of adolescents that thought of themselves as rejects from their social group and were discouraged as a result. They realized that what they liked to do didn't fit with the mainstream, or with the kids who were "popular." Most were intelligent and willing to cooperate, but not to conform to school social group dictates. Creating art in the group once a week helped them learn about each other, be in touch with their inner lives, find a sense of fulfillment and their own truth; as a result, they began to bond and to feel good about themselves. They took this secret bond back to school where they now functioned successfully and were glad for their sense of autonomy. Some of these students were with me for the two years I worked at the Response Center.

INFERIORITY FEELINGS AND EATING DISORDERS

Eating disorders can be thought of as the expression of inferiority feelings, and can be life-threatening. Mistaken messages a teenager, especially a girl, might be giving herself are "I am a failure," "I can never live up to the expectations of others," and so the symptoms of an eating disorder provide a distraction and even relief from the intense feelings of inferiority. When we feel in a position of extreme inferiority, one way we try to compensate is by being perfect. The goal of the behavior (being perfect) is meant to defend or safeguard self-esteem and is self-focused. Turning unhealthy behavior into a healthy focus on eating right, exercising, and thinking positively are goals for therapy that can lead to being sensitive to the feelings of others and less on the possible goal of "perfection."

DEFIANCE/CONDUCT DISORDER AND ART THERAPY

Conduct disorder is one of the most commonly diagnosed psychological disorders among minors (Feehan, McGee, & Williams, 1993). Those children (9 – 14) and adolescents (14 – 17) diagnosed with defiance or Conduct Disorder seem not to be concerned for the welfare of others. Certain acts of violence directed toward others, such as physical cruelty, stealing, fighting, and then lying to avoid punishment, serves to hide the child or adolescent's vulnerability or feeling of inferiority. Seemingly to be "in power" over others functions to offset this feeling of inferiority and serves as a way to cope with the circumstances of life as the child or adolescent understands them (Sweitzer, 2005).

Adler proposed that any oppositional behavior occurs when there is a lack of trust or security, and is usually experienced by children who come from homes where there is already violence. This child or adolescent might believe that the only way to survive is to behave in a way that maintains the fictional goal of being "in power" over others. Lacking self-understanding and the ability to be socially empathic, the child or adolescent arranges, without conscious awareness, to safe-guard self-esteem through misbehavior. They believe that others perceive them as they perceive themselves, to be inferior, and that the only way to live is to fight to be in power over – superior to – others. Economic disadvantage can lead to unhealthy competitiveness and violence, but the great majority of the poor are not violent. There are risk factors, of course, that can lead to conduct disorders, but what statistics show is that approximately 6 – 8 % of children of all social classes and races show hostile conduct problems.

SOCIAL AGGRESSION
Social aggression is a nonphysical form of misbehavior that includes bullying, gossip, and social exclusion, leading to consequences for both perpetrators and victims. The need to form friendships is especially evident in middle school settings, where the student is looking for a way to find a place of belonging. In this environment, a child sometimes uses socially aggressive tactics to bolster self-esteem and mask feelings of inferiority. This unhealthy method of attaining superiority or status affects the mental health of all those involved, and is especially devastating to girls. Both perpetrators and victims of these manipulative acts may experience social isolation in the short term and relationship problems as adults, especially when there is a vicious circle of attention and revenge-seeking behaviors (Dreikurs & Stoltz, 1990). Other consequences include lowered self-worth, loneliness, self-doubt, school phobia and adjustment problems, anxiety, depression, and peer rejection. Socially useless behavior may also lead to drug and alcohol abuse, and peer ostracism, which has been identified as a factor in some of the recent school shootings and suicide (Froeschle, & Riney, 2008, p. 416-420). Tragedies like these make it imperative that everything possible is done to keep the school environment safe.

USING ART THERAPY IN A SCHOOL SETTING

Art Therapy Connection (ATC) is an inner-city, yearlong school art therapy program providing mental health services in Chicago to youth identified at risk of failing grades 3 through 12. The ATC program helps to address the social health needs of students living in impoverished communities and experiencing constant threats on a daily basis. ATC utilizes an Adlerian art therapy approach with an emphasis on developing group identity, group cohesion, and cooperation. In turn, a feeling of belonging and trust can be established through social interest so that students feel encouraged to stay in school and succeed.

Most administrators and teachers at the schools where ATC is offered realize that it is one of the few programs that offer a therapeutic approach to support school success. ATC therapists communicate regularly with the teachers, which helps to provide continuity in mutual care and support. The synergy among the art therapists, staff, and teachers offers a model of cooperation.

Through the ATC program students gain a better understanding of what they need to change in their thinking, their lives, the school environment, and the community, by learning socially useful ways to take responsibility for making this happen. When students see improvement in school adjustment and academic achievement, they feel proud and are motivated to continue this work.

As the founders of ATC, we chose to take art therapy into the inner-city environment, not quite knowing that the depth of despair we would encounter in the lives of the students who came for art therapy was more than anything we had ever experienced before. The art therapy group serves as a social microcosm. Interactions among group members and the art mirror or reflect the important issues that the students struggle with every day. Eventually, as the student begins to feel a sense of belonging, he or she can become sensitive to the needs of others as well as to his or her own needs (Dreikurs, S., 1986).

We found that the best predictor of a student's success is the relationship or alliance between the student (client) and the therapist, (Hawkins,

Catalano, & Miller, 1992; Dinkmeyer & Sperry, 1987). Compared to no intervention at all, no one model of therapy is more successful than another. The student or client is the sole agent of change, nothing else. Alliance predicts positive outcome better than anything else and is consistent with what our students tell us (Rogers, 1957). "I used to be a bad, bad, boy – one you co(u)ld not tell me anything, but by coming to art therapy, I am better;" "I trust the people in art therapy and now I trust others more." (Sutherland, Waldman, & Collins, 2010, p. 73).

At the same time, students need to be reminded that any change comes from within, that they are the ones who decide what they will or will not do. A high school student, who had failed ninth grade for three consecutive years, explained that family problems and his gang-involved friends were pulling him down. Now, after two years in art therapy, he no longer uses drugs, is not in a gang, has stopped blaming others or life circumstances, and is ready to graduate.

In the ATC program we encourage students to actively take charge of their lives and to start questioning. Rather than live in a world where they feel inferior and victimized, they can learn what it means to respect human rights and to find a democratic approach to solving problems, and that dreams can come true (Sutherland, et al., 2010, p. 72)

THE ART DIRECTIVES

Some art directives designed to invite participation and encourage social interest are created and processed first by the graduate art therapy students in class and then with the young students with whom they are working in the school setting. They include the following:

1. Draw your favorite kind of day (Manning, 1987), or Draw your favorite time of day.
2. Bird's Nest Drawing (Kaiser & Deaver, 2009), art-based assessment to assess attachment security (Bowlby, 1969). Write a story about the drawing that includes a beginning, middle, and end.

3. Make a mask (as a way to open up discussion about emotions and how we may hide our feelings to avoid feeling vulnerable).

4. Make a puppet, and, with a partner who also has made a puppet, talk to each other about a situation that is a problem for each of you right now.

5. Draw three wishes (other than wishing for more wishes) (Ables, 1972).

6. Draw the way your life is now, then draw the way you want it to be.

7. Draw a road, which can be a metaphor to help us recognize that we each take individual paths, that we have the ability to make changes, and that we each own a part of the "truth" about life. (Hanes, 1995)

8. Sand Tray, in which small objects and toys representative of real life are provided. We are invited to create a sand tray by choosing, and arranging in the sand tray, whatever objects hold appeal for us. (Oaklander, 1988, p 159-179).

Process: The sand tray can be used with any age but can be especially useful with children, who can use the objects to "make a picture in the sand." The therapist notices which objects the child chooses or avoids from among the many items available for "telling the story." The child is invited to carry on conversations with the different object he or she placed in the sand tray.

Objective: The therapist directs the story back to what is happening in the child's life to learn where the child may be experiencing difficulty in real life situations. Just the act of expressing feelings through the objects in the sand tray helps the child integrate troubling experiences and minimize feelings of fear.

KEEPING ART IN THE CLASSROOM CURRICULUM

Viktor Lowenfeld believed that art "may well mean the difference between an adjusted, happy individual and one who, in spite of all learning, will have difficulty in his relationships with others" (1954, p. 9). The small sample done by the Art Therapy Connection shows that including Adlerian art therapy in the curriculum can improve school attendance leading to graduation. The students themselves who attended art therapy recognized marked improvement in math, reading, science, and other subject areas. Achievement in school can lead to success in other areas of life. Today, in a society organized increasingly around technology, Adlerian art therapy can be the means for greater self-awareness and improving human values in society, and, I believe, will keep alive a love for learning.

CONCLUSION

Our behavior reflects our experience of the world in which we live. "If that world is characterized by threat, chaos, unpredictability, fear and trauma, the brain will reflect that by altering the development of the neural systems involved in the stress and fear response" (Perry, 2000, p. 3). This results in any number of changes in ability to pay attention, impulse control, sleep, fine motor control, and blood pressure. Children and adolescents just becoming aware of their own independence and power need encouragement. The path from childhood through adolescence into young adulthood is full of doubt and ambiguity. It calls for parents, children, teachers, and students to respect each other in order to safely navigate this difficult transition.

May you always find
A clear path to follow
Filled with beauty and joy.

8

An Adlerian Approach to Couple and Family Art Therapy

In the Atira art therapy training program directed by Evadne McNeil I remember making clay sculptures of my family members, giving them voices and then arranging them in relation to one another. This experiential gave me clues as to what I remembered it felt like to be a first born child in my family. Over the years of growing up and into my marriage and becoming a parent, I slowly learned that some of my unconscious thoughts, attitudes and behavior created in childhood caused problems for my husband and three children. I learned that to be "right" meant that others were "wrong," that to be "perfect" made others imperfect and put me in competition with them. To be the "authority" meant that I demanded conformity or obedience rather than letting others think for themselves; to be overprotective invited dependency or rebellion; to be judgmental alienated others; and to be dependent meant giving up my autonomy. I learned that a sense of humor can take away the pain and put others at ease. I learned not to take myself too seriously although, at times, I still do.

I can say that I have changed certain attitudes and goals, but change comes slowly, and the changes I do make sometimes lead to resentfulness and misunderstanding. I more fully understand the choices I made as a child and realize that my younger sister and brother each saw the world from different places. I become more understanding of my parents as I learned to be a parent to my own children and a wife to my husband.

I think back to the significant people in my life and give descriptive words to each of them. My words include "nurturing," "sense of humor," "spirit of adventure," "independence," and "resiliency." My thoughts turn to a great-grandmother who played the piano for others in the nursing home where she lived, even though she could no longer see the keys. I'm reminded of my grandmother who used colorful scraps from our outgrown clothes to piece together butterflies forming the pattern on the quilts that my mother used to cover us at night. I remember laughing at my father's jokes, listening to the adventures that went with traveling to other countries, playing in my grandmother's beautiful garden, and watching both grandmothers face life with resiliency and independence after my grandfathers had passed away.

EARLY RECOLLECTIONS (ERS)
The basic attitude toward life, the thoughts, the feelings, the behavior, and the goal, are all reflected in ERs. These ERs, along with the birth order and Family Constellation can help to give a consistent pattern of a person's lifestyle. As we adapt to life, we unconsciously (and sometimes consciously) change ERs to more accurately reflect our current social situation, or even sometimes forget them when they are no longer useful to us. Birth order, too, can change, as children are born or brought into a family. As a therapist I look more for the way a person understands his or her position in the family. I was a first born, but I favored being partners with my sister.

COUPLES
In the first meeting with a couple in a troubled relationship I ask each partner to "Draw what keeps you and your partner apart." From these two drawings the three of us can see, talk about, and have a subjective understanding of the underlying power struggle, where both of the partners feel defeated and have created distance in their relationship. Again, ERs are important to understanding the underlying dynamics in the relationship. Drawing the ER makes it easier for the couple to see and take

responsibility for the meaning they give to their own lives and to their current life situation.

With two or three more ERs we can come to a better understanding of the couple's lifestyle pattern (CLP). It takes practice to interpret the ERs and how they fit with the CLP. Together we make note of the thoughts, feelings, attitudes and behaviors in order to make it easier for them to see and take responsibility for what they have each contributed to the current life situation. As each partner begins to understand their own and each other's perception of the relationship and provided each is willing to work toward a common goal of trust and respect, changes can slowly take place.

Couple distress is the single most common reason for seeking therapy. It undermines healthy family relationships and can lead to depression, anxiety, and addiction disorders. Millions of couples seek therapy, yet couple counselors are the least successful among providers of mental health services in achieving results (1995 Consumer Report). In the 21st century there are not as many early marriages, some people decide instead to live together, and some couples decide not to have children. Marriage is left over from a time when we needed an arrangement to manage property and reproduction. In many countries marriage has nothing to do with love. For some, the church has tried to project perfectionism in marriage, but no matter what the arrangement, any intimate relationship can be hard.

Couple relationships can be especially difficult when each person has certain thoughts and values that interfere with the goal of the partner. One can want order and comfort while the other might like to create excitement and chaos. One might want close friends while the other holds in high esteem those he would never know. A lack of common ground can create trouble for both partners especially as each determines to do their own thing in their own way. One might yearn for intimacy and maybe want too close a connection, while the other might want a caretaker and autonomy. Unrealistic expectations are fatal for the relationship if taken to the extreme. To find balance, to reach unity and harmony, to achieve wholeness while maintaining individual identities: Is it possible? Yes, when couples can live with the knowledge that love takes profound work, that each needs space in the relationship, and that marriage or partnership calls for respect and trust when coming to agreements.

PARENTING CLASSES

The balance between attachment and separation seems to be the hardest task for children in a family. Then again, it is the child's ability to adapt to the family environment which might be the most important piece in how a child learns to deal with the frustrations of everyday life. Parenting classes helped me learn to be more encouraging and less discouraging, and ideally, to prepare my children to take care of themselves and to help others.

I learned from Parent Study Groups that it is our task as parents to create a safe environment for encouraging children to choose their own paths. This does not imply that we will do it perfectly, nor will they, or that there is even a formula. Children will know you love them when you say "I really want to hear about what happened for you today," or ask, "What will you do the next time?" This attitude is one that can promote self-confidence and a sense of security. Children will do best if they understand that they have choices and are allowed to do things for themselves within the limits of their ability. And yes, we all make mistakes, but that's how we learn and it takes courage to try again. Sometimes you can say to the child, "We can work this out together." Happiness comes from a feeling of belonging, knowing that we can solve our own problems, and being useful to others.

The goal of parent study groups is to understand the purpose of the child's behavior and to gain skills in democratic approaches for coping with the daily problems of living together. We learn not to reinforce unacceptable behavior, how to encourage cooperative behavior, and that misbehaving children are discouraged children. We experience the difference between what it means to be a "good" parent (well-intentioned, but denying the child opportunities to make their own decisions), and what it means to be a responsible parent (one who uses encouragement to let the child experience the consequences of his or her own behavior). We learn that rewards and punishment teach children to be dependent on the opinion of others, while encouragement fosters independent thinking, taking responsibility, and a spirit of cooperation.

Family meetings are useful in making decisions about issues that involve all family members, for problem-solving, or just to be together at a certain time every week. One of the hardest questions to answer is "Who owns the problem?" especially as it impacts the well-being and reputation of the family.

Teaching my children to balance dependency with the need to be self-sufficient and develop skills was not something I thought about very much as a young mother. I thought it came naturally. I just was glad they were healthy, growing, learning to do things for themselves while I was busy trying to figure out my own path to maturity. In my own imperfection and emotional insecurity I know I created difficulties for my children. And yet, just as we all do if we are invested in the process, we have the most important growth where we have made mistakes.

FAMILY SCRIBBLE AND COMING TO AN AGREEMENT PRACTICED IN GROUP ART THERAPY TRAINING

An experiential based on *Family Therapy and Evaluation through Art* directs a group of us "scribble in the air," and then on a large piece of paper taped to the wall, with our eyes closed (Kwiakowska, 1978). Opening our eyes we look at the "mess" we created. First we noticed the differences in the scribbles. Some scribbles were smooth and round, others jagged and irregular. Some were done in bright colors; others were done in pale shades. Some took more space than others. Some of us worked fast, some slow, some intensely, some worked high on the large piece of paper, some low. We looked at these differences and made guesses about what the scribbles "said" about each of us and about how we found our place of belonging in the group. References were made as to how we behaved or created our place in our own families based on our perceptions and beliefs. We learned about birth order and that it really does not determine anything, except how we each understand our place in the family.

Then we came to an agreement about what we would do and chose one scribble as the starting point for a picture. Together we decided on an underwater scene. We began to work, each contributing something. The feeling of shared responsibility, of knowing that we could not have come up with so many ideas individually, gave us pleasure. But then, in processing the work we had done together, one person was irritated when she saw others drawing outside of the original scribble. She felt we had not lived up to our agreement. Eventually she tied this feeling of being irritated and sad to a current separation issue – her son going off to college, i.e., leaving the boundaries of home.

Another person felt discouraged when her scribble was the one we had chosen to elaborate into a theme, and wondered where she would fit in if we all took over her space. Yet another found that the rules she gave herself were too focused and boring. She was disappointed in the color she had chosen for her scribble and critical of the group work, but felt that working together was less painful than doing art alone. Some of us were concerned about pleasing others, or invading someone else's space, and some did not want to take the initiative. One person heard "rules" and was afraid of breaking them, but then gave herself permission to join the fun. Another heard the directive as "do your own thing" instead of "come to an agreement." Coming to an agreement means cooperating without compromising our own ideas (Dreikurs, S., 1986).

Afterwards we asked the following questions: "Did you learn something about yourself?", "In what ways does being in this group remind you of how you were in your family of origin or in your family today?" One person was surprised that she felt scared yet knew she wanted to be part of the process. Most of us were not concerned about success or failure and just wanted to be playful. When it came to signing our work, one felt it would be good for her to do so because it would give her an identity which she had not felt in her family of origin.

The dark side, or the side I like to keep out of my awareness, is my resentment, lack of tolerance, and being critical when life and others don't measure up to my expectations. Then I wonder why I have expectations at all? Isn't it preferable to trust that I will be able to creatively respond to the moment rather than trying to plan ahead and be disappointed? I can do this more easily when the outcome is not tied to my self-esteem.

We decided that doing work in this group was different from doing work together as a family. Our group was like an "ideal family" even though we could see our individual differences; leader, peace-maker, baby. One group member said, "In this group I can be understood — my family never understood me." All of us could find ways that reminded us of how we learned to relate and respond to parents and siblings. We felt successful in completing this task, something to remember when working with families who may never have realized that they can, in fact, function effectively as a team. Of course, the family constellation, the family atmosphere, and the basic attitudes influencing family behavior patterns differ greatly across cultures. In the group, looking at our families from a holistic-systems perspective began to take precedence over just looking at our symptoms and how we experienced life in our families. We realized the importance of exploring the dysfunctional interactions between the family's lifestyle pattern and the "problem child," rather than letting the child be blamed for the family difficulties.

We talked about the lack of success with couples counseling and how distress in the relationship creates problems for the family. What would happen while working with families where there are power struggles, violence, abuse, criticism, or blaming? The art provides ways to recognize issues of hostility, fear, control, dependency and ambivalence due to feelings of inferiority as well as positive qualities of concern, joy, and cooperation. Kwiatkowska (1978) wrote, "Art is a tangible, visible form which makes it difficult for the family to deny or ignore the symbolic messages it contains" (p. 128). Through the family group art process, reality often confronts denial, and reveals information that one might not be able or willing to express verbally. The family also has an opportunity to observe their own interactions and to have an active involvement in the therapeutic process (DeOrnellas, Kottman, and Millican, 1997, p. 452).

FIRST MEETING WITH A FAMILY FOR ART THERAPY
When meeting with the family for the first time, the members might each be asked to "draw yourself as you want others to see you." This gives family members a chance to understand how they see themselves and well as how others see them. Mother might see herself as providing care when the children might see her as overprotecting and controlling. Resentment can build up when the children are not allowed freedom to do things for themselves. Father might feel anger because mother is spending time with the children and not with him (Kerr, Hoshino, Sutherland, Parashak, & McCarley, 2008, p. 167). Mother might feel threatened or alienated, and could even try to increase her attempt to control.

In the above example, when the private logic seems rigid, and mother is having trouble adapting to her current life situation, it is possible for the therapist and family members to encourage change by offering different perspectives. This allows mother to free herself from continuing in a mistaken direction by offering not only a change in perception, but also a change in the attitude and behavior towards the family. Mother is now in control of making new choices or remaining in the previous state of fear and vulnerability. If encouraged, she is ready to find new responses to replace the old behaviors that were creating difficulties for the family.

The family atmosphere results from the relationships between the parents and the children. The atmosphere may be overprotective, overindulgent, authoritarian, rejecting, permissive or competitive. These labels can help the therapist to understand the discouraging dynamics, but in no way can alleviate the frustration, confusion, and resentment of the family members. It takes time to open the family discussion and it needs the cooperation of the entire family to be able to turn a discouraging situation into one of encouragement. For instance, because art does not have an agenda, painting the family atmosphere could put into visual image the dark secret of fear that might never have been explored verbally. This fear might show up in an angry child's drawings providing insight and encouragement for a family who have been held hostage by the child's angry outbursts and the reason for coming for art therapy. Fear of failing in school and not getting needed tutoring might be recognized in time to turn a frightening experience into one that is more helpful, sparing the child from the current painful "identified patient" position (Sutherland, 2011).

Art materials can be used to help the family members clarify the roles and perceptions they have of each other, to highlight patterns of interaction, and to explore ways to create a family atmosphere in the spirit of social interest, one where there is no superior role. "With insight, it is possible for the family members to move from being discouraged to feeling encouraged, to move from being closed down to becoming actively creative" (ibid, p. 178). Art is also one of the most powerful interventions the therapist may use for resistance; for those who talk too little, talk too much, or intellectualize, allowing the family to see for themselves the evidence of their family dynamics. The art itself is the agent of change; the therapist may make helpful observations, but the family members must acknowledge, accept and take responsibility for making changes to the family lifestyle pattern.

The family therapist must be able to understand the concept of the unity of the personality, for the individual, and also for the marital and the family system; and then to know to treat the style of life and not the symptoms (Adler, 1963).

These Art Directives are done first in the Couple and Family art therapy class with the students, and then with families in supervision:

ART DIRECTIVES

1. Draw what Family means to you.
2. Draw the Family Atmosphere in Your Family of Origin.

3. Draw yourself as an animal in relation to a conflict or problem you might have had in your family of origin (Papp, 1982). Draw other family members as animals to the same problem. Give each animal a descriptive word.

4. Draw a picture of your family doing something together (Burns & Kaufman, 1970, 1972). Look for who is left out, distance, or togetherness in relationships.

5. The Nine-Square – Take a large sheet of paper and fold it so that there are 9 squares. Each square contains a word for you to illustrate. Choose 9 words from the following list: "life," "play," "love," "hope," "me," "work," "spirit," "death," "safety," "hope." Put a word in each square with a drawing for what that word means to you (Farrell, 1999).

6. Draw the family as you would like it to be. Address the question "What does each of you need to do individually to make that happen? (This helps to indicate that each person needs to concentrate on changing his or her own behavior.)

7. Family Clay Ring: The therapist puts a ring of clay and extra clay in front of the family members who are seated in a circle. Each starts by adding something in clay to the clay circle. The circle is turned to the right and each again adds something to the circle without destroying the original art. This continues until all have had a chance to add something. The family can continue until they feel they have completed the piece and are content with the way it looks. This may be the first time the whole family has worked together on a project and often they are surprised at what they can do (Farrell, 1999).

OTHER COUPLE/FAMILY ISSUES TO EXPLORE

Remembering that the presenting issues are rarely the real issues, we look at Communication Patterns; Loneliness; Sex; Emerging Adults, The Role of Power or Control; Divorce and Child Custody; Adoption; Caring for Elderly Parents or In-Laws; Addiction; Physical Illness; Disability;

Families with Returning Military People, Mental Health; Parents in Prison; Unemployment; Resistance, Social Equality, Homosexuality; Transgender; Gender Identity Disorder.

Divorce is complex in its consequences for family members with no simple answers. It can be heartbreaking, but it can also rescue families from domestic abuse, addiction, betrayal, and offer opportunities for life-transforming personal growth. We need to continue to shed light on the suffering of women, and to expose the power relations in both the home and the workplace for the welfare of both sexes, and to provide children with the best possible care.

Same-sex marriage is just now becoming legal on the state level. Discrimination in this area is no longer legally tolerated, and yet, like civil rights for African-Americans, the struggle is slow and costly. We have yet to turn the point of prejudice in American society.

Trying to reduce or prevent violent crimes in Chicago is an ongoing struggle. Deborah Gorman-Smith (2013) writes that "decades of research on preventing violence points to a few key lessons. One lesson is that strong families are essential to preventing youth violence." Continuing support can come from programs developed for helping families make better lives for their children while encouraging education and parental responsibility.

CONCLUSION

Adlerian family art therapy seeks to enhance the feeling of cooperation and to better understand how family members find a place of belonging. The focus on the art task is done with agreement, and becomes more important than the focus on the individual, although each contribution is recognized for its uniqueness. Imperfections are overlooked as the shared art project focuses on working together (Dreikurs, S., 1986).

A bridge from me to you
Over years of forgetting
Pain and resentment

To connect means to stretch
Beyond fear and doubt
To a place somewhere in the middle
Is it possible still in the time we have left?

9

Art Therapy with Older Adults

This course explores ways to create community with older adults by inviting them to join in the creative process of making art. We follow the group art therapy model created and described by Tee Dreikurs in her book, *Cows can be purple* (1986).

As older adults in group art therapy we learn that we are not expected to produce a work of art, nor is our art going to be used to test us in any way; we are here just to enjoy putting color on paper. We start simply enough just listening to music, and when we are ready we choose colors and express the rhythm on a sheet of paper with a paintbrush. When we are finished we display our work by taping it to the wall in our art room. We experience a sense of freedom and are surprised at how the music and painting can so dramatically change what we were thinking and feeling, so different from when we first came into the art room. We all seem to be pleased with what we created. We tell others how much we like their art. We talk about how thoughts influence attitude, and how both influence behavior. We all help to put things back in order and clean up the art room.

This is the ideal, but it hardly ever works this way. Some of us might refuse to join in, or are depressed, or we don't like the music. We might be afraid to try, thinking we can't do anything, or we are disappointed with what we have painted. And yet, when we watch the others having fun, achieving something, not afraid to fail, complimenting each other's art, we, too begin to participate. Immediate attitudes and behavior change and we learn to trust ourselves to work alongside others and be part of the group – just not always everyone, and not all the time.

Adlerian psychology supports the belief that unconscious motives and ideas can influence thoughts and behavior, and that our self-determination can give us the creative power to change our life through changing our perception of it, no matter what our age. Current mind-body work on aging echoes this belief (Cohen, 2000, p. 32-37). Longevity has increased by 30 years in the last century. With many older adults now in assisted living homes, nursing homes, or coming to senior community centers, management recognizes the value of using creative arts to bring a sense of completion to the lives of the elderly as well as inclusion in a group. Education is a lifelong process while brain impairment is the result of disease, not age.

Alzheimer's disease is a progressive and fatal type of dementia that causes problems with memory, thinking, and behavior. At the most severe stage of Alzheimer's there is an inability to recognize oneself or family, and an inability to communicate or take care of oneself in any way. There are differences between senility and Alzheimer's disease. Senility may begin with minor forgetfulness and states of mental confusion and may progress to senile dementia. Senility may be due to a series of small strokes or neurological ailments, Huntington's or Parkinson's, or to any number of other causes such as depression, over-medication, malnutrition, an infection, or even a thyroid problem. When asked, the greatest concern for six out of ten of us is the loss of mental capacity.

THE USE OF ADLERIAN THERAPY TO OPTIMIZE STRENGTH OF OLDER ADULTS

According to research done by Brink in 1979, the Adlerian approach is not only the most integrative but also the most effective psychotherapeutic approach to use with the older adult (Sperry, 1992a). Brink noted that, since aging is a developmental process, the goal of therapy is to help the older adult cope with everyday problems and losses. The developmental tasks of older adults can include adjusting to decreasing physical strength or health issues, to retirement and reduced income, and to the death of a spouse and friends. Older adults must also grapple with establishing satisfactory physical living arrangements and affiliation with peers, meeting social responsibilities in living arrangements with others, and preparing philosophically for death, which might raise unresolved issues from the past.

Brink also mentioned that the problem-centered focus of the Adlerian approach is hopeful because it optimizes the strength of the older adult toward compensation for the many losses that come late in life (ibid.). Creating art, when it is done in a group setting, can be used to share responsibility for a task through division of labor as well as to create community (Dreikurs, S., 1986). Research indicates that social bonding can slow the process of aging and that the creative spirit is active through decline and loss (Chopra, 1994).

Aging does not change the basic personality style, but there are physical challenges that need to be recognized. Moving "from a minus to a plus" will include helping the older person learn to accept help while acknowledging choices, and finding constructive ways to be competent even as they become more dependent.

"All human behavior has a purpose and is movement toward a goal. If we want to help someone change direction, we must understand the purpose of the behavior" (Dreikurs, 1964). Possible goals of older people include getting Attention (love, service); Power (to hold on to status); Revenge (getting even); and to Withdraw (to show helplessness and hopelessness). Positive ways the therapist can meet those goals are to give love and service before it is asked for, to let the older person take the initiative, or to give comfort when appropriate (Dinkmeyer, D. & McKay, G., 1976).

Many older adults want to tell their stories and want to hear your stories as well. Stories expand self-awareness and awareness of others, and keep people connected to those around them. Sharing stories about pets, neighborhoods, and siblings offers opportunities to change and grow (Moon, p. 61). They can encourage each other and be open to solving some of the new problems they are encountering in their lives. According to research reported in *The New York Times,* (Tierney, 2013), nostalgia can help ward off depression, anxiety, and loneliness.

With older adults, we assess what is needed. Steps to take on the journey with them include putting value on their stories and experiences, offering encouragement in the form of assurance that they have lived useful lives, actively listening to the reality of the life situation by reflecting back to them what we hear them saying, respecting what they don't want to say, avoiding judgment and criticism, affirming their emotions, accepting but not reinforcing negative feelings, and recognizing our own emotions.

Some older people like to knit or sew. Sitting in a circle and talking to each other, they can make beautiful items for those who might need them, a kind of compassionate social action. It is helpful to the older person to still feel useful. If there are children nearby, in a preschool or day care center, arrange to have them come and visit. The children and adults can sing songs and read stories to each other, play games, or paint together. Children express a sense of innocence and wonder about life. Seeing these qualities in the children may help to keep alive their own faith in the mystery of the universe. And maybe the children will learn a little about what it means to be a part of the circle of life. If photographs or albums are available, encourage the group members to bring them. The photographs can help them remember their stories and might even inspire drawings.

Help the older person stay close to nature as much as possible. Encourage them to feel the warmth of the sun and the softly falling rain, then maybe to watch the millions of stars in the sky and the moon as it changes with the seasons. Bring them snow and let them paint with it in winter, and sand when it is summer. Both might hold special memories for them. And let them feel the air blowing around them; breathing in playfulness, trust, a spirit of adventure; breathing out fear and judgment; breathing in feelings of harmony, acceptance; breathing out the feelings of anger, doubt, or hate.

Some of the older adults will be suffering from Alzheimer's or dementia, but they still might be able to feel a connection to the group just being with others. No matter what the limitations, people with dementia can still express their inner subjective world through art. The choice of color, lines, shapes, and themes closely mirrors the individual's personality, and can be a way to participate when words no longer work. For most of the group members, art enhances self-esteem and minimizes loneliness.

The video *Art Therapy: The Healing Vision (Ault, 1986)* features Joan Erikson in her 90's talking about the psychosocial life stages of development that she and her husband Erik designed. While there are stages across the life span, they don't necessarily happen in sequence: most of us experience an ongoing attempt to balance between knowing and not knowing what to do next in adjusting to the challenges of life. Both Erik and Joan lived into their eighties and nineties, and that is when Joan found it helpful to add a ninth stage of psychosocial development that reflects the experience of very old people. She and Erik had titled the eighth stage "Integrity vs. Despair." In Erikson's publication The *Life Cycle Completed (Extended Version)* (Erikson, E., Erikson, J., 1997) Joan wrote: "To face down despair with faith and appropriate humility is perhaps the wisest course" (p. 106). It is important to remember that there is no battle between two sides in which one side wins, but that conflict and tension are the source for growth, strength, and commitment at any age.

Growing older is not an easy task, and with it comes end-of-life challenges: sometimes crippling pain, sometimes poverty, sometimes debilitating illness, and most likely dependence. The potential for suicide is high, and issues about the right to die concern the field of psychology as well as medicine. We can all hope for a meaningful old age, to continue to make choices, to find ourselves in a safe place, but circumstances may dictate otherwise.

The Art Directives help us recognize our own creative process. "Art follows the spirit of life" (Henri, 1923) and we can pay attention to our own dreams, symbols, images and metaphors. Art experientials can awaken our creative spirit and keep us in the "here and now." It can objectify and amplify life's experiences, especially current struggles. Art, like memory, is not the representation of things or events but expression of the subjective experience we have with them. "Memory is what lies between what happened and what is remembered" (Blos, 1979). In our memory, our perceptions are filtered by our personal biases and even our mood at the moment.

The following Art Directives done in class give way to discussion:

ART DIRECTIVES

1. Draw the memory of your first encounter with an older person
2. Draw an image of what old age looks like to you.
3. Draw a garden that you would like to have, or use old garden catalogs to create a collage.
4. Listen to music, stand up and move to the rhythm of the music without talking. Draw the image that comes up for you. Name the emotion that evolves out of your image. Our feelings are the most accurate mirror we have of our relationships with others. Let others guess the emotion you are portraying.
5. Draw yourself as an older adult. What does your eighty-year-old self say to your younger self?
6. A large circle is drawn and cut into as many pieces as there are participants. Each person decorates their puzzle piece and then all of the pieces are fit back into the circle shape.

When done in group art therapy with older adults, the finished circle is displayed where others can see and enjoy it. Being one of those who contributed brings pleasure and a feeling of being connected to others.

I am learning to
Let go of whatever was
On the wings of birds

10

Art Therapy Studio: Professional Development

In 1957, I read Herbert Read's *Education Through Art* (1949), where he stated that the purpose of education is to expand the uniqueness as well as the social consciousness of the individual. The democratic thinking that formed these words appealed to my sensibilities. To me, this meant that there can be progression toward healthy human relationships and that art can make it visible. Ever since that time this ideal has formed my philosophy for a lifetime of teaching.

Years later, we can provide evidence and research to support how we want to look at education, whether it is in art or any other subject (Dweck, 2006). We know that it is through education and having the right experiences that every child can achieve, and it is through effort and perseverance that they succeed. We want to establish a model of "growth" in education which not only allows room for conflict and failure, but welcomes it. In contrast, a "fixed" model means that not only do we have to succeed, but we have to reach the point of perfection; a discouraging model for most of us. The secret to learning is not necessarily the outcome but the struggle, to make mistakes and learn from them. While art satisfies a need for expression, it also reflects the approach we take in becoming more conscious human beings. "The real drawing teacher is the inner life" (Read, 1931), but it is our connection with others that encourages us to keep on drawing (R. Dreikurs, 1976, unpublished manuscript). Even the youngest children know this intuitively. The challenge becomes one of weaving together our unique gifts as expressed in our creativity, our need for community, and our individual need for freedom. I learn from the dialectical creative process of achieving perfection in one moment but experiencing imperfection in the next. It encourages me to go on, to do better, whether in my art, my work, or in my relationships with others.

ART THERAPY STUDIO
Different activities involve understanding the value of movement or dance as warm-up for creativity; of contour line drawing to strengthen confidence and ability; of art as a problem-solving technique – to create new ways of relating to the world; and of art as a way to connect to the earth through seed paintings – to remember the abundance of possibilities we have. We talk about the persona as mask, how masks mirror our innermost self.

THE ART DIRECTIVE: Creative Process
Homework: Describe your creative process, including the steps you take to solve a social problem. Use quotes, if you wish, and a drawing.

THE ART DIRECTIVE: Silence
Draw what silence looks like to you. In class we discuss when "silence" might be useful in our work with clients – not as punishment, but to give clients time to think for themselves. When is emotion not expressed? When there has been an early association between showing emotions and pain such as rejection, betrayal, or severe punishment, then concealing emotion becomes a way to not let others have power over us.

We experiment with t'ai chi, haiku, and sand tray. T'ai chi is a spiritual form combining inner strength and balance. Haiku are short poems of seventeen syllables (five-seven-five) used to capture a feeling; sand tray allows us to create a miniature world where we can imaginatively play out situations of conflict.

DEPTH IN PLASTIC ILLUSION

"Depth in plastic illusion" is another term for linear perspective. The seven forms of linear perspective are transparency, shadow, big, small, in color, overlapping, or the position on the picture plane. Unlike art from other cultures of the world, art using linear perspective is usually only found in western societies. Symbolically, perspective does not fit the Taoist or Zen philosophies of the East or the Indigenous cultures. Art work from these cultures expresses a center-less continuum that renders perspective unimportant. In the language of art history, the term "classicism" refers to a style of art that tends toward simplicity, symmetry and the reduction of tension. Conversely, "expressionism" strives for the increase of tension by heightening irregular lines, the unusual, the unexpected, the asymmetrical, and the complex. Both styles epitomize the continuum found in all visual art and, when thought of in psychological terms, can also describe the artist's movement in life.

THE ART DIRECTIVE: Create a simple symbol to represent yourself

Process: Take time to think of a symbol to represent yourself. What personal meaning do you attach to your symbol?

Take a large sheet of paper. Fold it in half lengthwise, then fold it again crosswise two times. When you unfold the paper, you will have eight sections, one of which you will leave blank. Use your symbol to experiment with depth in plastic illusion. Using the seven forms of linear perspective (transparency, shadow, big, small, in color, overlapping, or the position on the picture plane), draw your symbol so that it represents one for each section.

Objective/Rationale: To observe how the meaning of your symbol changes when you observe it as transparent, in shadow, big, small, in color, overlapping, or where it is on the picture plane (up close, or in the distance).

Using perspective is a realistic way of representing space, but it involves deforming the normal shape of what we see. In order to draw a building in perspective, two sides have to be made shorter than they are in reality. "Deformation is the key factor in depth perception because it decreases simplicity and increases tension in the visual field" (Arnheim, 1954, 1974, p. 259). A deformation conveys the impression that "some mechanical push or pull has been applied to the object, as though it had been stretched or compressed, twisted or bent" (Arnheim, 1954, p. 259). Deformation invites us to compare what is with what "ought to be" and leads us to examine what symbolic or metaphoric message our own art perspective might hold for us.

Similarly, in psychological theory, we find that we unconsciously "bend" or "deform" the truth to fit what we choose to believe. Often we live our lives by what we think should be true, and we act "as if" it is true (Vaihinger, 1925). We can even consciously act "as if" something is true to give ourselves courage when trying out new behavior.

Memory plays a role in distorting reality, in that what we have unconsciously chosen to remember shapes our lives. We create memories of our experiences to fit with what will best help us to adapt to the current life situation. These memories provide practical and useful constructs, or imperatives, that simplify making sense of the world we live in. The world then fits with what we expect it to be. This self-deception is revealed in our dreams, wishes, Early Recollections (ERs), and art. Self-deception informs the attitude, the beliefs, and the behavior and, from my experience, can even over-ride childhood memories. In therapy we find out that "the private logic appears to justify mistaken behavior and prevents one from seeing that many difficulties and disappointments in life are the logical consequences of mistakes in the life plan" (Dreikurs, R., 1950, p. 45).

OTHER STUDIO ART TECHNIQUES

While depth in plastic illusion is one exercise, we also experiment with other art techniques. Using a piece of fruit as a model, we practice using dots to create value in three drawings: first to create shadow, then one to create daylight, and the third to give the illusion of night-time. We discuss "light" and "dark" as symbol, and form creating feeling. We make a picture within a picture, we practice metamorphoses or transformation where one object changes into another, reconciliation of opposites (day turning into night), word imagery (attaching words to images to convey meaning in the art), use of appropriation (using pictures from magazines or photographs), and dislocation (putting something in a place where we wouldn't expect to see it – e.g., Rene Magritte's train engine coming out of a fireplace).

A mental connection, or "the recognition of elective affinities," was Magritte's term for making a conscious combination of objects revealing similarities which are often overlooked. His aim was to reveal connections between objects that might seem strange but were there just for the looking (birds drawn in place of leaves on a plant.) Slides of Magritte's art can act as a catalyst to look at things in ways we had not imagined before.

We bring objects to class that represent something about ourselves – something significant to us. We make contour line drawings of this object from two or three perspectives and paint or draw our feeling response to the object. Sometimes when we choose an object we are not even sure of its significance for us and we find out something new when we talk about it in class.

ARTISTS

We study the selected works of artists as a way to explore the psychological dynamics of artistic creativity so that we can practice recognizing form and feeling in our own art work. We experience the meaning behind words such as balance, shape, form, space, light, color, value, movement, symbol, intuition, metaphor, and expression as they relate to what we perceive in art work.

Magritte invites me to look at the environment using more consciously created symbols, while Marc Chagall seems more interested in creating a vibrant atmosphere. With Chagall's work, I feel as if I am participating in a "marriage of the real and the imagined." Chagall calls this "other reality, unreality, or supra-reality" (Meyer, 1961, p. 15). The visual metaphors, the symbolic significance of the imagery, the color and form used as symbols to represent this "other reality" all speak to me of the unity found in the dualities we experience in the world: inner/outer, dependent/indepen-dent, good and evil.

Chagall paints life in its simplicity and in its hidden complexity. He presents places, people, and objects from memories of his own experi-ences in life. Everywhere in his art reason is crowded out and the uncon-scious holds sway, as if Chagall is attempting to restore our equilibrium which might be endangered by too much logic. Hasidic teaching, a fun-damental source of Chagall's art, holds that reason alone alienates us from the world, and stands as a genuine obstacle to the knowledge of God learned through faith. Students study the work of different artists, devel-op practice in designing art experientials, and then take turns presenting these experientials in class.

SEEKING INNER PEACE AND WELLNESS BY OBSERVING NATURE AND CREATING ART

Following the idea that everything we experience shapes our lives ac-cording to how we remember it and give meaning to it, we read Joseph Campbell (1988) who explains that early myths were based on the sur-rounding vegetation. Creation myths show the intuition and logic behind the meaning which evolved from one's experience of connection with the natural world. Nature is a source of inspiration and I invite the students to join me outside.

I ask students to notice what attracts their attention and to draw what-ever that is: a certain place, a tree, a rock, a plant, a flower, water, or an animal. Our drawings make our thoughts visible in a single metaphorical image. For instance, we free associate to our images and then talk about how what we say might resonate with the way we are experiencing life at the moment. "A continual (dialectical, creative) process goes on between world and self and self and world; one implies the other and neither can be understood if we omit the other" (May, 1975, p. 51).

Ocean waves can bring comfort, but also excitement: they rise, until curling over the top, they fling themselves upon the sand and then, find-ing themselves being pulled back into the ocean, they get ready to do the same thing all over again. Birth, life, death, and maybe even the hereafter, are seen in rapid, energetic motion. Meaning comes easily when I use waves to reflect whatever is going on in my life at the moment; happy, sad; finding and losing my way; lifting up, falling down; belief, doubt; silence, noise; moving from a minus to a plus; steady, rogue; creative, destructive; retreat, return; change, changing; life goes on, and on.

THE NATURE OF ART AND ITS RELATION TO FEELING

Rudolf Arnheim (1974) states that art functions to visually organize experience into an integrated structure. Vision is not simply a mechanical rendering of what we see, but rather a creative and imaginative reflection of our own reality. Visual perception, as with any other sensory perception, is indivisible and fits with our holistic way of understanding life.

Visual experience is dynamic. The eye intuitively senses BALANCE. In art we create balance with size: the larger object will be heavier; bright colors are heavier than dark ones; black must cover a larger area to balance a white area; an object isolated in space seems heavy as do shapes that are compact. Vertical forms seem to be heavier than oblique ones. When an image seems off-balance we wonder about the meaning it has for the artist and what it might bring up for each of us in our own lives.

Visual balance can be obtained through an intuitively felt direction of a piece. The force of gravity with which we live gives reason to our perception. If the form in the art rises up, we get the idea of overcoming resistance; if the form moves down it might mean surrendering to the pull from below. The first might be experienced metaphorically as victory, while falling down might be experienced as defeat, failure, giving up, or letting go. The artist's culture may influence whether a picture is meant to be "read" from left to right or right to left, reminding us to always check with the client to understand the direction they wish to project and why.

We strive for balance, homeostasis, in all phases of our physical and mental existence. The law of nature is about balance, harmony, and equilibrium, and can be observed in all organic life. It is known as the Law of

Compensation, the same Law of Compensation that Adler incorporated into his psychological theory. When we have physical imperfections, we tend to overcompensate with another part of the body, i.e., losing our eyesight might make us compensate by strengthening our sense of hearing. One of us might compensate by having the courage to be imperfect, while another of us might use our disability to put others in our service and feel cheated by life (neurotic behavior, phobias).

In psychological terms, Adler theorized that when we feel off-balance (e.g., inferior, inadequate) we strive to become equal to or even superior to others in order to gain balance and recover our self-esteem. Anxiety is normal to any kind of a threat. If the stress is too much it can paralyze us or take its toll on our health, but research tells us it can also help us summon energy to function at our creative best. One person might perceive life as highly stressful and too difficult, another may view it as an invitation to meet the challenges of life.

COLOR can have metaphorical meaning as can MOTION and LINE. Colors range from warm to cool; motion seen in art can be from fast to standing still; a straight line can represent strictness, rigidity and frozenness, while curved lines can represent gentleness, flexibility and a more natural feeling. The path of movement may be straight and direct or flexible and indirect. Line and movement can express something to the viewer but the viewer also brings meaning to what is seen. Adler said to trust only movement. We move on a continuum from a minus to a plus, looking for balance. Agitation or calm can be expressed in a line movement and so can the concept of chase and escape.

SIZE often gives clues to the meaning we either consciously or unconsciously want to express. When mother and child are the same size we perceive an equality that might not be true in reality but is true in the artist's experience and feeling.

Psychologically, LIGHT is one of the most powerful of human experiences and, in combination with darkness, represents a dualism of antagonistic powers found in the mythology and philosophy of many cultures. We can think of light as symbolizing goodness, while darkness represents evil. The Bible identifies God, truth, and salvation with light and the Devil with darkness. Light can stand for enlightenment and knowledge, but also for innocence. Black may be used to represent sickness or death, but also for mystery or something that we don't yet understand.

Without light we cannot observe shape, color, space or movement. Light creates space but also the "shadow" referred to in Jungian psychology as that part of ourselves which we may unconsciously choose not to recognize. By keeping the undesirable part of ourselves "in the dark" or out of our consciousness, we can avoid taking responsibility for it. An Adlerian might say that we unconsciously arrange to keep this part of ourselves a secret in order to safe-guard our self-esteem.

The principle of SIMPLICITY, a basic guideline of Gestalt psychology, holds that any visual pattern will tend to the simplest configuration in terms of wholeness and understanding. This system fits with closed systems and keeps us from bringing too much information into our lives. However, if we are mentally healthy, we tend to live in an open system, looking for new information once the hierarchical motives for attachment, security, and competence have been met (Forgus & Shulman, 1979). Arnheim (1974) says it this way:

The living creature replenishes its fuel for action by absorbing information through the senses and processing and transforming it internally. Brain and mind envisage change and crave it; they strive for growth, invite challenge and adventure. Laziness, far from being a natural impulse, generally is caused by infirmity, fear, protest, or some other disturbance. At the same time, the tendency toward simplicity is constantly at work. It creates the most harmonious and unified organization available for the given constellation of forces, thereby ensuring the best possible functioning both within the mind and body and in their relation to the social and physical environment. We envisage the human mind as an inter-play of tension-heightening and tension-reducing strivings (p. 411).

The art process and product tell us through the intuitive language of our inner reality what science cannot tell us and what religion was created to tell us – who we are, why we are here, what we hope for, why there is suffering, the meaning of life and death (Rader, 1961). "Art is the representation, science the explanation of the same reality" (Read, 1949, p. 11).

THE LAW OF DIFFERENTIATION

Arnheim (1974) describes The Law of Differentiation from the artist's point of view (p. 179). The shape remains undifferentiated until the artist makes it a more complex statement by giving it details, by adding color or by putting it in a setting thereby giving it subjective meaning.

In psychological thought, the law of differentiation is relevant to how we create our personalities, especially how we develop self-esteem and identity separate from others. Yet, we don't want to isolate ourselves but to remain open and connected to others. We need to understand and appreciate the differences between cultures and nations, religions and spiritual traditions of the world. Without diversity we will not survive and without understanding of others we will continue to have wars and the violent destruction that goes with it.

Some artists ascribe to the ideal that art can and should play a role in transforming society. Yes, art can be used to influence attitudes, beliefs and behavior regarding social justice, segregation, women's rights, advocacy for literacy, poverty, health care, economics, and any other form of social disadvantage. We can only make changes when we become aware of the myths we have created to maintain inequality. Art makes visible what is invisible (Arnheim, 1974).

CONCLUSION

All art becomes the visual projection of who we are. We acknowledge the uniqueness of the individual approach to life as well as the unity of the personality as it is reflected in our art product and process. Our truth, then, as made visible through art, can help to reveal the ideas we have about ourselves and about life, and encourage change both privately and toward the injustices of life. Besides having the opportunity to learning more about what we believe, the interactive interpersonal relationships students have with each other in the classroom can mirror many of our relationships outside of the classroom, and can also provide a model for doing group therapy beyond graduation (Dreikurs, S., 1986; Yalom, 2005).

Art opens my heart
To the world again as it did
When I was a child

11

Art Therapy and Psychodynamics Surrounding Life Challenges

While the stigma on mental disorders is slowly lifting, even students in a psychology program can be frightened at the idea of emotional disturbances. "Mental disorders are crippling, and can even be fatal, with as many as one in five Americans suffering from them. It can keep those who suffer its more devastating form from being able to live a normal life at work, in families, or at school" (Byrne, 2012). Only a few turn to violence, but our jails are full of those who suffer with mental disorders, with very little access to professional help and almost no hope for recovery.

MENTAL DISORDERS

Mental disorders are biologically-based brain disorders that cannot be overcome through will power, and are not related to a person's character or intelligence. Multiple factors interact with each other to produce a disorder that may include a genetic vulnerability. Although genetic inheritance may potentially play a role, it still does not determine who will develop a mental disorder. So far, no underlying genetic patterns or brain scans can prove a causal relationship to the severe mental disorders such schizophrenia, bipolar disorder, major depression, autism, Alzheimer's disease, addiction disorders, or dementia that are capable of disrupting relationships with others. The diagnosis and treatment of a mental disorder is left to the subjective opinion of the psychiatrist who determines the disorder based on the descriptive behaviors and diagnostic labels found in the *DSM-V* (2013).

Today we know that DNA is not destiny. It responds to social connections and other life experiences (Watters, 2006). While we understand that both nature and nurture play different roles in shaping our personalities, and while we need both, I believe that it is actually nurture that plays the bigger role when it comes to our health. In other words, the connection we make with others and how we think can dramatically alter the way our body fights disease and physical or mental disorders, and possibly can affect our genetic make-up as well. It works both ways: any effort to understand how genes affect thinking and behavior must also take into account how social experience affects our genes.

"The cure of the part should not be attempted without treatment of the whole," according to Plato in the fourth century B.C., meaning that all mental life is related to the physical body. According to Adler's holistic concept, maladaptive behaviors and many physical illnesses are preceded by what the individual considers significant life events (Adler, p. 301). Strong negative emotions can alter endocrine balance, causing physiological changes that can lead to disruption in the sense of adequacy. Maladaptive behaviors are unconscious attempts at compensation. Besides acting in ways that create distance in relationships, the symptoms of illness or disorder can even sometimes be inappropriately used as an excuse for not working or for claiming disability, affecting all of us.

DETERMINISTIC/HUMANISTIC APPROACH
TO UNDERSTANDING BEHAVIOR

In my first graduate class at the Alfred Adler Institute, Dr. Bernard Shulman used the term, "entelechy," a philosophical term credited to Aristotle that is translatable to mean something like "inherent goal-directedness." All living things, all plant and animal life share with us an impulse to achieve completion of an ideal pattern. "It is the entelechy or life force of an acorn to be an oak tree with every twig and every leaf that it produces in response to that impulse to perfection" (Houston, 1994). Each human life is also shaped according to the unfolding of this innate and intrinsic force, to achieve completeness or perfection.

In psychology, this is an example of determinism, a belief that all behavior is determined by external and internal forces acting on the person that can be subjected to scientific inquiry. More theories in psychology are based on determinism than on free will. Those of us who believe in free will believe that life is too complex to be based simply on external and internal factors, although we agree that these factors exist. Adler's theory is humanistic, and calls for a social approach to understanding human behavior. It is a soft determinism in that we are self-determining: we have free will to choose our behavior, which makes us responsible for our actions. Our laws are guided by ethics, and so implicitly our society supports the concept of free will. If we expect moral responsibility we must also accept the concept of free will.

As with plants and animals, our physical bodies are mostly determined before birth, but personality traits are more flexible and available to consciousness and change. These personality patterns develop only as we grow and experience social life around us. Competition, cooperation and other features of human behavior such as social interest and social justice are among learned behaviors. Essentially everything about our interaction with the social world rests on the process of this mostly unconscious learning.

Adlerian personality theory is based on unconsciously self-created inner goal-directedness to achieve completion or perfection similar to the innate force, entelechy. The goal orientation is forward movement toward a goal of significance, superiority, or success. It can be a realistic goal to solve the problems of life leading to useful behavior on a continuum or it can be unrealistic goal of exaggerated superiority over others leading to useless behavior. We subjectively create our own personalities to fit our social experiences in life. Once established, we have a set of consistent characteristic behaviors which basically stay the same regardless of the situation, until something significant happens to change our thoughts. We will always be striving for completeness, wholeness, perfection in body, mind, and spirit in order to overcome the feeling of incompleteness and to help us find our place in society. Adler called this "striving from a felt minus to a felt plus."

As we know, perfect fulfillment is made impossible by adverse circumstances both in nature and in our minds where we seek to fulfill ideal patterns. We know little about what leads one person to succumb to adversity while another rises above it to respond to life challenges. When there is conflict with damage to the psyche in the drama of social living, entelechy (the life force) acts as a vector and restores the integrity of the individual into a whole. In response to a loss of power in a relationship (a feeling of inferiority) we might overcompensate by unconsciously creating unhealthy or somatic responses, even psychosis, which might be the best we can do at the time and can be life-saving. Eventually these dysfunctional responses call attention to the need for an adjustment in the way we have given meaning to our lives (Shulman, 1980, in-class notes).

THE ART DIRECTIVE: The Open Door

Process: Pretend that your paper is a door that you have just opened. Paint whatever it is that you see on the other side. Look for the surprise. Spend some time journaling about your painting.

Perhaps paradox and the emergence of the unexpected are the keys to the healing aspect of art therapy. According to Edith Kramer, "This – the element of surprise – I believe to be the hallmark of the exceptional both in art and in art therapy. No matter how carefully it has been planned and prepared for, every good work of art and every memorable art therapy session bring forth something unexpected" (Kramer, 1996, p. 180).

Objective/Rationale: that we can use art for a corrective emotional experience, to ventilate negative feelings, and find alternative ways to cope with life circumstances.

DIAGNOSTIC & STATISTICAL MANUAL OF MENTAL DISORDERS (DSM-V, 2013)

The original goal for creating the *DSM* was to establish psychiatry firmly on the disease model of medical practice so that symptoms could be treated with medications. It was an attempt to get psychiatrists to make the same diagnosis for a given set of symptoms and then to prescribe the same medical treatment. The diagnostic labels are descriptive rather than dynamic and are useful to drug and insurance companies but do nothing to help understand the purpose of the client's behavior.

For those of us who believe that our problems are not all based on genetics or a chemical imbalance, but rather on an existential one, whether life has any meaning, purpose or value, we realize that medication will not necessarily bring about healing. A clinical diagnosis might give the therapist an orientation as to how a client is responding to a problem in life but does not help in understanding the client's uniquely subjective process, the client's private logic.

Today, an assessment for mental distress using the *DSM-V* will still assign a diagnosis, but the diagnoses are called disorders, rather than diseases or illnesses. The *DSM-V* uses this term "to acknowledge the complex interplay of biological, cultural, and psychological factors involved in mental distress" (Nussbaum, 2013, p. 4-6). *DSM-V* improves the accuracy of psychiatric diagnoses by measuring the severity of a disorder, aligning diagnoses with the International Classification of Disease (ICD), and incorporating recent advances in neurosciences (Regier, Kuhl, & Kupfer, 2013). The *DSM-V* still considers human sickness to be beyond human control whereas now mental disorders are considered to result from a combination of biological, genetic, environmental, social and psychological events. This new wording takes mental disorders out of the deterministic model into the humanistic, holistic model as defined by Alfred Adler and his followers.

The word "disorder" takes into consideration the social role mental distress has for the person. It is defined as a disturbance in physical or psychological functioning, and reinforces a distinction between mental problems (disorders), and physical problems (diseases) (Nussbaum, 2013,

p. 7). From the Adlerian perspective, "psychopathology is fundamentally a disturbance in attitude, a false belief regarding one's own limitations and a mistaken set of ideas about life which prevent one from full participation and contribution. The individual shuns cooperation and avoids solving real-life problems" (Ferguson, 1995, p. 29). The similarity between these two definitions is clear. An Adlerian therapist would still want to know to what purpose an individual would put mental disorders, and physical illnesses as well.

"THE QUESTION"
Tee Dreikurs (1986) adapted an art directive to the "Question" (Dreikurs, R., 1954) by asking clients to: "Draw what would be different in your life if I could wave a magic wand and take away all of your symptoms." Whether the symptom is physical or psychological, the therapist can find out to what purpose the client would be putting his or her illness or mental disorder. Perhaps nothing would be different indicating possible organic pathology or perhaps the disorder or illness indicates against whom or against what conditions the symptom is directed. And again, possibly the symptoms of the disorder are the best that one can do in the face of overwhelming stress and serve to keep one alive at that time. "Any crisis situation is created by the impact of a given life situation on a certain personality. What upsets one (however) may not upset another" (Dreikurs, R., 1953). This thought echoes the statement of Epictetus, a philosopher born a Roman slave in 55 C.E.), "Man is troubled not by events themselves but by the views he takes of them."

CASE EXAMPLE
A middle-aged man begrudgingly came to art therapy, angry, upset, and ready to leave his marriage. He was suffering from serious physical ailments, severe back pain, and depression. I told him that drawing his current situation might be helpful; he agreed, and so I asked him to "Draw what you are experiencing in your life right now." His drawing showed him trapped beneath a huge boulder with his arms and legs flailing about.

I then asked him to draw "What needs to be different?" The next drawing showed him sitting in his own studio at his easel with his drawing supplies around him. With these two drawings done in the initial interview, he knew immediately that we both understood his situation and that I was there to help him make some positive changes in his life as well as give up blaming others for his discouragement. He was then willing to enter into the therapeutic alliance.

Having quickly perceived his situation and knowing what he needed to do, he moved away from being a victim and into taking charge of his own life. He built a studio over his garage where he could spend time alone. His wife told me later what a gift his art therapy drawings were to him, and how understanding and acting on the message he gave himself had improved balance in his life and their relationship.

Adler did not believe it was helpful to assign a diagnosis, but rather to help the client understand the subjective meaning, the private logic, created for living in community with others. Without understanding what brought the client to treatment, the life situation and the lifestyle pattern, we may never understand the underlying symptoms.

Depression in the *DSM-V*, for instance, has been defined in a way that includes normal sadness, although it does exclude bereavement. Sometimes sadness is the appropriate response to a life situation, and suffering can be helpful, even necessary, to the healing process. Without some kind of conflict or suffering, we would not know the value of healing or happiness, nor would we be open to insight into or willing to take responsibility for our own behavior. The art work can sometimes "say" what we have yet to understand; that part of self that comes uncensored from the unconscious. Clients can begin to feel understood once they can discuss and make some guesses about what the art work reveals to them; and a therapeutic connection to the therapist can lead to trust and cooperation.

ADAPTING ADLERIAN THEORY TO THE DSM-V
Even though Adlerian therapists do not consider diagnostic classifications to be essential in the treatment of individuals, we have adapted Adlerian

theory to fit the *DSM-V* in order to stay current with the language used by those who practice other theoretical approaches. Using the same language to report to insurance companies ensures that our clients receive the same benefits as others who share the same diagnosis (Sperry & Carlson, 1996). Rather than just accepting the crisis situation and a description of the symptoms as found in *DSM-V*, an Adlerian therapist believes that the whole life situation needs to be explored, with the client's consent, in order to understand the lifestyle pattern. By completing a Life Style Inventory (Shulman & Mosak, 1988) we supplement what we feel is missing from the *DSM-V*.

As part of creating a relationship, the first interview involves listening to what the client has to say about his or her condition, symptoms, and discomfort, what Rudolf Dreikurs (1954) referred to as the subjective condition. The list of complaints is matched up to diagnostic criteria. The complaints might be about things happening to them such as unfounded fears, sleepless nights, or bizarre thoughts. As Adlerian therapists we would look at the movement in the behavior: Is the client retreating from social relationships into addiction or depression? Is the movement passive or active, weak or strong, dependent or independent, withdrawn or gregarious – possibly indicating degrees of social distance versus social participation?

The Life Style Inventory supplements the descriptive language found in the *DSM-V* by including information about the family constellation, birth order, sibling relationships, parent-child relationships, family atmosphere, and outstanding achievements, or any deficiencies or failures. This gives us a description of personality traits and the way the client arranges to define and defend him or herself. Drawings can also help to clarify the family atmosphere, the Family Constellation, family relationships, and Early Recollections.

We document physical conditions or disorders such as diabetes, heart conditions, and chronic pain problems. We find out if the client uses any organic inferiority (such as intellectual disability or brain disorder), medical problems, or other disability to feel in an inferior position, a minus position. We do this not to blame, but to understand the client's position, whether he or she puts himself or herself above or below others. We assess psychosocial stressors. In many situations clients are bringing problems into therapy which they have tried to resolve themselves without understanding the purpose of the symptom or behavior. It is sometimes difficult for them to do this without help.

The summary of the Life Style Inventory, using both the Family Constellation and Early Recollections, is done with the client and provides a sense of the client's movement in life; toward, away from, or against others; above, below, or equal to others; hostile, friendly, depressed, or optimistic (Dreikurs, R., 1967, p. 39; Dreikurs, S., 1976, p. 79). The significance of symptoms can sometimes be understood in light of these movements as well as the art, and can be illuminating to the client.

Freud later came close to socio-teleological thinking, but he saw conflicts in life as primarily intrapersonal rather than interpersonal. Freud studied pathology and focused on human sickness and weaknesses. Freud gave us the disease model, while Adler and Dreikurs focused on well-being and "preventing trouble before it begins." Adler was aware of the relationship we have with ourselves in terms of our private logic (the unconscious), self-guiding ideals, and feelings of inferiority. He also recognized that we sometimes create self-serving distortions of the truth to make life circumstances more amenable not only to ourselves, but to others as well (Stone, 1997).

USING ADLER'S HOLISTIC FRAMEWORK
TO EXPLORE THE PSYCHODYNAMICS
SURROUNDING LIFE'S CHALLENGES

Adler's holistic framework recognizes that the unconscious process (private logic) is dependent on the deeply held core beliefs of the individual, which underlie mental or social disorders, even eating and addictive disorders. Adler believed that the organs of the body are induced to cooperate with the purpose of behavior, and that a change in behavior changes the thoughts of private logic. Conversely, if the thoughts change due to therapeutic insight, so does the behavior.

What may appear to others as irrational thoughts and actions may really be an unconscious act to save our lives when our dreams are crushed by forces outside of our control. When it is depression, all the processes of the body begin to cooperate with the purpose of the behavior. Sleep eludes us, digestion is a problem, our immune systems shut down, we get sick, and illness can take over our lives. Our emotions overwhelm our ability to think clearly. Even to cry may be impossible. For the time being, we cannot even hear the words that might help us make sense out of our world or learn new coping skills. The purpose of this behavior is to arrange, without our conscious awareness, to take ourselves out of circulation so that nothing, not even our own thoughts, can continue to hurt us.

Depression can be described as "a silent temper tantrum" or protest about the way life is proceeding (Mosak, cited in Sperry & Carlson, 1993, p. 144). Depressed adults and children learn early in life to put other people into their service possibly due to a feeling of inadequacy or in cooperation with faulty training; that is, being spoiled or over-protected in one way or another. By becoming depressed and producing distressing symptoms, they have an excuse for not cooperating and to be free of responsibility (Sperry, et al., 1993). Mental disorders and healthy functioning are not either-or, all-or-none, dichotomies, but instead form a continuum between optimum positive attitudes and extreme discouragement and disillusionment.

POTENTIAL SUICIDE

A crisis situation may bring a client to the hospital or to therapy. The therapist looks at what the client anticipates and expects. It is especially important to assess for potential suicide and when necessary, stop all interviewing and work only toward stabilizing the client. Suicidal ideation can result from the death of a loved one, divorce, separation, the breakup of a relationship, serious illness, pain, or perceived failure.

If the suicidal behavior is thought to be manipulative, Kurt Adler (1980) believed in confronting the client to uncover anger and the goal of revenge, goals that don't often fit with self-ideals. Suicide is the ultimate escape from solving life's problems and feelings of guilt and blame only serve to act as an excuse not to cooperate.

When one of my clients saw that she drew herself as a deer running toward "freedom" and away from responsibilities, she knew that suicide was not the answer and that she had to make some new choices for her life. She did and found satisfaction as a high school English teacher.

There are several pioneering groups, such as Compassion in Dying and the Final Exit Network, which value the individual's right to self-determination in matters of life and death, but the field of psychology does not share this stance. In fact, a therapist who does not take reasonable action to prevent suicide can be cited for a wrongful death action (Vorus, 2013).

In time, others having suicidal thoughts choose to move beyond their deep discouragement and recognize the preciousness of life. Loving someone, a child perhaps, can help to bring about healing, even if not being loved by a divorcing partner is no longer a reality. Rather than looking outside of oneself for validation or security, one can learn to trust, maybe for the first time or maybe again, his or her own ability to meet the challenges of life.

MOTIVES FOR BEHAVIOR

Attachment, security, competence, and cognition are all motives for behavior. When we mistakenly believe they are being severely threatened, we might unconsciously find ways to escape through mental disorders, physical illness, or a combination of both. Possible threats or discouragement to attachment include loss of a loved one, rejection by significant others, and being alone in a strange place. Life-threatening danger or loss of income or property threaten security. Competence is threatened by loss of ability, such as in aging, or personal failure. Threats to cognition include loss of stability in any of the perceptual areas, or derailment in the pursuit of the guiding self-ideal. (Forgus & Shulman, 1979, p. 326).

SOME BASIC MISTAKES IN PERCEPTION

Some basic mistakes that we might make in perception are overgeneralizations ("life is dangerous"); impossible goals of security ("in order to be safe, I have to please everyone"); meeting the demands of life ("life is too hard"); minimizing self-worth (I'm not good enough"); faulty values ("money equals power"); and exaggeration of the personal ideal or fictive goal for behavior ("I have to be perfect, right, good...") (Mosak, cited in Corsini, 1979, p. 67). We are not usually aware of these mistaken goals, but they have unconsciously become part of our lifestyles, our private logic. They might have been appropriate responses to the situation in our childhood, but only bring difficulty in adult relationships.

Adler (1956) categorized personality into four types: ruling, getting, avoiding, and the healthy, socially useful person (Sperry et al., 1993, p. 602). Mosak (1977) defined what he called the most common lifestyle themes: getter; controller; driver; to be good, perfect, right; martyrs, victims; "aginners" (against others); feeling avoiders, and excitement seekers (pp. 183-187). These personality types are not used as definitive labels but only to help understand the dynamics of the individual. The therapist can sometimes focus on how each of these types can also be a measure of strength in the role it plays in our health and in the social world.

Over-ambition, discouragement, and pessimism can cause stress and bring about mental disorders. "The loftiest goals are found in the most pathological cases, that is, in the psychoses," (Ansbacher & Ansbacher 1956, p.314). Psychosis creates distance from others. Excessive or inappropriate affect results in behavior which keeps others away. No one event in childhood can cause any particular symptom or psychological disorder. "Rather, when people develop a 'neurosis', (now called "neurotic disorder") they bring up from memory events long past to give explanation to their current position" (Ansbacher & Ansbacher, 1956, p. 289). Symptoms of neurotic behavior, such as excessive anxiety, depression, obsessive-compulsive behavior, or physical complaints without objective evidence of disease are not caused by organic malfunction. These symptoms can be thought of as a form of protest, and need to be understood for the purpose they serve in a social context, including attention, revenge, power, or inadequacy in dealing with life situations.

Dreikurs (1967) noted that the difference between psychosis, neurotic disorders, and personality disorders is the degree of common sense in relationship to private logic. Psychosis is possible when there is a positive family history for a major psychiatric disorder, a biological genetic predisposition, child-rearing practices that lead to extreme feelings of inadequacy, and/or self-training in discouragement. Psychotic behavior can be thought of as a cry of powerlessness. "One becomes schizophrenic over a period of time in response to cumulative life stresses and a feeling of failure. The choice to behave this way is neither conscious nor planned ahead of time," (Sperry et al., 1993, p. 33). The individual responds to inner reality (sense of self) and outer reality (sense of who others are) in a way that interferes with and even shuts out satisfying or loving relationships. In psychosis one is not able to make connections with others.

Shulman (1993) expects a person diagnosed as schizophrenic or suffering from bipolar disorder to hold superhuman goals and a lack of common sense in trying to achieve them, along with psychotic symptoms. Only medication can reach through to the person trapped inside the intensity of the psychosis. Sperry and Carlson (1993) remind us that "research has shown that schizophrenics have a higher level of aspiration than non-schizophrenics, and they tend to raise these levels after repeated failures rather than lowering them as normal persons do" therefore subjecting themselves to repeated failure and depression (p. 44). The goal may be very high: to reach perfection and maybe genius levels in any area of life which, for some, is their way of contributing to society. But it also may be extremely inappropriate when it brings about constant feelings of failure and isolation from others. In psychosis, one is unaware that common sense is discarded and only feelings of omnipotence prevail. These individuals act "as if" their private logic were fact rather than fiction, and say "no" to living in cooperation with the social order of life. People with neurotic disorders say "yes, but" to life and move with hesitation in meeting the tasks of life, finding excuses and wanting to blame others for not achieving success (Mosak, 1977).

There is a similarity between schizophrenia and the acutely disordered state of the manic phase. However, those who are manic seek close rather than distant relationships and their behavior is designed to keep others busy with them. The person with bipolar disorder acts to protect him or herself from the danger of loss of self-esteem by establishing a "good" relationship with others, fitting in with their wishes, fearing that not to do so, love will be withheld. "Individuals with bipolar disorder usually accept the human role whereas schizophrenics do not" (Sperry et al., 1993, p. 48).

Most of us want to bring balance back into our lives so that we can participate usefully in life again. Even as children we will do so if we are not deeply discouraged. For children, the issues might be separation anxiety, loss or death of a parent, feelings of isolation from peers, sexual abuse, power struggles, or depression due to either a real or perceived crisis situation. Whether pathology is found in children or in adults, the effect of the behavior on family members is profound and also needs to be addressed.

And the mystery in understanding human behavior: "Everything" we think, either for ourselves or for others, "can also be different. The uniqueness of the individual cannot be expressed in a short formula" (Ansbacher & Ansbacher, 1956, p. 194). But we can guess, with empathy as a starting place, to make sense out of what we as therapists are experiencing or what our clients, with luck, tell us they are experiencing.

It can be legally difficult to get someone to treatment, especially when the client is an adult. There is always the possibility of damaging the trust holding together a relationship. Once in therapy, most of us resist insight into our own behavior and will only attempt it when we feel we have a chance to make life better for ourselves. The creative process of art-making, either individually or in groups, can encourage awareness of the changes we can make that will help us move away from safeguarding behaviors we use when life doesn't go the way we wish. Adler was optimistic and believed in the creative nature of human beings, only that we need to train ourselves in the direction of social equality and social interest, but he also knew that we need to recognize what might be unjust situations and to help correct them in a respectful way.

PUTTING OURSELVES AT ONE WITH OTHERS

When learning to become art therapists, we don't separate ourselves from the lives of those suffering mental disorders because, given certain circumstances, we could just as easily find ourselves in the same discouraging life situations. We participate in the art experientials in the same way we would if we were the clients. Self-disclosure is always an option, as is asking for responses from others in the group. We understand that what we say about the work of others also says something about ourselves. I need to tell you about my art, not for you to diagnose, but just to have you help me understand where I am at the moment. This can help me face the reality of my current life situation. By this time in the program students know that the drawing they create will express their in-the-moment thoughts, feelings and attitude, that there is no right or wrong way to express ourselves in art, and that we learn from each other in open communication.

LOOKING AT A RESEARCH STUDY

For over one hundred years the most persistent question has been whether accurate diagnostic information is systematically encoded in the art of psychiatric patients.

THE FORMAL ELEMENTS ART THERAPY SCALE

Linda Gantt (1990) gave me permission to show slides of the art work that she had collected from art therapy sessions for her dissertation research. Her study included the art work of patients suffering from schizophrenia, bipolar disorder, paranoia, substance abuse, major depression, organic mental disorder, and dementia, as well as non-patients. She decided to use a single-picture assessment for researching diagnostic information in the art of those patients with mental disorders. The Formal Elements Art Therapy Scale (FEATS) is the title of the 14 scales of assessment she developed with Paula Howie in 1979 that they correlated with the a-theo-retical descriptions of specific diagnoses from the *DSM*-III.

The art therapy students were given a list of the psychiatric disorders being used in the study along with the 14 rating scales. As the slides of the art work were shown, we talked about each one to see how the rating scale applied. The students then made guesses about the diagnosis of the disorder based on how they understood each of the disorders. I wanted the students to see for themselves if there were any distinguishing differences between the art of patients and the art of non-patients. And if so, could they demonstrate that the art of patients contains at least some information or something distinctive which could be understood without a verbal explanation from the artist.

It was agreed that the drawings done by controls were significantly different from those of patients with organic disorders on some of the scales. Drawings of controls were significantly different from those with mania. Drawings of both controls and patients with major depression were significantly different from those patients with schizophrenia and drawings of patients with major depression were significantly different from those with schizophrenia. And even though we were searching for diagnostic clues, and we could recognize a certain idiosyncratic peculiarity or strangeness, we could not determine that accurate diagnostic information is systematically encoded in the art of patients suffering from mental disorders.

Caveat: Anti-psychotic drugs and anti-depressant drugs act quickly and a difference of a week between the making of one piece of art and another could change the way we think about a client. Also it is important to consider the culture's art style especially as it relates to those patients who come from non-western settings.

THE ART DIRECTIVE: "Draw a person picking an apple from a tree."

This drawing experiential was first described by Viktor Lowenfeld (1939) in a study he conducted on a child's use of space in art, and is the same one that Linda Gantt used for her research study.

An Adlerian art therapist will not use art work for psychological testing (Dreikurs, S., 1986) nor will we label behavior according to the *DSM-V.* Diagnosis, even when it is done by a psychiatrist, contributes little to the well-being of the client. The explanation of the drawing's meaning is left entirely up to the client, or to the student in this case, so we look at each other's drawings and give each other the opportunity to integrate inner thoughts (self-understanding) and outer or social reality from our own art work. Invariably, the students found ways to be encouraging to each other.

CONCLUSION

The art experientials we do in class can lead to reconciliation of the seemingly never-ending continuum between the real and the ideal, between what we hope for and what we get, between lacking self-esteem to earning self-respect, from being dependent on others for help and learning to take care of ourselves. "The unconscious often works in unexpected ways" long after class is over, when students have taken their art work home, taped it to the wall, and continue to find meaning in it. (Lydiatt, 1987, p. 9). What we see in our art work on a day-to-day basis can be astonishing. In this way, there is no end to the art we can create in response to an art directive done in class.

I believe that change is possible for me, and for my clients: we are all capable of making positive changes in our lives. Recognition of a behavior pattern can be immediate, or it can take time, sometimes years. Reconciling the inner world (how we really feel) with the outer world (meeting the challenges of life in useful ways) requires the willingness to first acknowledge and accept and then to change whatever beliefs, attitude, or mistaken goals keep us from enjoying our connection to others in our lives.

Art becomes the bridge
Between the self we know
And the self we keep secret

12

Loss/Grieving: Art Therapy and Psychodrama

This chapter begins with an Art Directive that reminds us that there are many different types of loss, some that the students have already experienced, such as loss of a parent, a sibling, a job, a friendship, a relationship. Loss is something we experience every day in many ways, big and small; the loss of health (when illness comes), a dream, a pet, economic security, when a child grows up and leaves home, loss of home, belongings, and community which can happen, after all, due to disaster or moving to a different place. We learn not to even acknowledge some losses, there are so many.

THE ART DIRECTIVE: Draw what "loss" looks like to you.
Process: We share our drawings with each other.

Combining the communicative and healing power of psychodrama and art during times of loss helps students to recognize that all creative therapies employ spontaneity as part of the healing process. Art and psychodrama revolve around the issues of grief that students bring, and the most troubling of these are about death. Both the art done in class and the psychodrama evoke emotion; together they invite insight and transformation from grief to acceptance.

Grieving is a uniquely personal process. Sometimes we want our story to be heard and our feelings to be understood but there is little evidence that "telling our story" will help to alleviate our suffering. As humans, we attempt to put meaning on every kind of death, from illness, a fatal accident on the highway, suicide, from gun violence, or soldiers dying on the killing field. Death can come in so many "unnatural" ways that we sometimes find it hard to accept.

LEARNING ABOUT LIFE AND DEATH

As small children, we learn from nature and from our parents that all living forms, plants, animals, birds, fish, loved ones, eventually die and that we, too, will die someday. Of course, we don't understand what that means until we are older. It is natural that life comes to an end, and this does not need to be unhappy; but grief is a natural reaction in people and even some animals. Even when death is expected, the task at hand is to learn how to integrate that loss, which can be more difficult when it is someone we have deeply loved.

In preschool children learn songs about the seasons and how the year goes round and round. It is a time when children learn compassion and how to take care of all living things.

We had a funeral for a rabbit that died and I let the children tell me their ideas about death. We got another bunny and, guess what, the children named that one "Honey Bun," too. And when one child's baby brother died from a heart defect, we found we didn't have an answer for that, but only that we couldn't go to the cemetery and bring him home again. For another child's uncle to be killed in the war, the only reason I could give was that "Freedom isn't free," and that her uncle fought in a war to keep us safe. "Why" is the first question children ask when they are told that life does not last forever, and it is the last question we all ask when someone we love dies.

LOSS

Borrowing from ancient cultures, I sometimes like to bring a beautiful stone to class. We pass the stone around and when it's our turn, we tell the story of a loss and what we did to survive it. As we remember our own moments of resiliency, we feel encouraged by our strengths. Many times loss does not fit with our picture of how life should be. Loss can be due to a traumatic event; war, a terrorist attack, an earthquake, a tsunami, floods, a hurricane, a plane crash, a ship sinking, or a house destroyed by fire. Loss of innocence, boundaries, self, might be due to sexual abuse or sexual assault. These losses stay with us for a lifetime in one way or another and can even change the configuration in our brains. In the group process, we express our thoughts in a drawing or create a piece of art that helps us to be open to the process grief. In turn, we witness the creative process of others as they find ways to integrate or transform loss and grief in their own lives.

THE ART DIRECTIVE: Drawing Another's Experience of Loss
Process: Choose a partner, listen to each other's story of loss, and then draw it. With the help of your drawing and with your partner's permission, tell the story of your partner's loss to the class (McAbee, 1992, demonstration at a NASAP convention).

When a student seems "warmed up" to the loss, a psychodrama takes place. Psychodrama expresses in action what often does not translate easily into words. Psychodrama gives the student a chance to act out the story of loss with the help of other group members taking on different roles and also sharing the feeling of what loss was for them (for more on psychodrama, see Chapter 14).

SOME BRIEF CULTURAL AND RELIGIOUS PERSPECTIVES ABOUT DEATH

The socially responsible therapist is aware of cultural bias for self as well as for others when we pay attention to the art, the psychodrama, and the meaning of a death for our clients. Even though art is less dependent on words, we still need to be sensitive to what the art uniquely expresses about the other person. We put our own thoughts on hold and then check out the meaning of the art with the client by listening to his or her story. Different cultures have much to teach us about the grieving process when illness and death are involved. We can offer each other comfort if we understand, for instance, that the belief in the value of prayer can sometimes bring relief during a loved one's long debilitating illness or death.

Religions offer a response to death, while science is quiet on a possible afterlife. Some general guidelines for how religions view the afterlife include the following: Judaism places more focus on the proper actions in this life and has little to say about possible afterlife; Christians believe in heaven and hell, and that your destination depends on faith and your good deeds during life; Muslims are similar to Christians in believing there will be a day of judgment when the dead will be divided between paradise and damnation; Buddhists usually claim the doctrine of reincarnation, ending only in the final liberation known as Nirvana; Hindus also believe in reincarnation, with the status of your next life depending on your actions in this one; and life and death are the flip sides of the Tao (Taoism) with death being a transformation from being to non-being. Some cultures have a funeral to celebrate, as in China's Donghai region where a funeral is considered a status symbol. Americans mostly see a funeral as a way to pay respects and say goodbye to the one they have lost.

JAPAN'S SUICIDE CULTURE

As a therapist, it may be important to know that suicide in Japan has historically been seen as an acceptable option in a strongly hierarchical culture. Rather than being considered pathological, the Japanese have viewed suicide as a gesture of moral integrity and preserving honor, or even an act of beauty. In Japan, there has never been any kind of religious prohibition against suicide as there is in the West, leaving people the right to choose their own death. This is the cultural theory of suicide in Japan, but for most of the past hundred years, the rate of suicide in Japan is much the same as most countries in the West.

In Japan, a Buddhist monk leads death workshops for the suicidal at his temple (MacFarquhar, 2013). He first asks them to imagine that they have only three months left to live, and wants them to write down what they want to do in those three months. Then he wants them to imagine and write down what they would do if they have one month left, then a week, then ten minutes. Most start to cry. One man realized he had never considered what he might want to do with his life. He felt liberated from the desire to die and went on to live a useful life.

In American society there is a tendency to see death as a failure. When we are older and near death, we are sometimes encouraged to hang onto life well beyond the time it makes sense to let go.

TRANSFORMING THE PAIN OF LOSS

The shattering despair of some deaths leaves no room for negotiation, and almost no room for hope. We want our old lives back, with the same dreams and hopes for the future. We learn that nothing lasts forever, good or bad, and that nothing goes exactly as we might have planned. The art gives form to our images of loss and grief. Psychodrama can help to relieve the pain of loss associated with a death as it did with a woman who had suffered a miscarriage. In psychodrama, she was able to hold her baby, give her a name and love, and say good-bye to her.

Another client showed resentment against the elements when he lost his parents in an earthquake while he was away. His drawing showed the collapse of the home where they lived, with his parents now buried under the rubble. In psychodrama, he was able to hold his parents, comfort them, and tell them how much he loved and honored them. Psychodrama was able to transform his feelings of loss into a loving memory.

MEMORIALIZING THE LOSS

The memory of any significant death never leaves, but love continues. Sometimes we can use that love to help someone else: start a scholarship fund, plant trees, donate to a cause, charity, or research important to the person who has died. We watch "Carved from the Heart" (Frankenstein & Brady, 1998), a portrait of grief, healing, and community. Filmed in Alaska, it is the story of a man who, with the help of his community, carved a totem pole in memory of his son who died of a drug overdose.

We find there are different ways to transform our grief experiences by creatively finding ways to memorialize the loss. On Memorial Day at Ala Moana Beach Park in Hawaii, people send more than 1,000 paper lanterns, glowing orange, out to sea. This is a centuries old Buddhist ritual which centers on small lanterns believed to ferry spirits on a safe journey over the ocean to their spiritual home. Those of us on the beach fill out individual prayer slips that we attach to the lantern frames. Powerful drumming and chanting resonates over the surf as we release the lanterns into the water. Watching the lanterns move toward the horizon and seeming to disappear over the earth's edge brings us solace as we grieve for our loved ones who have died. The feeling among us is one of shared contentment. Without even talking we share a connection with one another.

THE ART DIRECTIVE: Listen to the Guided Meditation

You are walking on a country road in late afternoon. On one side you see meadows filled with wild flowers, animals grazing, and a barn in the distance. On the other side willow trees outline the passage of a rippling stream. You feel the gentle breeze, and become aware of your breathing, grateful for the powerful gift of renewal.

You come to some fields, freshly plowed and newly sprouted. Rocks, pried out of the land, create a natural barrier. You wonder what it must have been like for those first farmers to grow crops in this rich soil, warmed by the sun and nourished by rain, to harvest the food and to prepare a meal for their families. As a child, you remember helping to plant some corn and, learning to be patient, you saw the miracle of life appear as if by magic, food for the table, and then death at the end of the season when the snow came.

Looking beyond the fields you catch a glimpse of deer in the shafts of sunlight before they blend into the shadows. You listen to the sound of birds calling to one another as the shadows lengthen. Before long, the road brings you to within sight of the inn where you are staying. Others have stayed here before you, leaving a legacy of many stories within its walls. It reminds you of home, where the heart is.

Process: Make a drawing of what you heard that inspired you. When everyone is finished with their drawing, I ask the students if they are willing to tear up their drawing and make a collage with the pieces. Not everyone does it.

Discussion follows, and sometimes psychodrama.

Objective: How does this experience fit with your experience of loss? Is it possible that out of the old or what is "lost," you can create something new and beautiful? How does this drawing/story/process fit with how you understand loss in your life?

For death of a loved one, the pain of grief is never constant but never fully goes away either. Two major tasks need to be accomplished during the time of mourning: to acknowledge and accept that death has occurred, and learn to integrate the emotions and problems this loss creates. There is no set time-table; it is different for each of us.

Rationale: Drawing our grief and using psychodrama can be a means to get to a less conscious level of knowing ourselves and bring light to some of our deeper thoughts and beliefs about any loss. "So it seems the materials of renewal are always at hand, deep within the artist's imagination and the longing of the heart. To stay vibrant and alive, we need to make a clear and open space from which to awaken and see the world differently" (Kapitan 2003, p 61).

It is sometimes as simple as drawing a milkweed pod or a pine cone and seeing the abundance of seeds ready to spill out to start new life. The metaphor in nature can bring comfort. We understand once again that life is temporary and that within every ending there is the promise of a new beginning, maybe not in the way we expect.

HELP WITH LOSS AND GRIEF

A friend who lost her brother to suicide founded and named an organization called Loving Outreach to Survivors of Suicide (LOSS) in his memory. It is now part of Catholic Charities, serving as a free, non-denominational program that supports individuals who are grieving the suicide of a loved one.

There are veterans returning home from military service where they experienced severe trauma and life-threatening moments. No longer are they living with a group of soldiers with a common purpose. Many of these veterans are suffering from posttraumatic stress disorder (PTSD), traumatic brain injury, depression, and anxiety. Some have turned to addiction, alcohol, drugs, or overwork, as a way to escape tormenting thoughts. The number of veteran suicides is rising.

Some veterans want to protect their families from the brutal combat stories where they had no control over what was happening and found themselves witnessing their friends being horrifically injured and dying. Art therapy students working in this field have been trained to do the intense work involved with helping veterans transition back into civilian society. In the art therapy group, veterans can replace the isolation and emptiness they are experiencing by telling their painful stories and supporting each other in their search for a new sense of community.

Art therapists, through the International Art Therapy Organization and locally, have gone wherever there is trauma and loss, providing relief in recovery from disasters, both natural and man-made. Probably the most important path toward healing is being able to share and be witnesses to the art done in group. Viewing our experiences as expressed through our art can bring our emotions into conscious awareness, possibly making it easier to communicate those feelings in words and integrate the trauma into our lives.

A small minority in any age group will have a hard time and experience complicated grief (*DSM-V*) and need help from a therapist. Having done their own experiential learning regarding loss and grieving in this course, students will be better able to focus their efforts on tailoring interventions when working with loss, death, and trauma.

Research is ongoing. Perhaps someday neuroscientists will be able to tell us that the creative process of making art and encouragement from group members can help to heal the effects of traumatic memories, making PTSD less threatening in our lives.

CAN NEUROSCIENCE HELP?

For almost one hundred years scientists have studied the way long term and short term memories are imprinted upon our brains and the neural systems involved in learning, emotion, and memory. A neuroscientist studies the intricate biology of how emotional memories are formed in the brain and, most recently, the connection between memory and fear. Fear is an instinct that helps us respond to dangerous situations; known to us as the "fight, flight, or freeze" response. We need fear memories to survive. But what happens when fear takes over our lives? Over five percent of us experience some form of post-traumatic stress disorder. For combat veterans the figure is even higher. "Others suffer from severe anxiety, debilitating phobias, and the biologically-based cravings of addiction. Emotions appear to be formed in the same neural pathways used to create memories. This might mean that a successful treatment for fear associated with traumatic memories could also work for these other conditions (Specter, 2014, p. 36).

Behavioral therapies can sometimes work, especially teaching people to overcome their fear through presenting negative memories over and over again without anything bad happening, which psychiatrists refer to as "exposure therapy." I learned it years ago as "extinction" theory. Unfortunately, people sometimes experience a particularly stressful situation in the future and the fear memory can often return to overwhelm the calm memory.

We change our memories, sometimes on a daily basis. It is nothing new and something we may do unconsciously or sometimes even consciously. We remember only what is useful to us, sometimes even making it up, but it is debilitating to us to be trapped in a life where we are constantly reminded of the overwhelming fear attached to trauma.

Neuroscience may help us find a way to rewrite our darkest memories. We would still have the memory of the trauma, but the addictive emotion of fear would be blocked. To go beyond erasing or rewriting our memories, perhaps we could find new treatments to restore memories we have lost due to Alzheimer's or other trauma to the brain. These thoughts seem far off into the future, yet we already know that a primary function of the brain is the maintenance of health and psychological balance (compensating for feelings of inferiority). According to Robert Ornstein and David Sobel (1987), "the brain has evolved complex 'bodyguards' designed to ward off disease, and it may even be that our human tendency toward social connectedness may help keep us well." (p. 50)

Death has been with us
Since ancient dawn breaking
IT COMES AS NO SURPRISE

13

Addictive Behavior and the Use of Art in Recovery

The drawings we do at the beginning of this class help to establish a common ground for understanding and working with problems of addiction. We start with learning that addiction refers to an unhealthy attachment to one or more of the following: alcohol, drugs, gambling, sex, work, internet, and also to behaviors that include compulsions, eating disorders, and co-dependent relationships. The word "addiction" can be defined as devoting or surrendering oneself to something habitually or obsessively which is harmful to the person and to relationships with others.

THE ART DIRECTIVE: Draw what addiction looks like to you.

PROBLEMS OF ADDICTION

R. Dreikurs observed that susceptibility to addiction can begin with doubt and fear about meeting the challenges of life and often lead to the unconscious need to depend on something, such as a repeated activity or behavior, or someone else for security and reassurance. Thoughts of being not good enough and fear of failure keep us from cooperating and participating in life in healthy ways. The addictive process is a learned way of coping so that these feelings of inadequacy can be avoided.

Addiction involves a complicated mixture of personality, genetic factors, cultural forces, and our individual response to stressful situations in life. Alcoholism, drug abuse, depression, and co-dependency are at the useless end of compensating for the feeling of inferiority. So are stress disorders, compulsions, and eating disorders.

We choose to addict ourselves in spite of being "wired for survival," with some addictions leading to serious negative behaviors, brain impairment, criminal behavior, physical illnesses, and social consequences, e.g., DUIs, death, domestic abuse, divorce, bankruptcy, absenteeism from work. This can happen to any one of us at any time when feelings we don't understand take over our lives, making addiction hard to overcome, no matter how hard we fight. Addiction is not a sickness or a disease, but comes from an ordinary process that gets exaggerated and becomes a habit that controls our lives. Alfred Adler (1917) believed that "addiction is a form of the neurotic arrangement and could only be healed if community feeling increases and vanity decreases" (*The Neurotic Constitution*). This theory fits with the basic principles of Alcoholics Anonymous (1939), which calls for "a transformation of thought and attitude" (thinking less about self); being interested in and being useful to others (similar to community feeling and social interest).

Alcoholism is a progressive disorder. It begins with pleasure and then progresses to more than normal control over our lives and becomes self-destructive and potentially harmful to others. Always, it creates distance in relationships. As the behavior deteriorates into hurting, punishing, and risking-taking behavior, someone close may try to protect and take care of him or her. Taken to the extreme, this becomes enabling behavior even though the reward is often intolerable and abusive treatment. Co-dependence is an addictive behavior pattern that gives control of our lives to others rather than trusting ourselves and others to meet the challenges of life independently.

EATING DISORDERS

"Eating disorders are characterized by a preoccupation with food" which involve a refusal to eat, overeating and purging (Sperry et al., 1993, p. 567). Both bulimia and anorexia nervosa can lead to compulsive behavior, depression, and even death. Eating disorders can be considered a passive form of rebellion combined with a desire for what one considers an idealized body image. An anorectic has a distorted idea about his or her own body image and denies reality checks. Bulimics are overly concerned with body shape and weight. Both tend to deny the need for therapeutic intervention which could help them choose more useful means for coping with the feelings of inferiority that most likely initiated the addictive behavior.

Unresolved emotional issues leading to depression, rage, powerlessness and loss, faulty thinking about body size, and negative family environments, can all be used to explain the development of an eating disorder including inherited biological or genetic variables. Some possible mistaken messages a child, a teenager, or an adult might be giving themselves are, "I am a failure," "I'm not as good as others," "I can never live up to the expectations of others," and so "the symptoms of an eating disorder provide a distraction (and even relief) from the intense feelings of inferiority which include despair and feelings of helplessness" (Belangee, 2006, p. 5). Recovery from addiction or addictive behavior patterns requires breaking the unhealthy attachment and consciously working to create a healthy re-orientation to life. Some refuse to do it.

AN ADLERIAN PERSPECTIVE ON UNDERSTANDING THE PROCESS OF ADDICTION

THE ART DIRECTIVE: Draw yourself reaching out to your child self

Process: Select any art materials and create a drawing of yourself at any stage in life reaching out to yourself as a child.

Objective: To think of a time before addiction took over our lives. Using art can inspire us to go beyond the way we might habitually respond to life and others around us.

Rationale: That by reaching out to our child self we remember the innocence and purity but also the pain we might have experienced (due to rejection, abandonment, cruelty, abuse) but didn't know how to understand it. "Art is the creation of form and form expresses human feeling" (Langer, 1953). In class, we discuss what we do to compensate for the feeling of pain.

The social adjustment each child makes in learning to cope with the challenges of life begins in infancy. As the child starts "to make sense out of life," he or she begins to solve what Adler called "life's central problem – the attitude toward others," always on a continuum from being deeply discouraged to being encouraged toward developing independence and social interest" (Dreikurs, R., 1971, p. 66).

Trust begins in the connection with the primary caretaker. This leads to establishing mutuality and the capacity for giving to others, clearly a prerequisite to the development of social interest. The differentiation of self from non-self is another developmental step toward the discipline of social interest. The family can gently influence the innate potential of the child to move towards being more self-confident, more self-sufficient, and having a more positive and joyful attitude towards others and life situations. A sense of self-esteem increases feelings of being able to master difficult situations. If the child is not helped to handle frustration in a useful way it can lead to experiencing exaggerated feelings of inferiority, inadequacy, insecurity, or unworthiness that is sometimes compensated for by addictive patterns of behavior. The child becomes afraid of showing true feelings for fear of punishment (shame and guilt) or rejection (fear of abandonment). Children want to succeed and will do so if not discouraged.

Co-dependent patterns of behavior can begin in any family system where the child unconsciously decides that he or she is unacceptable, and that the opinion of others is more important than his or her own. The child's true self is hidden as the child tries out behavior that he or she hopes will bring the feeling of safety and the feeling of belonging that is the motivation for all behavior. The child might choose behavior that at the extreme creates over-dependency (moves toward); that defeats others (hostility, moves against); or that moves away from (isolation) the demands of social living (Horney, 1951).

Children, no matter what the family situation is like, will make their own decisions about themselves and life. Throughout our lives we continue to make adjustments in our social interactions with others. Sometimes we look to another person as an example or a mentor for how we want to live our lives. As adults we know that social conflict brings suffering but also gives the opportunity to become more aware of private, mistaken goals and how they stand in the way of healthy relationships. We can learn to compensate for feelings of inadequacy and loneliness, or hopelessness and helplessness, by changing our attitudes, thoughts, and behavior. We can begin by accepting responsibility for our own behavior without giving excuses, blaming others, or finding fault.

A pattern of addictive behavior usually begins with a perceived crisis situation leading to stress. The crisis for some might mean "not pleasing others," or not being "top dog;" while for others, it could be "the feeling of being controlled." Some might be in crisis when they believe they are "not getting the most out of people," others when they are not "the center of attention." Still others may experience crisis when they see themselves as less than perfect (Mosak, 1977, pp. 183-186).

One way we can become aware of and learn to counter these self-defeating beliefs is by drawing our feelings and sharing our stories. The art process, with the support and encouragement of the group, leads to a more active and intuitive understanding of the meaning we give to our life experiences.

THE ART DIRECTIVE: Draw your space

Process: Take a sheet of paper, put an image of yourself on the paper, and then draw what the space around you looks like

Objective: To become aware of what the space in your life feels like; the thoughts and emotions you experience when you see what happens in your space.

Rationale: to have a better understanding of how you compensate for the feelings evoked in your drawing.

ROLE OF DENIAL AND DISHONESTY IN ADDICTION

Denial is a method we unconsciously choose in order to avoid aware-ness of any perceived unacceptable reality. Denial of addiction keeps us unaware of unhealthy behaviors and their potentially fatal consequences. Denial serves the purpose of keeping anxiety at bay while addiction grad-ually develops, and also keeps secret any insight into the purpose of our behavior. When confronted, some of us will say that we don't have an ad-diction problem, or that the problem is being exaggerated, or we blame our job, lack of job, or anything else to justify our addiction. Although others might recognize the denial, they can only actively step in to stop it when there is danger of death.

THE ART DIRECTIVE: Draw your "wall of denial." (Chickerneo, 1993)
Process: If you are willing, take a sheet of paper and paint or draw a wall that you might be using to keep awareness of addiction in denial. We describe our "walls" and how they protect us from knowing the truth.
Objective: To let the intuitive self create the wall that keeps you from let-ting go of addictive behavior; to learn what feelings keep the wall togeth-er; to see how addiction creates distance in relationships and contributes to our feelings of loneliness and detachment.
Rationale: To look at our thoughts, emotions, and behaviors and begin to understand the private logic we use to give ourselves excuses for our ad-dictions, including co-dependency; to learn that it is okay to express our feelings and emotions; to gain understanding of how addictive patterns of behavior makes our relationships with others very difficult and sometimes impossible.

Treatment for addiction can fail when one resists or is excused from the need to understand the private logic of the denial pattern which is intrinsic to the nature of any addiction. The philosophy of Alcoholics Anonymous (A.A.) places the greatest importance on conversion in the process of re-covery. What impressed me after attending an A.A. meeting as part of an assignment in the addictions class was the sense of community, where everyone was respectful of and encouraging to those struggling with feelings of shame and guilt.

ART THERAPY AND THE SPIRITUAL PROCESS

Alcoholics Anonymous (A.A.) was the first 12-step program designed for recovery from alcoholism based on spirituality. Being actively involved in the 12-step program is one way to encourage creative and spiritual growth. Achieving spiritual growth and personal growth are the same. Both call for self-awareness so that we can begin to accept and understand our perceived feelings of inferiority and learn to compensate for them in a useful way. For the partner or parent, Al-Anon meetings can help one to establish and maintain boundaries without becoming co-dependent with an addict.

According to A.A. philosophy, as we "let go and let God" in whatever way works for us, we will be able to free ourselves from addictive patterns of behavior. Spiritual growth happens best when we are able to acknowledge our addiction and to give up the mistaken goal of having to be "perfect," "the best," or "the most pleasing," the "fixer," the "hero," or even "the center of attention." Once we are able to identify a mistaken goal and recognize the illusion that it once provided security, it will be easier to let it go.

In A.A., "spirituality" refers to symbolic expressions of behavior that indicate personal awareness and growth. These expressions can indicate a change in behavior from obsessive dependency on or attachment to behaviors, things or people to living more in harmony with the social order of life. When there is recovery from an addiction we can sometimes turn useless compensation into useful compensation by helping others who want to recover. Social interest is the antitheses of addiction.

SMART RECOVERY

A secular alternative to A.A. is SMART Recovery (Self-Management and Recovery Training). Participants choose this approach because it treats addiction as a problem that can be solved through self-help and rational thinking. It borrows many of its techniques from cognitive-behavioral therapy; focusing on motivation to cope with urges, managing feelings and behavior, and learning to live a more balanced life. Those who support this alternative believe that sobriety is within their control and is a choice people are equipped to make.

DRAWING THE EARLY RECOLLECTION (DREIKURS, S., 1986)

A brief review: we draw what we know from within based on memories created by past experiences and adapted to fit our current life situations. Art can give form to these recollections stored as images in our memories. These few Early Recollections (ERs) kept at the level of awareness express our unconscious attitude toward life. The attitude, deeply rooted in unconscious feelings of early childhood, need to be re-experienced before they can be made conscious and understood in relation to the present moment (Miller, 1986). The process of making art actively involves us in our own recovery process.

THE ART DIRECTIVE: Draw or create an Early Recollection (Dreikurs, S., 1986) of a spiritual experience you had as a child.

Process: Take a sheet of paper, any size or color, or any art materials and create a visual image of an ER related to a "spiritual" experience you had as a child. If you are willing, share this experience with us.

Objective: to make visual an experience where you became aware of "a power greater than yourself."

Rationale: to practice and learn to recognize the truth of what you believe; a subjective experience which opens to some insight or awareness of how you have created meaning and value for your life.

THE ART DIRECTIVE: Self-Symbol and Torn Away Paper

Process: On a piece of paper create a symbol to represent yourself. Then tear away the paper from around the symbol you created. Place your self-symbol on a larger piece of paper. Use the torn paper scraps in whatever way works for you. Journal about your self-symbol and the torn scraps of paper.

Objective: To see what happens for you when you tear away the paper surrounding your self-symbol and how this process might reflect what is going on in your life right now.

Rationale: To become more aware of the responsibility we have for making choices and creating the meaning for our lives.

THE ART DIRECTIVE: The Willow Branch

Process: Choose a corkscrew willow branch and make it your own by decorating it or drawing it. Journal what the willow branch symbolizes for you.

Objective: To think and to talk about, if students are willing, how the plant world creates balance when nature brings about destruction and chaos and the parallel to our own lives when we feel threatened, vulnerable, or wounded.

Rationale: that by bringing into awareness ways in which we create balance in our lives (moving from a minus to a plus), we can practice "letting go" of unhealthy ways to compensate for feelings of inferiority, inadequacy, and loneliness. The branch can be used to attach prayers, messages of encouragement, "letting go" of some behavior that holds us back (willing to give up blaming others for unsatisfying relationships), asking for forgiveness, making amends to someone we have hurt, and to make a commitment to recovery.

There is no deterministic way for understanding human behavior. Stress does not cause addiction; it is always a choice, complicated by genetics and cultural forces. Those who choose addiction are motivated by their own need for security and the addiction itself serves only to help relieve or deny perceived feelings of inferiority. Addiction keeps us busy with behavior which can eventually destroy us both physically and spiritually. A mistaken and self-defeating view that "others owe me and can be manipulated to meet my needs" or "I'm not good enough as I am" keeps me from responding to life in a useful way.

All art therapy experientials are done as a group in the classroom as a way for students to experience how it is to work with clients in a group setting. Tee Dreikurs recognized that the group experience

> ...opens up the natural creativity and spontaneity which we all had in our childhood, which is frequently lost in the process of growing up. The group experience enhances cooperation and produces a feeling of belonging, the participants respond to mood rather than thought, (and) new relationships are established. Painting can be used as a medium to facilitate behavioral, emotional, and attitudinal change in the 'here and now' situation. No specific knowledge of past history or of diagnostic categories is required since the trained therapist can perceive the patient's immediate behavioral responses and can understand them in terms of social distance versus social participation, discouragement versus optimism, and competition versus cooperation. (Dreikurs, S., 1976, p. 79).

Without focusing on the symptom, we are treating the underlying purpose of addiction. I love how this works!

THE ART DIRECTIVE: On the Sea of Life
Process: Tear a large sheet of paper (approximately 4' x 12') from a roll and tape it to the wall. As a group design and create the "sea of life" to include open sea, stormy and calm, an island, a beach, a pier, a lighthouse, a first aid station, and a life guard. Then taking whatever materials you wish, create what you look like on the "sea of life."
Objective: To see life as a journey and how we keep ourselves safe but also open to adventure as we encounter different situations in life. To explore the choices we make, movement in life, originality, how we "surf" life or go deep.

SUMMARY

We end this course on a playful note, yet the art directive can lead to insight and inspiration as we learn to understand attitudes and behaviors that impact our lives.

What sustains the
Addictive personality is
The belief that addiction
Is a sickness

14

Group Dream Work Using
Art and Psychodrama

Working with dreams in the classroom is similar to the approach used when drawing Early Recollections (ERs) (Dreikurs, S., 1986), except that in this class we combine art making with psychodrama to explore the meaning of the dream. Objectives of this course are to become familiar with terms, concepts and the use of art, psychodrama, symbol and metaphor in understanding dreams. Students bring their own dreams to use in the didactic work we do in class. The instructors act in the roles of group facilitators; one as the art therapist, the other as director of psychodrama.

BASIC ASSUMPTIONS ABOUT DREAMS
We might be able to influence what we dream about (lucid dreaming) but never what we will dream for the mechanism of creating the dream is inaccessible to conscious influence (Freud,1932). Dreams are sometimes the shadow of the current life situation (Aristotle) and can help us understand how we unconsciously experienced a life event. Sleep and dreams come in the service of health and wholeness by bringing the body back into balance. Dreams follow the Law of Compensation…a psychological mechanism by which feelings of inferiority, frustration, or failure in one area are counterbalanced by achievement or positive feelings in another area (moving from a minus to a plus). Example: In waking life I was rescued from an accident; in my dream I found myself tending to and helping a stranger who had been in an accident.

For Adler, "the task of the dream is to meet the difficulty in life and to provide a solution, but often the solution or goal reveals a lack of courage" (1931, p.96). "Dreams are the factory of emotions" (Adler) and "all emotions in dreams serve the purpose of fortifying attitudes and actions; their strength lies in the fact that their purpose is not recognized" (Dreikurs, R. cited in Shulman, B., 1973, p. 63). Rudolf Dreikurs (1967) called this the "self-deception of the dream." We see what we want to see. We understand what we are ready to understand. Example: In my dream I found myself in a situation for which I was unprepared; I told myself that I was in the wrong place (avoidance). In waking life, I found myself facing a difficult situation and knew that somehow I had to find a way to make peace with it; that it would be impossible to avoid.

If it is important to the individual to maintain the "fiction" of his or her life, then the dream helps to maintain the unconsciously self-created goal. Dreams can be understood as attempts to reinforce and facilitate movement towards subjectively chosen goals and are a reflection of our lifestyle pattern. Others might have ideas for the meaning of the dream, but the dreamer is the final authority.

Our goals might be the "good part of ourselves, taken to the extreme, but they still might reflect "the private goal of superiority; that of being in control, being perfect, pleasing, or even being helpful when others can help themselves, that creates distance in our relationships with others (Mosak, 1977). It is the attitude, emotion, and purpose of the dream that is explored in the group dream approach. The dreamer decides if his or her behavior is useful or if it gets in the way of the relationship.

TELLING THE DREAM

One student volunteers to tell a dream that feels significant, but is not sure of the meaning. The dreamer tells the dream in the first person, present tense. The dreamer is asked, "When did you have this dream? Are the people in your dream real? What is their relationship to you? Is the dream still important to you?"

THE ART DIRECTIVE: Drawing the Dream

Process: Listen to the story in the dream and draw the dream "as if" it is your own. If you are willing, please post your drawings on the wall. When everyone is ready, you will each be invited to tell the story of "your" dream in the first person, present tense; the dreamer listens to the messages in each of the dreams and also tells the story of his/her "dream" picture. The dreamer is invited to tell us a little about his/her current life situation and possibly to relate it to what is happening in the dream. It is always the dreamer's choice to decide how much to share with the group. Others, too, may want to share what the dream means to them in their current life situation. The dream is acted out in psychodrama, either by the dreamer or by another student who seems "warmed up" to what is happening in the dream. There might be more than one psychodrama for the same dream.

Objective: To provide options for the dreamer; to provide the warm-up for the psychodrama; to help bridge the gap between the dream images and waking reality with our drawings and/or in psychodrama; to help clarify how we unconsciously experienced a social situation; to understand the purpose of emotion created in the dream; to possibly provide a "wake-up call" to change our behavior, to take responsibility for the meaning we give to our own "dream" story.

Rationale: that each of us has a different approach to life which may or may not be useful to the dreamer; dreams hold the answers to understanding ourselves and can best be understood by relating them to what we are experiencing in waking life. Dreams help us clarify the direction we are seeking in life, our lifestyle pattern and can compensate for feelings of frustration, loss, and failure.

A DREAM CAN SOMETIMES WARN US OR ENCOURAGE US

I tell my dream: "I don't remember what is so important about what I am going to do or see, but I am told that I have to drive the car really fast to get up the hill or I would lose momentum and will have to back down. My daughter and husband are in the car with me. I am driving when halfway up the hill the car would not go any farther. I say, 'Oh, this is what they meant when they told me to drive fast up the hill.' I try to back the car down a little way and start up again, but it does not work. I lose momentum, so I give up and am slowly backing down the hill by keeping my foot on the brake. Coming at us are many kids on bikes and skateboards and they speed pass us on their way down the hill."

Most Vivid Moment: Keeping my foot on the brake as I slowly back down the hill, knowing I had lost the momentum, but not over control of the car.

Feelings: Scared that my foot would slip, and disappointed when I realized I could not get us to where I wanted to go

Dream Symbols: car – symbol for self, metaphor – moving (death) trap; driver's seat – unconscious position of power and control, "taking others for a ride." In looking at the drawing of the dream, it is possible to enter into conversation with the dream characters and to listen to their responses. Husband: "back off;" daughter: "lighten up;" the car: "I won't go where you want me to, but you still have control;" the hill: "I'm making it an uphill struggle for you;" the road: "I can lead you to a better place;" kids on skateboards and bicycles: "we don't need anyone to help us live our lives;" "we are free to live our lives the way we want to." The dream suggests a helpful attitude change in my relationship with family members by making me aware of what I would like to keep secret: that I want to be in control and have things go my way. I make a conscious effort to adopt a less controlling position, and work more toward cooperation and coming to an agreement when there are decisions to be made or problems to be solved in our family.

BASIC CONCEPTS OF PSYCHODRAMA

There are three parts to Psychodrama: the Warm-up, the Action, and the Sharing (Moreno & Fox, 1987). The use of personal symbols in dream working helps to warm up the group members to many issues concerning significant relationships, or the lack of them (Wadeson, Durkin, Perach,

1989, p. 331). This phase also allows students to express thoughts and feelings, the early stages in the process of group cohesion. When an individual seems warmed up to his or her own drawing, the psychodrama "action" takes place (Dushman & Bressler, 1991, p. 519). The protagonist becomes that individual, not necessarily the one who told the dream.

WARM-UP
Telling the story and drawing the dream serves as a warm-up to the drama. The purpose of the warm-up is to provide some means for the emergence of the protagonist and to foster spontaneity necessary for the action. Drawing the dream helps the other students get the "feel" of what is going to be acted out. Group members play the roles of significant others (auxiliary egos) in the enactment of the dream. "Tele" refers to the unspoken vibes that go between people based on intuition and insight that makes it possible for protagonists to select those they feel will best fit to play roles in their psychodrama.

ACTION
The action portion of the psychodrama starts with an incident or emotion from the dream of the protagonist and is the heart of the enactment. The action takes place in the here and now and involves the role-playing portrayal of key scenes in the dream. The director makes use of various psycho-dramatic techniques necessary to reveal the problem, to clarify and objectify the feelings being expressed by the protagonist and to move toward its solution (Yablonsky, 1976, p. 96).

One technique is Role Reversal. The protagonist becomes the significant other and the auxiliary takes on the role of the protagonist so the protagonist sees one's self from the perspective of the other. "Role reversal is the operational way to implement the Golden Rule" (Blatner & Blatner, 1988, p. 98).

A Social Exploration takes place when it is necessary to investigate the role of the auxiliary in the protagonist's life and to understand why the auxiliary acts in certain ways. Future or past projection means that the scene is set in the future or past in order to help the protagonist more deeply explore the meaning he or she gives to a particular event.

Symbolism is used to concretize what the protagonist is thinking or feeling. Dreams create mood through metaphor as found in the image or symbol which are unique to the dreamer. We have the most direct access to the dreamer's symbol system in the dream (Gold, 2014, p. 31). Meaning can be determined by the affect attached to the symbol (Ibid., p. 104).

SHARING

After the psychodrama, the students share the ways in which they identify with the action, and discover that this creates many "psychodramas" occurring in the room simultaneously. The group sharing process helps to bring about the feeling of belonging and reduce feelings of isolation or alienation. Being able to share dreams through the art and psychodrama, a clearer picture of ourselves can emerge through the real and imagined, the conscious and the not-yet-understood. Both allow the metaphoric dream symbols to become concrete in the present moment, stimulating new perceptions that may provide a catalyst for insight. Just as dreams are a "rehearsal for living" (Shulman, 1973), so too, is psychodrama a "rehearsal for living" (Starr, 1977).

ART AND PSYCHODRAMA

According to Socrates, the primary objective of man is to care for his soul. Jacob Moreno used Socrates' word "daimon" to describe the inner, private voice, divine guide or guiding spirit (Blatner & Blatner, 1988). Adler used the term "guiding self-ideal" to describe the inner source. Psychodrama comes from the Greek words "psyche," meaning spirit or soul, and "drama," meaning action. Psychodrama literally means "the soul in action" (Grant, 1981, p. 1).

Dreams and one's art contain tacit knowledge, and "intuition arises out of the tacit dimension" (Polyani, 1967, p. 6). Intuition is a deeper knowing which is holistic and personal and mostly not understood by the dreamer. We begin to realize that we know more than we are able to explain in words. With practice in recognizing the emotions we have created in our dreams we can begin to see how they serve the purpose of strengthening our attitudes and supporting private logic.

Adler taught us to "trust only movement" (Ellenberger, 1970, p. 576). A person's words may say one thing but it is the action or behavior in the dream made visible through the drawings and enacted in psychodrama that expresses how one relates to others. Allowing ourselves to enter into the dream through psychodrama by giving voice and action to the metaphors found in the images and symbols can, in effect, bring the secrets (hidden goals) we unconsciously keep to ourselves into conscious awareness. Paying attention to our role in the dream, e.g., actor, observer, healer, victim, is also important to understanding the dream.

"The dream is simply the clearest picture we have of our inner world," (Gold, 1981, p. 30) and is consistent with an individual's style of life. Sometimes the dream is one that keeps repeating itself, possibly reflecting an unresolved issue. Although symbols in dreams are not universal, social issues and problems are common experiences. Uncovering similar themes within the group creates connection and a feeling of safety.

Art making and psychodrama move rapidly and powerfully to the core issues of one's life evoking strong emotions and an inner search that can add a rich therapeutic dimension to the group experience. With self-disclosure and support from the group, students have a chance to recognize, accept and possibly change a thought, attitude, goal or behavior that might be creating conflict for them in social situations. (Dushman & Sutherland, 1997). In the spirit of giving and receiving, everyone has an opportunity to become more intimately connected with others in the group (Dreikurs, S., 1986).

LINK BETWEEN ADLERIAN THEORY, ART THERAPY AND PSYCHODRAMA

Adler (1930) believed that "the individual is thus both the picture and the artist. He is the artist of his own personality..." (p. 5). Moreno (1953) called psychodrama the "science which explores the 'truth' by dramatic methods." No process demonstrates Adler's metaphor more completely than an integration of dreams, art therapy and psychodrama. All are expressions of one's inner reality, one's guiding self-ideal. The integration of these three forms of expression provides the dreamer with a creative method for exploring a dream.

The crucial link between art making and psychodrama is Moreno's "concept of spontaneity-creativity" (Moreno & Fox, 1987, p. 40). Spontaneity-creativity is an innate ability which can be developed and has an inverse correlation to anxiety (ibid.). Spontaneity, done without premeditation or the desire to control the experience, is the catalyst to creativity necessary to coping with life.

The goal in psychodrama is to increase the person's role repertoire. Telling and drawing the dream helps to reduce anxiety and increase spontaneity (Sirotka, 1982). Playing the part of the antagonist in psychodrama can help give our dreams a clear example of how the conscious and that which is kept secret emerges through role-play.

A DREAM LEADING TO SELF-AWARENESS AND CHANGE

In a dream group, I tell my dream following surgery: "I am walking in a war zone where buildings have been destroyed and broken glass is everywhere. Streets are littered with garbage. My three children are with me. We go into a restaurant where we are served a delicious meal. Later we go outside and find ourselves in a beautifully ordered landscape. In the distance we see a peacock, strutting down the road to meet us. He gives me three feathers from his tail. I take them, so pleased with the gift."

Most Vivid Moment: "Taking the three beautiful feathers from the peacock"

Feelings: "Happy, peaceful"

Current Life Situation: "Recovering from surgery and feeling discouraged concerning a troubling relationship with my husband"

The group members finish their drawings of this dream and post them on the wall. Taking turns, they each tell the story of the dream, first person, present tense, and sometimes just give their drawings a title. One simply says, "gift," another says, "from trash to beauty," "from imperfect to perfect," "hope," "from illness to gratitude."

After looking at the drawings the other participants have made and listening to their stories of the dream, I then acted out the dream scenes.

After the psychodrama, I am asked if I would be willing to bring meaning to my dream symbols and connect them to what is happening in my life at the moment. Very simply, I saw the trash as the cancer removed from my body; the restaurant as nourishment for life, health, and movement from chaos to order; the children symbolizing a gift of life and love; while the peacock to me meant beauty and sacrifice. In connecting my dream to my current life situation, I said the dream gave me hope for recovery from surgery and also for the relationship with my husband, that he (the peacock) was coming toward me with a gift of himself and that was all I wanted from him. The dream encouraged me to remember that order come out of chaos, growth comes out of disappointment and conflict, and that I need to learn to live with the ambiguity of the perfect and imperfect, pleasure and pain.

In exploring this dream and gaining insight, I am able to better understand how I use discouragement and powerlessness, and even illness, as way to defend against my inability to live up to my ideals of a perfect life and perfect relationships. I see how this dream can compensate for negative feelings, and how that which is kept secret emerges through the dream images and psychodrama. This dream is encouraging but also deceiving. I have to look beyond the dream to find the mistaken idea or expectation; that sometimes I might be expecting others to give me what I want, i.e., peace in a relationship or to make my life okay with a "gift" or "sacrifice" without having to contribute anything of myself. If I were to change the dream, I would be meeting the peacock with a gift of my own love. Growth for me comes at this moment as I decide to find ways to encourage the one I love rather than dreaming about unrealistic expectations.

CONCLUSION

In working with dreams, as in learning from any life experiences, we can begin to acknowledge and take responsibility for our unrealistic expectations. It's hard to separate the truth of who we are from what we want to believe about ourselves, and how our own selfish desires for peace and harmony create suffering, even illness, when we don't get what we want.

Group dream work, if it is to be successful, is not something imposed on another, but is an intimate process between individuals. Each must be willing to risk uncovering secret goals which might be creating distance in relationships. Working together cooperatively in a safe environment can bring about new learning and the willingness to try out new strategies to bring about equality in the relationships we seek with each other. It also takes courage to let go of the attachment we have to the way we want our lives to be, and be able to accept life for the gift that it is – and know that this is our challenge for the rest of our lives. And the biggest gift is that group work can reduce social isolation and discouragement which, in itself, can bring about psychological well-being.

A dream provides an
Image for a felt experience
In waking life

15

Group Art Therapy Supervision

The decision to become an Adlerian art therapist is also a commitment to personal growth. The art therapy program at Adler provides an integration of counseling psychology and art therapy and also calls for the student's active involvement in the community. Supervision continues to focus on both personal and professional growth as students begin to practice with clients in "real life" the theory and practical skills they have been learning in the classroom. Unjust living situations will also need to be recognized and understood. When community leaders ask for help, students need to find ways to get involved in supporting them in their effort to transform unsafe and problematical conditions in their communities. Required supervision continues as graduates prepare for registration as Licensed Professional Counselors (LPC), art therapists (ATR), and Licensed Clinical Professional Counselors (LCPC) beyond graduation.

The theoretical concepts of art therapy are still not very well understood among administrators, psychologists, social workers, and other therapists who may think that the intention of art therapy is to provide art as an activity or as a way to keep children and clients entertained or busy. Sometimes this lack of understanding creates an added dimension to what a supervisee needs to do once they are out in the field. In whatever setting, school, hospital, nursing home, group practice, the supervisee "must sense the aim of the institution and fit (his)/her particular skills into facilitating and implementing the agency's mission" (Robbins & Sibley,

1976, p. 71) while at the same time demonstrate, by example, workshop, and explanation, the value of using art as a therapeutic intervention.

Supervisees meet as a group on a regularly scheduled basis, usually once a week. Supervision almost always takes the form of meeting the students or graduates wherever they might be in that moment. The goal is to bring the group together to share the process of solving any counseling difficulties while, at the same time, making sure that no harm occurs to them or their clients. The student brings information about the relationship being developed with a client, the subjective experiences of the client which have brought him or her into therapy, a lifestyle summary of the client, if possible, any assessment, intervention or plans for treatment, and process notes to date. Supervision also involves the relationship they have with their supervisors, the particular unit or group of patients with whom they are engaged, even the physical building and/or space in which they work. Supervisees are expected to be aware of their own lifestyle patterns in the client-therapist relationship.

Seeing ourselves clearly in relationships to others is difficult. When we look at others we often see ourselves, a projection of our own thoughts, or the way we would like others to be. We can fool ourselves into thinking that clients are meeting or not meeting the goals of therapy. As individuals, we decide whether we can trust others or feel betrayed by them, whether we are too focused on getting things done or solving problems for others, too obsessed with getting ahead, too optimistic or too pessimistic. Eventually we find the balance that feels right to us in certain situations, only to know that life will change again.

As the supervisor, I also need to be aware of the potential influence my own lifestyle has on the supervisory process. My job in supervision is to establish an atmosphere of respect and trust so that there can be a "give and take" of how we understand ourselves and each other in the group. The plan is to develop a deeper awareness of our own ideas and attitudes, strengths and weaknesses, when working with clients. Providing therapy is not part of the supervisory role, but sometimes the work done in supervision feels like therapy.

We look for the unique way each client relates to the others in the setting where they are providing therapy; the classroom, hospital setting, a safe place, or counseling center. The therapeutic approach needs to focus on the strengths of the client, while at the same time offering hope through connection and collaboration. The aim therapeutically is to help clients learn to take responsibility for their own behavior and to encourage relationships with others as they learn to creatively take control of their lives and minimize self-defeating behaviors.

Just as we encourage each other in supervision, we can also encourage our clients so that they can learn to recognize how their perceptions and behavior may be leading them to discouragement, and then to encourage them to experiment with more useful approaches to the challenges of life. Rather than labeling the symptoms of our clients, we can do a Life Style Inventory to explore with them how they have subjectively created the meaning for their lives. Rather than ignoring unjust living situations, we can encourage clients to work together to improve life around them. By changing some of the oppressive social conditions under which they are living, they may be able to enhance the quality of their personal lives. As the lives of our clients improve, so do the lives of others.

Some of the images made by clients in the art therapy room can be threatening both to the client and to the new therapist, sometimes bringing about anxiety, fear, and anger. This can create situations where both the client and the supervisee are feeling inadequate, vulnerable, and helpless. This is the work that usually comes to supervision. When a crisis arises, I advise supervisees to talk to their immediate on-site supervisor first, and then to call me. It is up to the supervisee to create a therapeutic alliance with his or her clients while still maintaining professional boundaries. As the supervisor, my goal is to honor the supervisee's integrity, knowing that eventually he or she will come to understand that the answer lies within and not in what I or others have to say.

Those in supervision make art in response to the community, workplace, field supervisor, and clients in their practice setting. These drawings can evoke feelings that otherwise might remain unknown to the supervisee. The goal of making art helps to keep alive the images of recent experiences and to clarify the troubling reactions that arise in any new learning situation.

I remember that, when I was in art therapy supervision, Evadne McNeil would sometimes ask us to copy the art work of our clients. Making the identical picture gave me a different feeling about a client. I could be more empathetic even when these were not my own clients' drawings. Sometimes I experienced sadness, anger, or fear; or I might be confused by my replica drawing. My perception of a client would change as we talked about our drawings in a group. This process helped us to come to a better understanding of our clients as well as creating a closer connection with them. Evadne attributed this approach to understanding a client's art work to Edith Kramer. Because I, too, found it useful, I continued the practice with my students in the M.A. in Counseling Psychology: Art Therapy program.

Honoring my own truth means to trust the learning process even though it can sometimes be painful for both the supervisee and for me. I also do my own art in response to my supervisees. Seldom are there easy answers to complex problems, nor is there a formula. To pretend that there are simple solutions would fail to prepare supervisees to see human behavior as it really is and quite likely to build up false hopes for the future.

CONCLUSION

Using a peer consultation model, supervision provides students engaged in practicum training with an opportunity to discuss professional development and the work experience. We discuss specific cases as a way to illustrate general principles of counseling and group art therapy interventions. The focus is on professional development by expanding knowledge, skills, and self-awareness needed to provide competent and ethical counseling.

In our image of
Each other, perceiver and
Perceived become one

16

Thoughts about Research

One of the ways we learn to understand ourselves and the world is through research. This, in turn, generates new knowledge and leads to new products, methods, and techniques which can improve the well-being of the earth and all of us who inhabit it. The historical and philosophical foundations of research reach back to Plato (385 B.C.E.) who used the allegory of the cave to help us understand that what we see are only shadows of reality; that we need to escape the cave (the confines of our minds) and see what is creating the shadows.

Some believe we only find truth through a worship relationship with God; that truth may be found only through faith. Believing in something without good reason to do so is called faith. Inductive reasoning (The Empiricists, John Locke, 1690) recognized that simple ideas become more complex upon reflection, and Bishop Berkeley (1710) observed that reasoning begins in the particular individual thought process and moves into "something more common" with others. There was a separation of faith from reason in the early part of the 19th century when Harvard became a secular school. What was then called "rational inquiry" became the means of pursuing "truth."

Dialectic thought, a process most associated with the German philosopher Georg Hegel, recognizes that once we have a thought (thesis), it is challenged by another (antithesis) and this results in synthesis. This happens either in ongoing conversations with others publicly or with ourselves privately. The role of scientific investigation is to validate intuitive thoughts or "deep truth," what we think we know. We want to believe that whether we apply inductive reasoning (empiricism – the idea that the source of all knowledge is to exist in sensory experience) or deductive reasoning (rationalization – testing the validity of truth through logic) that we are working to prevent trouble before it begins, or to find ways to fix it, and that we are always progressing toward the truth. Today we know that no amount of experimentation can ever prove that something is forever right; but a single experiment can prove something wrong.

Deductive reasoning does help in the areas of advocacy, ethics, education, diversity, medicine, poverty, and social responsibility, leading to healthier social environments. It is temporary and always ongoing. We also continue to measure the value of family systems therapy, drugs used in the therapeutic process, humanistic and other theoretical approaches to therapy, including the creative arts therapies. Replication is the foundation of modern research which can correct for flaws due to subjectivity. A wide discrepancy suggests that scientists sometimes confirm what they think is true, disregarding what they don't want to see. Beliefs can be misleading, sometimes even deceiving.

INTUITION – THE FOUNDATION FOR INTEGRATING SENSORY INFORMATION AND REASON

Intuition has been an acceptable mode of knowing since ancient times. The idea that we know more than we are able to speak about or explain (Ansbacher & Ansbacher, 1956), refers to what Michael Polyani (1967) called the "tacit dimension" (understood, but not stated or expressed). From the tacit dimension, a "bridge" is formed between the implicit knowledge (unexpressed but implied) inherent in the tacit and the explicit or clearly visible components of knowledge which are observable and easily described. Moustakas (1990) called this bridge between the explicit and the tacit, the realm of the intuitive. We rarely question the truth of the senses and of human reason in regard to scientific and philosophical systems of truth; intuition is not so easily subjected to scientific inquiry.

Intuition makes knowledge immediately possible without the intervening steps of sensory information and logical reasoning. Intuition makes possible the perceiving of things as wholes, a holistic approach, rather than separating the whole into parts. Scientific exploration or research seeks to validate what Mishlove (1994) calls, "deep truth," that which we implicitly "know" as the truth beyond what our senses tell us and beyond reason (p.31). Intuitional insight usually comes after we have exhausted our efforts to find the truth through sensory information and logic and sometimes comes to us in dreams, e.g., Elias Howe's invention of the sewing machine needle came in a dream after days of struggling to build a successful machine.

Intuition has also been the starting place as the source of truth for many great discoveries in the history of human thought; science, art, philosophy, religion, ethics, and technology, even though it does not always guarantee the truth. With art therapy, the content of the drawing is important in diagnostic standardized testing while expressive movement is noted in free drawings and depends on the use of intuition in understanding the possible meaning

Intuition calls for "active imagination" (Jung) or "free association" (Freud, Adler, S. Dreikurs) and goes beyond conscious awareness. The artist and the observer (therapist, scientist) are each seeing the work according to their own bias. It is difficult to separate out the emotional self when projecting or giving meaning to the art of others. If the art work is done in a class setting, all members dialogue, with the student's permission, until the student is satisfied with the meaning. The student who gives us permission to discuss the art work is always the final authority. It takes courage to do this kind of work in a group, and sometimes insight or new learning is the reward.

USING THE INTUITIVE APPROACH TO UNDERSTAND HUMAN BEHAVIOR: HEURISTIC RESEARCH

Hermeneutic, heuristic and phenomenological research captures the creative moment in a way that opens to integrating ideas about social interest and self-awareness that is more fitting with the postmodern approach to understanding human behavior. Postmodern thinking asserts that "objective" analysis of our clients is very likely skewed by our own perceptions and therefore may not be a valid method for gathering information. Empirically-based (scientific) interventions are those frequently required by most third-party payers even though we've found that testing does not necessarily give us an accurate summary of things, and we end up wasting a lot of money treating patients based on results that are misleading (Lehrer, 2010). We need more than just data when studying the complicated behavior of human beings.

Qualitative approaches respect the complexity of human experiences and allow for the emergence of the unique and infinite number of ways human beings can find meaning for their lives. Research designs that give us information about the efficacy of using art therapy with clients are usually heuristic and phenomenologically-based. Heuristic research cannot be proven, but together in a group, co-researchers can create consensual meaning (Chickerneo, 1993). Themes emerge which help clients realize they do have the power to take responsibility for their own lives and make appropriate changes to their thoughts, attitudes, and behavior. This approach is helpful to the client, but does little to satisfy the demands of the insurance companies who are looking more for diagnosis and a treatment plan based on an accurate assessment as well as quick healing for the client.

It has been said that aesthetic associations are intuitive. "Art is perfectly defined when simply defined as intuition" (Croce, 1921, p. 33). The non-scientific approach calls for imagination. Imagination is a creative process and, as such, has its source in intuition ("the source of true knowing") and is different for each of us. I ask myself, "What meaning do I give this image. "What is the message I give myself?" Does this message stay the same or does it change over time? I remind myself to stay open to the surprise in the art.

When we open to the image in our own art work we give meaning to its message through projection. Sensory perception, reason, or verbal speculation alone cannot give us insight. Intuition, by itself, can easily lead us astray, but it can also more instantaneously approximate the truth. An integration of all three (sensory, intuitive, and reasoning or verbal) needs to happen if we are looking for "the truth."

FROM INDIVIDUAL TO COLLECTIVE CONSCIOUSNESS
Collective intelligence brings together researchers from a variety of fields to confirm that what determines the creativity and cultural change of a population leading to consciousness is the amount of interaction between individuals. Evolution in consciousness is a collective enterprise that relies on exchange, rather than on what is inside one individual's head. New ideas come from each other. When individuals come together with a common purpose to solve a problem, all of their collective resources, knowledge, experiences, and perceptions become available to the other group members. Bringing together new and different ideas to awareness closely parallels Hegel's theory of dialectic thought where new ideas emerge from a combination of ideas or a synthesis (Hegel, 2005).

Adlerian group art therapy fits this model as we each help the other to find the "truth" in an exchange of ideas in the moment. Validity on this anecdotal "proof" might be improved by having group members answer objective pre- and post-test questions relevant to the design of the research problem (Kapitan, 2010, p. 69).

Research in all areas of life continues to offer the hope that we may be able to resolve, maybe even more hopefully, prevent, some of the world's oppressive social problems and provide answers to our everlasting questions about social conditions and health. The results of research may only be temporary leading to improvements in some areas of life or mostly inconclusive, but the ability to have ongoing conversations with others is what most distinctly separates us as human beings from most animal and plant kingdoms due to only a slight difference in DNA. And, at the heart of human genetics, research shows the interconnectedness of all human beings which generates to mean that our ancestry is all intertwined, no matter what the laws of segregation say. Progress evolves slowly, if at all, yet ethical research needs to be ongoing in the direction of truth, understanding that there is no one solution to the problems we encounter nor will there ever be.

RESEARCH IN THE MEDICAL FIELD

Fear of disease and death and a desire to understand and overcome this fear were the motivating forces behind most early research in the medical field. One hundred and fifty years ago, we had no idea what even caused disease. Science and technology identified bacteria and viruses. Now we know that we are not completely helpless over the forces of disease, but also that we will never be completely free from them either, even when more preventions and cures are discovered.

The question remains: why do some people stay healthy, some get sick and recover, and others die even though all are exposed to the same bacteria or virus, or even the same "overwhelming" stress and even, sometimes, trauma? In 1862, Alfred Russell Wallace, an English naturalist, developed a theory of evolution by natural selection similar to the theory that Darwin had developed. He answered the above question: "Those variants best fitted to their circumstances survive" (Quammen, 2008, p. 133). So, is the ability to adapt the only key to survival? Do Early Recollections help us in the ability to adapt?

Even though there is little research on this subject, Adler believed that we retain from childhood "only those memories that support our direction of striving for significance and security." (Kopp, 1995, p. 38). Adlerian therapists recognize that the significance of the ER lies in the fact that it has been remembered or thought to be so, knowing that remembering is more a process of construction than one of reproduction. We create the ER to fit our lifestyle pattern. ERs contain omissions and distortions, are exaggerated and minimized in accordance with our inner needs. In other words we adapt our ERs to reflect intervening experiences and such revision actually helps us adapt to our environments.

Neuroscientist Joel Voss (2014) reports that "memory is designed to help us make good decisions in the moment and, therefore, memory has to stay up-to-date." Can science explore memory as part of personality shaped by the dynamic forces of the unconscious (private logic)? What thinking and feeling take place that lead to dysfunctional attitudes and behaviors? What happens to Early Recollections when people experience anxiety? "How can individuals become aware of, take control of, and change dysfunctional attitudes and behavior" that have formed the personality and create distance in relationships? (Patton, 2002).

RESEARCH ON MENTAL DISORDERS

We have research on many of the physical realities of illness and disease making it easier to diagnose and treat the patient. We know a lot about viruses and bacteria; we can study x-rays, cat scans, body temperature, and blood tests to determine what is wrong with the patient; i.e., a broken bone, a kidney stone, cancer, or pneumonia. But what specific scientific evidence do we have to help us "determine" the cause and effect of bipolar, schizophrenia, major depression, autism, attention deficit hyperactivity, Alzheimer's or addiction disorders, or even what it looks like in the brain?

A recent study finds that there are genetic risk factors shared by patients suffering from neuro-developmental disorders (Kolata, 2013). This is a breakthrough on the way to providing scientific evidence for diagnosing mental disorders but does not determine that one will suffer these disorders or even how to treat them. Genetic factors alone cannot account for brain disorders or how to prevent them. Human behavior is too diverse to rely on genetic evidence. There is no scientific research to date that will tell us what a mental disorder looks like in the brain (like there would be in a brain scan for a tumor or even Alzheimer's); at least not enough to warrant the diagnosis of a mental disorder. And we are still a long way to finding effective ways to use technology (other than ECTs which are not always successful) to improve the health of the brain, both a scary and exciting thought.

The *DSM-V* (2013) is all we have right now to diagnose and describe the symptoms of mental disorders. It gives us descriptions of behavioral symptoms for clinical use but there is nothing except the subjective opinion of a psychiatrist to prove the existence of a mental disorder. The impact of the *DSM* on the field of medicine for psychiatric disorders is huge, affecting both psychiatrists and their clients. For lack of scientific evidence, drug and insurance companies have had to rely on the *DSM* for diagnosis, treatment, and the subjective opinion of the prescribing psychiatrist. Is the patient suffering from a mental disorder or distress that occurs normally in life? If the psychiatrist or family doctor determines that there is "clinical significance" both the patient and the doctor are entitled to the benefits of insurance and drug treatments for mental disorders. Without the "label" of a specific type of psychiatric diagnosis, the provider organization does not get paid and the patient is blocked from access to mental health services. The *DSM-V* is helpful, but we need scientific evidence beyond subjective opinion.

COGNITIVE DISSONANCE

Research today is based on our belief in two contradictory assumptions. From a legal standpoint, many believe that humans are equal and have free will that allows them to take responsibility for their actions. From a biological or medical point of view, however, humans are just organisms that respond to stimuli. We live with these two contradictory models. To believe in both models brings about cognitive dissonance. Until we resolve this dilemma, we will continue to have trouble finding answers through research into the etiology of disorders or the sources of health.

ART THERAPY RESEARCH

Students preparing for work as art therapists need to understand the clinical therapeutic approach of interviewing techniques, developmental theories, how creativity is used in the process of healing, a psychological theory to support the work they do with clients, writing up reports, and current research. Art therapy is currently being researched in prisons, with cancer care, PTSD, elder care, family therapy, in community settings and in schools, especially with those children identified at risk of failure.

Students quickly realize how the field of art therapy struggles to conform to the clinical or scientific approach in theory, research and practice. As art therapists, we also use research within the guidelines of a professional set of ethical standards to develop methods that might help people better understand and change those attitudes, beliefs and behaviors that create distance between themselves and others.

We remember that science was originally conceived to study only one dimension of our reality; the physical process, and that the solutions to particular health problems deal with only the symptoms, and not personality that is shaped by the dynamic forces of the unconscious. I agree with Lynn Kapitan (2010) that it has been "a contemporary challenge for art therapists to find paths of inquiry that reflect their core values and allow them to see and to act upon the therapeutic enterprise with both an artist's and scientist's way of knowing (p. xviii)." We need to be able to scientifically define the perplexing problem of consciousness, and how art might help to illuminate it.

Scientific thinking finds the concept of consciousness difficult to study. From a biological perspective, science agrees that consciousness is not some part of the brain that orders behavior, although a scientist agrees that what the brain does do, awake or asleep (dreams) is make images. These images correspond to external reality as we experience and give meaning to it and can be evidenced visually on paper. This happens everywhere in the world and with every culture, making words adjunctive to art therapy but not available to diagnostic labels.

Without scientific evidence to verify the effectiveness of art therapy, be it done individually, in groups, in combination with talk therapy, we will continue to rely on phenomenological experiments, personal testimony, and observation to determine the benefit of art therapy. How will we know when we are successful? We look for improvement in attitude, beliefs, feeling, and the goals for behavior. Will we ever be able to scientifically prove that using art as a therapeutic intervention works with clients?

Possibly, once we have brain imaging to support a corrective change in the brain leading to improved social relationships.

Linda Gantt developed a Formal Elements Art Therapy Scale (Gantt, 2009) and realized the limits of the research potential when looking to find support for her hypotheses: using the patient's art to measure for diagnostic information through assessing formal variables. Pat Allen (1992), as spokesperson for many art therapists, believed that a scientific approach using standardized testing in the creative arts therapies "disparages our identities as artists and ultimately weakens our unique contribution to therapy (cited in McNiff, 1992, p. 3). Shaun McNiff considers himself a practitioner-researcher who goes beyond "predetermined criteria or approved scientific research" to do his research (ibid., p. 3).

Harriet Wadeson focused on "emerging data" as opposed to "elicited specific data" in her research policy. It can be said that one's art "reflects the individual's emotional state at the time" (Wadeson, 1980, p. 188) but that, to date, there is "no systematic procedure sufficiently refined to diagnose a patient simply on the basis of art expression" (Wadeson, 1980, pp. 197-198). Judith Rubin acknowledged that many art therapists "may have gotten caught in the empiricist numerical web" and that it is important to recognize the "phenomenological subjective nature of the creative experience" (1987, p. 184). Some art therapists encourage single-case research, but believe that many aspects of the human experience cannot be studied mechanically. Most art therapists would express the idea that all knowledge is a construction of the human mind. This is a good fit with the social constructivist point of view, congruent with Adlerian theory and existential philosophy where the primary focus is on the significance of individual choice and freedom, how we continuously strive to give our lives meaning and to find our place in the world (Scott, Kelly, & Tolbert, 1995).

Many art therapists like to use "free" drawings in which the client chooses what to draw, but this does not lend itself to a systematic study. Harriet Wadeson (1980) found it difficult to point to common symbolic content but she did find a "similarity in characteristics of art expression" (p. 61 – 62, such as lack of color, more empty space, less investment of effort, and "a pervading emptiness" among depressed patients (ibid., p. 66). From an ethical point of view, Wadeson warns us against "labeling" with good reason. We are not medical doctors trained to diagnose and treat mental disorders.

The use of color has always fascinated me. Can color be subjected to scientific inquiry and correlated with mental disorders? If we look for only the myth, metaphor, or form, we miss the emotional or feeling part that color can evoke. But like other projective tests, we find that color cannot be translated into words or concepts with fixed categories of meaning. We know that color and light impart energy and influence us, and that the response to both is much more apt to be individual than universal. Like the sound listened to in music, color can soothe, irritate, give us courage, and inspire us. Color, or lack of it, is probably the most elusive when we try to subject it to a codified meaning, yet the most subjectively powerful when we give meaning to it in a work of art.

I'm reminded of Mark Rothko's paintings, especially those done in the latter part of his life that some said seemed preoccupied with nothingness and non-being. He was depressed and committed suicide in 1970 after completing a series of paintings in browns, blacks and greens. Rather than emptiness, I saw in those abstract paintings a simple beauty that spoke to me of peace. And indeed, maybe he had already come to a sense of peace on his own terms – or maybe that's where I was at the time.

We still have to choose what to believe, about ourselves, about our clients, and continue to research the value of doing art therapy. We have been able to rule out finding a one-to-one relationship existing between any specific drawing and color is too elusive to indicate any particular social disorder, but still we need to demonstrate the effectiveness of its techniques in order to maintain and increase art therapy as a treatment modality. We need to be clear that art therapy is a form of psychother-apy and is different from occupational, physical, or activities therapies. Whether it is art as therapy or art psychotherapy, group or individual, we need to produce significant positive outcomes so that we, as art thera-pists, can continue to be counted as equals in the field of mental health.

ART IN THERAPY

Since all art done by clients needs to be understood in relationship to the troubling event(s) that brought them into therapy, they are the ones to receive a healing benefit. Shaun McNiff calls what one learns from his or her own art, "medicine" which is aligned with traditions of healing that treat the soul or mind as well as the body (1992, p. 297). My own art, like my own life, can be used as a projective technique, but "it is more than the sum of its parts and cannot be fully labeled with words or systematized into codified speech" (Ibid., p. 299). The art work can sometimes "say" what we are not ready to understand or accept about ourselves. These are the images that have the most to teach us (ibid., p. 300), but are difficult to subject to a research model.

I'm reminded of a client who came for art therapy when she was suffering from breast cancer. Her drawing took up a small space in the lower right had corner of the paper where she revealed herself as a sick person in bed. She told me the figure above the bed was her mother hovering over her. As she said this, she was shocked as she came to the realization that "my mother has always controlled my life." I only nodded my acceptance of her "truth" and then we talked about what that meant to her.

Clients can begin to feel understood once the therapist acknowledges the "truth" revealed in the art. The hidden goal reveals the method by which one tries to achieve a sense of belonging while the hidden purpose reveals the private logic that one might use to justify his or her behavior. Using the example above, the "hidden goal" might be "I need to be sick to feel significant and in order to have a place in life" and the private logic might be "I need my mother to take care of me."

In my experience with clients it is "being understood" that is the key to a therapeutic alliance leading to improved social functioning (validated by research). I have found that most clients, if given time, will understand what is revealed in their own art work without any help from me. Knowing they can come to their own conclusions gives them confidence to solve their own problems in life and also helps in establishing trust and mutual respect necessary for a therapeutic alliance between the two of us. If "being understood" is the most important factor leading to insight and a more positive adjustment in life, what does the art work contribute to this process? The art work "is in the space between inner and outer world, which is also the space between people – the transitional space – it is in this space that intimate relationships and creativity occur" (Winnicott, 1971).

I believe that group art therapy provides the same benefit; the art fills the space between inner and outer reality and between client and group members and takes the focus off of the individual. It is in the connection to others that leads to a shared understanding of one's own art work and also confidence in being able to solve problems that allows for connection and creating new approaches to social living.

OPEN STUDIO

The Open Studio Project in Evanston, Illinois was founded in 1991 and is another therapeutic approach using art. A participant/director provides the space and art supplies, but does not interfere with the creative process, does not assess the art work, and offers no suggestions. This is a not-for-profit program that can be found in communities open to everyone; any age. Even though Open Studios have been around for a very long time, in Europe and elsewhere, there is very little or no current research in place that validates the Open Studio as a therapeutic approach to healing. The practitioners of this approach intuitively "know" there is no one right way to find the "truth" or the value of making art except as one finds it in the art for him or herself.

In class we watch a documentary featuring M.C. Richards, "whose career from Black Mountain College to Creation Spirituality, from Rudolf Steiner advocate to philosophical artist, engages us in contemplative questioning regarding the nature of art, imagination, wholeness, community, and our place in the cosmos" (Kane, Lewis-Kane, & Richards, 2003). Her teaching and her work inspired the many who were with her to live creatively and to believe in themselves; "that art is a gate, not a product, wisdom a source, not a judgment" (ibid.). Richards talked about the "crossing point," that which we know about ourselves and that which we unconsciously keep secret (in the dark), and how we cross over from one into the other at any given time.

In 2013 I was in Scotland and bought a book titled *The Silent Weaver: The Extraordinary Life and Work of Angus MacPhee* written by Roger Hutchinson (2011). It is the true story of a man who went to war in 1939 but returned home before the fighting was done. War had broken him and Angus McPhee retreated into a silent, private world impenetrable to those around him. He quietly spent fifty years of his life at Craig Dunaid Hospital in Inverness where he created a large number of objects woven out of grass, sheep's wool and meadow flowers which he gathered. These objects included clothes, footwear, caps, hat, and bridles for animals and were either left to decay or were burned. Joyce Laing, an art therapist at Ross Clinic, discovered many of Angus McPhee's amazing creations and was able to preserve some of them for posterity. "Laing devised the term 'Art Extraordinary' for her collection of art done by patients because she thought the term "outsider art" was both derogatory and inadequate," (Hutchinson, 2011, p. 125). What this book tells me is that in spite of human frailty, the creative process survives, and that there are many ways to honor the process of art therapy.

THE ART DIRECTIVE: The Bridge Drawing: A Projective Technique for Assessment in Art Therapy *(Hays, 1981).*
Process: Draw a bridge going from one place to another. Draw yourself in the picture.
Rationale: Ron Hays designed this art experiential to explore "problems of communication with others." We process this experiential in class, with students volunteering to say what they see in their drawings and how it is a reflection on their current life. This is the last course we have together besides supervision, and students know each other very well. We can remind each other of what we have learned as the "truth" about ourselves while building close connections and the feeling of being understood.

Objective: This art directive brings up the difficulty of communicating the value of art therapy to the places where we work, to troubled communities, and to licensing officials. It might even show us where we "feel" or "intuitively know" where we are on the bridge of moving from academic life to work life.

The Research Methods Course integrates the students' academic program of study and clinical interests along with an introduction to research design, methodology and statistics. Students are expected to conduct an extensive review of psychological literature and research from the field and prepare a major research paper in an area of special interest which may result in an Independent Study. This is a self-directed study under faculty supervision in any theoretical or clinical aspect related to the art therapy curriculum. The required reading today would be Kapitan's *Introduction to Art Therapy Research* (2010). It gives a comprehensive overview of all previous art therapy research and invites answers to questions thoughtfully asked.

CONCLUSION

What real or imagined feelings of fear have become overwhelming and have convinced the person that he or she cannot measure up in the social situation? What fears are being experienced, such as those of abandonment, rejection, failure, isolation, being controlled by others? What is the emotional pain or sadness that leads to overeating, substance abuse, somatic complaints, or biologically based mental disorders? We all can and do experience the feeling of inferiority, inadequacy or rejection at different times in our lives, and become discouraged, but *discouragement is not a disorder.* The feeling of inferiority (or discouragement) is what we need to keep balance in our lives. It can stimulate us to grow and develop in harmony with our social and natural environment in socially useful ways (moving from a minus to a plus) (Adler, A., 1929, pp. 96-97).

It seems that no amount of testing or scientific research can explain everything we need to know about someone, nor can we think in terms of a causal orientation. Adler's (1964) early concept of the "creative power" or the creative role of the individual is what distinguishes his theory from other early personality theories, but does not lend itself very easily to research as we know it today (*Superiority and Social Interest*). Multiple viewpoints must continue to inform our interpretation of evidence, and we must develop a greater tolerance for ambiguity. Art therapy can certainly benefit from research, but essentially consciousness is so much more than what we can learn from scientific investigation.

In DNA's famed spiral staircase structure
Are hidden the mysteries of
Heredity, of growth, of dis-ease, of aging,
But choice and chance will often conflict with
Determination

Inspired by James Watson and Francis Crick, 1971

17

Conclusion – No Easy Answers

Some say that there is very little value in therapy, that people do not get better, and that therapy is an impossible profession. And that may be true, or it may be that we don't have a way to measure progress over the years that it will sometimes take to provide satisfying results.

There are no easy answers and there is no formula. Research tells us that medication may bring relief, but that a combination of medication and talk therapy will be of the most benefit. The unraveling of mistaken ideas takes time. We don't "hear" or "see" or "understand" anything about ourselves until we are ready. Until then we are on the path of resistance and refuse to seek or gain insight into our thoughts and behavior.

Only I can make the decision to begin to free myself from the prison of those thoughts and feelings that I unconsciously keep private and cause me to suffer in my relationships with others. I can approach my fears, doubts, anger, and anxiety and befriend them. I can begin to learn more about myself and then slowly change those thoughts and behaviors that get in the way of living life in a useful way. Adverse conditions, inner conflict and incongruity, even biological limitations will continue to interfere with fulfillment so the task of being on the path to self-awareness is always at hand.

The practice of psychology emerged from the field of philosophy, and originally was meant to be the study of the soul. The Greek word "psyche" means breath, soul or spirit. Spirituality then is not a religion but the process of learning about yourself and reaching out to connect to others and the world around you. It is through our relationships that we develop self-awareness and social interest, and find our place of belonging. It is here that Individual Psychology, art therapy, and social action meet on common ground. And until we are able to use words in a natural language common to people all over the world, art is, for now, the most viable means of coming to individual and universal consciousness. Science will eventually meet art to heal the brain from the addictive emotion of fear due to trauma, and possibly restore memories lost to dementia.

I have no illusions about having the final word on any of the subjects in this book, but only hope to continue where Tee Dreikurs left off. She used art combined with Individual Psychology first at Jane Addams Hull House, then at St. Joseph's Hospital, finally at the Alfred Adler Institute, where I first met her. The name of the school changed to The Adler School of Professional Psychology and is now Adler University. Following me as Chair of the art therapy program in Chicago is Jennifer Lacivita. In Vancouver, the Chair is Duanita Eleniak. The Adler Graduate School in Minneapolis, MN also offers a M.A. degree in art therapy and is chaired by Craig Balfany. Many of my students have already taken leadership roles in art therapy, and others are continuing the work that was started by Tee Dreikurs, each of us linking the past to the future.

To give freely without hope of reward or recompense:
it's far easier to follow the other road and ignore the needs of humanity.
But the greater joys of life lie down the road less traveled.

M. Scott Peck, 1978

Glossary

Adlerian Therapy: Two factors are vital to the effectiveness of Adlerian therapy: revelation of the accustomed life plan and encouragement in increasing awareness of the meaning we give to life and how we find our place of belonging with others. It is only in understanding the life plan and the consequences of our behavior that will bring about change (Dreikurs, 1936, p. 54).

Anxiety: "normal" anxiety, something we all experience at different times, might include fears, worries, discomfort, feelings of inferiority, frustrations which can lead to inner turmoil but not unduly interfere with social relationships. Anxiety can also be a disabling disorder to include panic attacks, phobias, somatic complaints, and social anxiety. Anxiety calls for and invites a creative response to the troubling situation.

"Arrangement" can be thought of as rationalization (Freud): the way we arrange our thinking, feeling, and/or behavior to justify self-serving objectives.

Art can function as a transitional object, but also project through image and metaphor the meaning we give to life and awareness of how we negotiate social relationships; through creating art in response to conflict we may find ways to change the way we experience a life situation by adapting our thinking and attitudes to fit with what feels more positive or healthy; art making bypasses safe-guarding defenses that impede understanding of self and others. The work of art symbolizes all the levels of reality that lie between what we experience in life and our perception of it (Ansbacher & Ansbacher, 1956, p. 180).

"As if": Hans Vaihinger's philosophy of "as if" influenced Adler's thinking about goal-directed behavior. We act "as if" something were true even though there might not be proof. These partial truths, called "fictions," become useful constructs for our behavior. Adler called this "fictional finalism." The "fiction" is a belief about the future, and "finalism" refers to the goal.

Basic Mistakes: "flaws in logic" that we most likely developed when we were young and without much experience in life. Usually we are not aware of these basic mistakes until they interfere in our relationships with other people. Basic mistakes can be about self, others, or the environment; they are "irrational, inappropriate, intolerant, egocentric, vindictive, compulsive, and insatiable (Shulman, B., 1973, quoted in Dreikurs, S., 2009, p. 110).

Behavior: all healthy behavior is purposive and motivated by a wish to be successful, to find a place of belonging, and make a significant contribution to society.

Belonging; security, the feeling of being at one with others usually begins with the mother in the family of origin and is carried on through life by taking care of yourself, caring for your loved ones, and caring for others in useful ways.

Biased Apperception: Reality is perceived in line with our intentions, in keeping with our goals.

Birth order: Adler suggested that birth order influences personality. Characteristics for five birth positions are outlined in his theory: first born, middle born, youngest, only, and twins. However Adler made it clear that the ordinal position was less important than the psychological position each child perceived for him or herself at different times in family life. Factors that might influence the perceived position include the spacing between the children, gender, childhood illness, and death of a sibling.

Cognitive dissonance is the mental stress or discomfort we experience when our beliefs and attitudes are in conflict with or are incompatible with our behavior.

Common sense: Inherent wisdom; can be thought of as a form of practical ethics that focuses on perceiving and acting on truths commonly shared such as democratic ideals, trust and respect. It includes using our gifts to promote the health and welfare of the world by working together in peace and friendship.

Compensation for feelings of physical or psychological inferiority may lead to a healthy fictional ideal; to be at one with others, to contribute in healthy ways at work, and to the community. Thoughts, emotions and behavior lead to goals that are on a continuum from useful to useless. Depending on the goal and ability of the individual, over-compensation might lead to failure (over-ambition) or to goals of "genius" in sports, scientific, or academic pursuits. Under-compensation might lead to creating emotions and symptoms that can be used to avoid responsibility or excuses for not living in the spirit of social equality.

Connection: Our quest, our earth walk, is to look within to know who we are, to see that we are connected to all things, that there is no separation, only in the mind (Native American belief); that each of us is forever socially embedded and responsible for the wellbeing of every other person; that when working with a new client, we strive for a connection (therapeutic alliance) when we are gathering information and planning the treatment process; that space when one creative person (the therapist) connects to another creative person (the client). Insight, acceptance of responsibility, cooperation with the agreed upon treatment plan, and changing the fictional final goal might not happen without a sense of connection between the therapist and client.

Consciousness: awareness of subjective meaning given to the purpose of our behavior in social relationships.

Consequences: A healthy child/person will come to a better understanding of his/her behavior and learn to take responsibility for it when he/she experiences the natural or logical consequences of his or her behavior; to encourage useful behavior and to be effective the logical consequences must fit with the behavior. From an Adlerian perspective, the use of praise and/or punishment might encourage dependent or rebellious behavior.

Control: Attempts to control the behavior of others may include threats, punishment, bribes, criticism, blame, complaining or rewards (Glasser, 1998). Trust and respect are necessary in order to win cooperation with the life tasks (Adler, Dreikurs).

Counseling is not the same as therapy although it could involve a life-style change. It is simply to be responsive to a current life problem or conflict by exploring strategies for dealing with a difficult life task or social situation.

Courage: It takes courage to be imperfect (R. Dreikurs); Creating art, music, poetry in response to our life events gives us courage to cope with our world when there is conflict. The real goal of the creative process is to change our consciousness so that we become more aware of the larger mosaic of which we all have a role. Mental health increases when individuals feel a sense of belonging and equality. This equality extends to relationships among groups and well-being increases when groups feel a sense of belonging in the larger circle of human life (E.D. Ferguson, 2010)

Depression: a real or imagined felt awareness of our inability to live up to the ideals we have created for ourselves; may have a genetic component and require medication (clinical depression).

Development: Our genetic code guides our biological development but might be influenced by the way we create meaning for our lives either positively or negatively.

Discouragement: A discouraged child might act in unhealthy ways by misbehaving. A discouraged adult may be feeling inadequate or unworthy (feelings of inferiority) and will give up or withdraw from social life possibly expecting others to take care of him/her. Faulty perceptions about self and life may be due to magical thinking, childhood abuse or trauma convincing one that he or she cannot measure up to the tasks of life. Adler preferred to use the term discouragement rather than personality pathology in response to feelings of inferiority. Discouragement can be described as enduring patterns of cognition, emotions, and behavior that negatively affect a person's adaptation to social living. When we are discouraged we tend to unconsciously create fictional ways to relieve, rather than overcome, our feelings of inferiority.

Disease can be thought of as a reaction of the body against a painful mental image or an illness brought about by stress, hatred, lack of attachment/loneliness, desire for unavailable or unattainable goals, fear; may include arthritis, asthma, rheumatism, heart trouble. As our minds receive messages from our bodies, so our minds can give guidance to our bodies.

Diversity: We each bring our own unique thoughts and ideas to the group and explore them in an atmosphere of trust and respect to bring about a desired change in response to unrest and conflict. It is only in diversity that we have collective strength to go forward and effectively make changes that will be of benefit. Survival requires a toleration of differences and cooperation as we learn to recognize our need for dependence on one another.

Dreams project the felt experience/conflict in symbolic language and are metaphorically reflective of our lifestyle; can sometimes be self-deceptive by irrationally expressing what we unconsciously want to have happen (wish fulfillment – Freud) rather than a useful way to solve a conflict (Adler, Dreikurs).

Early Recollections (ERs) are memories that help us to live our lives. We remember only that which fits with our self idealized goal for behavior and it is around this goal that personality is organized. ERs express our attitude toward life. The attitude is deeply rooted in unconscious feelings of early childhood. When these feelings are re-experienced we can make them consciously available to us and understand them in relation to the present moment (Ansbacher & Ansbacher, 1956). With consciousness we can keep them, or change them to serve us in a more socially useful manner.

Encouragement: communicates support and motivation by focusing on strengths, effort, and progress; is optimistic in that it makes a task more appealing by inspiring determination, hope and confidence.

Evolutionary psychology: the theory that memory, perception, and other psychological traits can be thought of from a Darwinian evolutionary perspective; that is, psychological traits are evolved adaptations to resolve recurrent problems in the quest for survival and are consistent with the theory of natural selection such as the ability to communicate, ability to cooperate. Over time it is believed that the most successful solutions for survival evolve into instincts and no longer need conscious thought to be put into action.

Family atmosphere refers to the unique relationship family members have with each other creating the "climate" in the family system. It usually starts with the older members of the family and can range from autocratic to permissive to democratic. Some words to describe the family atmosphere may include playful, loving, nurturing, hostile, frightening, critical, demanding, *laissez-faire*, controlling, cooperative, and competitive.

Family constellation: includes parents, children, and significant other family members; personality (lifestyle) develops out of the young child's family constellation, the relationship the child has with parents and siblings. As the child gets older, individual identity is forged in the context of peer relationships.

Family values commonly include religion, trust, respect, education, money, ethical behavior, status, and achievement.

Fictional or final fictive goal, usually just referred to as "the goal": In mental health, the forward movement of life is toward a significantly useful goal to compensate for childhood feelings of inferiority when meeting challenging social tasks. The goal subjectively seems to promise security (a feeling of belonging) and success. In mental disorders exaggerated feelings of inferiority lead to unrealistic or useless goals of superiority over others and a lack of social interest. The goal becomes the "final cause" of behavior, is self-determined and unique, and may be influenced by family stories, cultural factors, and the child's experiences in life. Encouraging a client to change the final goal toward one that is more useful can happen best in an atmosphere of social equality and trust.

Gestalt: The parts of the whole are understood within the context of the whole. "The whole is **greater than the sum of its parts" (Aristotle).**

"Gold Mine": "Listening for the gold mine," a term used by Rudolf and Sadie Dreikurs to understand the hidden intention of the behavior; usually discerned by the word "but," e.g., "I would write this book, but I don't have enough time," thereby negating the positive intention (1986, p 112).

Haiku is a form of Japanese poetry that keeps to the discipline of using only seventeen syllables in three lines of five, seven, five syllables for a total of seventeen syllables. We are inspired by observing the physical world, and using only seventeen syllables we find ourselves becoming aware of a deeper meaning that evokes emotion about something that is going on in our lives at the moment.

Happiness: To be happy means to be at home with yourself, with your family, at work, with those in your community and with others in the world; grows out of commitment and responsibility to others and letting go of infantile expectations.

Heuristic research: taking a theory that cannot be proven, but together creating meaning that will have value for those co-researchers involved.

Homeostasis: the tendency of the mind-body to maintain psychological balance by compensating for felt inferiority with unconsciously created safe-guarding mechanisms, which can include useful goals, or internal stability such as body temperature no matter what the external conditions present.

Immune system can be adversely affected by negative feelings. By deliberately changing our internal image of reality or view of the world, we can strengthen our immune systems that may have been weakened by significant events.

Inferiority: Most of the time feelings of inferiority are normal and motivate development and positive change. Exaggerated feelings of inferiority may lead to fear of abandonment or rejection, and sometimes lead to excusing oneself from risk to a fictional ideal or from effort that seems too difficult.

Lifestyle (or **Life Plan**): Our style of interacting with others commonly known as personality. We create our lifestyle in order to find a place of belonging or security (R. Dreikurs) by striving for superiority/significance and the freedom to have control over our own lives (Adler). It is a fictional life plan uniquely created to maintain movement and support toward our self-creative fictive goals; the way we have chosen to contribute to life around us. It includes thinking (cognition, attitudes), feelings, emotions, and acting; goals that are often revealed in our artwork as metaphor, image, symbol, and movement. We move toward the future, toward our goals; we are self-determined rather than being driven mechanistically by our past experiences or instincts, or determined by factors such as family, culture, biology, or genetics.

Mental disorders can be thought of as a radical protest and a complete inability to communicate with the social world. Feelings of insecurity and isolation lead to feelings of inferiority or an attitude of superiority and goal behavior that is self-centered and emotionally exploitive of other people. Medication is usually needed and therapy involves correcting mistaken ideas about self and others, learning to cooperate, and striving for more useful goals.

Metaphors: "express unconscious fictions through analogy rather than through logic" (Kopp, 1989). Metaphor is a form of symbolization that bridges the gap between what we know and what we are yet unaware of about ourselves, between intellect and intuition; metaphors integrate and evoke feelings that are congruent with how we live our lives.

Mistaken goals: All behavior has a social goal and is purposive. Emotions and symptoms all serve the hidden goal. To become aware of the intention of the goal and to learn to take responsibility for it becomes the work of therapy when we find ourselves suffering in our relationships with others.

Movement can be thought of as personality made visible. The main directions in life can be thought of as moving toward, away from, or against others. Any direction might be exaggerated and lead to difficulty in social living.

Neurotic symptoms may bring some success toward achieving fictional goals and homeostasis, but also give evidence of mistaken ideas for social living such as phobias, depression, and obsessive-compulsive behavior.

Passive aggressive behavior: an adaptive strategy that includes procrastination, pessimism, delaying tactics, inefficiency, obstructionism that serve to vent hostile feelings while simultaneously permitting an individual to appear ingratiating, friendly, and even submissive (Mosak in Sperry & Carlson, 1993, pp. 335-336). This behavior only tends to confuse and frustrate others.

Perception and reality: The way we perceive life and the way life is are two different things. All of our experiences are images of reality that we create in our minds. We create the world by the way we think. Perception of reality is sometimes blocked by emotional tension.

Perfection: completion, wholeness, overcoming difficulties; striving to perfect our self-ideal but taken to the extreme can create distance in relationships.

Positive attachments are a neurological necessity to further growth; lead to a feeling of safety and development of the brain.

Power is the primary goal, not happiness; that is power over our own lives, and not having to conform to the wishes of others (Nietzsche). When power is used in useless ways over others it needs to be redirected toward goals that contribute to the improvement of life for self and others.

Private logic: is that thought process carried out below the threshold of consciousness (Vaihinger, 1911 cited in Ansbacher & Ansbacher, 1956, pp76-100) and includes our attitudes, feelings, emotions and behavior as we move toward our self-created fictional goals. Symbols and metaphors found in our art work can be considered short cuts to understanding the private logic, lifestyle (personality).

Psychodrama There are three parts to Psychodrama: the warm-up, the action, and the sharing (Moreno & Fox, 1987, p. 40). Telling the story and drawing the dream can serve as a warm-up to the drama. The purpose of the warm-up is to provide some means for the emergence of the protagonist and to foster spontaneity necessary for the action.

Psychological integration of thoughts, beliefs, emotions, attitudes, and behavior is the capacity to establish enduring interpersonal relationships.

Punishment: judgmental treatment by one in power over another; no proof that punishment, isolation, deprivation or force corrects misbehavior or puts a stop to criminal activity. The only way we change is through compassion, trust and respect.

The Question: When we are experiencing symptoms and distance in our relationships with others, we need to ask ourselves "What would be different in our lives if we did not have these feelings or symptoms?" Our answer can frequently reveal what challenge or responsibility we are trying to avoid. If nothing would be different, we need to have our symptoms evaluated by a medical doctor. (Adler, Dreikurs)

"Regression in the service of the ego" (Kris, 1952) the specific means whereby unconscious material can be made conscious. i.e., sand tray, play, and art.

Self-deception about one's intentions is a normal, human process found in dreams and also in our private logic. It serves to keep hidden the goals of behavior until we are prepared little by little to take responsibility for how we created the meaning for our lives and the private logic needed to fulfill the mostly unconscious lifestyle plan.

Safe-guarding tendencies can be understood as unconsciously developed behaviors which may act as a side-show; blaming, depreciating, and accusing others as a way to retreat from unwanted challenges or responsibilities involved with social living. Adler and R. Dreikurs suggested that it is more useful to investigate defensive/safe-guarding tendencies from the point of view of advantages gained such as avoiding perceived personal failure and hiding the original problem.

Self-ideal: striving for one's self ideal is a healthy motivating force that we all have, but sometimes our self ideal gets us into trouble with others because it is taken to the extreme, i.e., helping others do what they can do for themselves.

Significance: A healthy striving for significance needs to be developed as part of the redirection of the lifestyle away from useless behavior and striving for power over others, and includes the goal of improving life for others through our choice of goals.

Social action: An organized process for improving or reforming policies dealing with unjust social issues such as education, wages, housing, living conditions, health care, prisons, food, with the goal of leading to the common good.

Social challenge: To become more aware of our thoughts, feelings, and behaviors and how they help us adapt to living in a democratic atmosphere.

Social feeling: the feeling of being at one in the universe, a feeling of belonging necessary for the development of social interest.

Social interest (*Gemeinschaftsgefühl*): innate potential arising out of a feeling of belonging (Dreikurs) that needs to be developed in a nurturing environment. It encourages the spirit of social equality and trust to bring about cooperation with and contribution (Adler) to the social order of life (E. Ferguson, 1999). It includes adaptation to the world of social relations as well as striving for perfection via *Gemeinschaftsgefühl*, both of which strengthen society and help lead to survival (La Voy, Brand, & McFadden, 2013).

Sublimation: The value of art lies in its ability to transform psychopathology and emotional conflict into personally meaningful action (McNiff, 1992, p. 30)

Superiority: a feeling of superiority (classical Adlerian theory) is compensation for a felt inferiority feeling and leads to socially useful behavior while a superiority complex is an exaggerated feeling of superiority to conceal inferiority feelings and leads to useless behavior that is usually annoying to others.

Teleology (Goal Orientation): Adler developed a teleological model (Aristotle) for his theoretical approach to understanding human behavior. We subjectively create goals based upon our ideals and values, and these provide motivation for our behavior. Adler believed that emotions generate behaviors and that emotional dynamics are "forward striving toward a final fictive goal" subjectively created by the individual based on his or her experiences in life. As Adlerian therapists we always look for the movement in life, for the subjective, unconscious goal of behavior created by the client to find his or her place of belonging.

Transitional space: the art work "is in the space between inner and outer world", which is also the space between people, sometimes the space between therapist and child. It is in this space that intimate relationships and creativity occur (Winnicott, 1953).

Traumatic or painful memories: I believe traumatic or painful memories are chemical and cannot be forgotten or erased even though they might be lost or repressed and therefore inaccessible. There are long-term ramifications of the traumatic event(s) throughout one's life even though we might not be able to recall them, but these memories, even if inaccessible to consciousness, might influence, but do not determine, our future actions.

"Trust the Process": Shaun McNiff (1998) says that "there is an unseen force (creativity) at work, alive within each of us, that gathers from the broad spectrum of our experience." This provides healing through the art process by illuminating doubt and fear, but also offering creative new options for living our lives. The art therapist offers safety and support throughout this process (p. 142).

Truth: Tee Dreikurs (1981, in class) reminded us that we each have a piece of the truth." "The idea that there is one people in possession of the truth, one answer to the world's ills or one solution to humanity's needs has done untold harm throughout history." (United States Secretary-General Kofi Annan, in his speech on receiving the 2001 Nobel Peace Prize).

References

Ables, B. (1972). The three wishes of latency-age children. *Developmental Psychology, 6*(1), 186. doi:10.1037/h0032210

Adler, A. (1929). *The science of living.* Garden City, New York: Garden City Publishing Company.

Adler, A. (1930). *The education of children.* New York: Greenberg.

Adler, A. (1931). *What life should mean to you.* Boston, MA: Little Brown.

Adler, A. (1963). *The problem child: The life style of the difficult child as analyzed in specific cases. New York: Capricorn Books.*

Adler, A. (1964). *Social interest: A challenge to mankind.* New York: Capricorn Books.

Adler, A. 1976. Individual Psychology and crime. *Journal of Individual Psychology, 32*(2), 131-144.

Adler, A., Ansbacher, H. & Ansbacher, R. (1956). *The Individual Psychology of Alfred Adler: A Systematic Presentation in Selections from His Writings.* New York: Basic Books.

Alcoholics Anonymous (1939). *Alcoholics anonymous: the story of how more than one hundred men have recovered from alcoholism.*

Allen, P. (1992). Artist in residence: An alternative to "clinification" for art therapists. *Art Therapy: Journal of the American Art Therapy Association, 9*(1), 22-29. doi:10.1080/07421656.1992.10758933

Allen, P. (1995). *Art is a way of knowing.* Boston: Shambhala.

Allen, P. (1995). Coyote comes in from the cold. The evolution of the open studio concept. *Art Therapy: Journal of the American Art Therapy Association, 12*(3), 161-166. doi:10.1080/07421656.1995.10759153

Allport, G. (1961). *Pattern and growth in personality.* New York: Holt, Rinehart and Winston.

American Art Therapy Association (2013). Ethical Principles for Art Therapists. Retrieved from http://www.arttherapy.org/upload/ethicalprinciples.pdf

American Psychiatric Association (1992). FactSHEET: Violence and Mental Illness. Washington, DC: APA. Retrieved from http://bipolarworld.net/pdf/violence.pdf

Ansbacher, H. L., & Ansbacher, R. R. (1956). *The individual psychology of Alfred Adler: A systematic presentation in selections from his writings.* Oxford, England: Basic Books.

Argüelles, J., & Argüelles, M. (1985). *Mandala.* Boston: Shambhala.

Arnheim, R. (1974). *Art and visual perception: a psychology of the creative eye.* Berkeley, CA: University of California Press.

Arnheim, R. (1966). *Toward a psychology of art: Collected essays.* Berkeley: University of California Press.

Ault, R. (1986). *Art therapy: The healing vision* [DVD]. Topeka, Kan.: The Menninger Foundation.

Bagemihl, B. (1999). *Biological exuberance: Animal homosexuality and natural diversity.* New York: St. Martin's Press.

Baker, B. (1994). Art therapy's growing pains. *Common Boundary, 12,* 42-48.

Baker, H. S., & Baker, M. N. (1987). Heinz Kohut's self psychology: an overview. *American Journal of Psychiatry, 144*(1), 1-9. doi:10.1176/ajp.144.1.1

Beames, T.B. (1992). *A student's glossary of Adlerian terminology.* [Ladysmith, B.C.]: [T.B. Beames].

Belangee, S. (2006). *Individual psychology* and eating disorders: A theoretical application. *Journal of Individual Psychology, 62*(1), 3-17.

Bennett, H. (1993). *Zuni fetishes: Using Native American objects for meditation, reflection, and insight.* San Francisco, HarperSanFrancisco.

Blatner, A., & Blatner, A. (1988). *Foundations of psychodrama: history, theory, and practice.* New York: Springer.

Blos, P. (1979). *The adolescent passage: Developmental issues.* New York: International Universities Press.

Bohm, D. (1992). On Dialogue. *Noetic Science Review 22,* 16-18.

Bowlby, J. (1969). *Attachment and loss.* New York: Basic Books.

Buck, J. (1948). The H-T-P technique: A qualitative and quantitative scoring manual. *Journal of Clinical Psychology, 4*(4), 317-396. doi:10.1002/1097-4679(194810)4:4<317::aid-jclp2270040402>3.0.co;2-6

Burns, R. C., & Kaufman, S. H. (1970). Kinetic family drawings (K-F-D): an introduction to understanding children through kinetic drawings. New York: Brunner/Mazel.

Burns, R., & Kaufman, S. (1972). *Actions, styles and symbols in kinetic family drawings (K-F-D): an interpretative manual.* New York: Brunner/Mazel.

Byrne, D. (2012, November 27). Fighting mental illness. *The Chicago Tribune.* Section 1, p. 17.

Campbell, J., & Moyers, B. (1988). *The power of myth.* New York: Doubleday.

Cane, F. (1951, 1983). *The artist in each of us.* Craftsbury Common, VT: Art Therapy Publications.

Cash. R.O., & Snow, M.S. (2001). Adlerian treatment of sexually abused children. *The Journal of Individual Psychology, 57* (1), 102-115.

Chickerneo, N. (1993). *Portraits of spirituality in recovery: The use of art in recovery from co-dependency and/or a chemical dependency.* Springfield, IL: Charles C Thomas.

Chopra, D. (1994). *The seven spiritual laws of success: a practical guide to the fulfillment of your dreams.* San Rafael, CA: Amber-Allen Publishing.

Cohen, G. (2000, March-April). c=me2: The Creativity Equation that Could Change Your Life. *Modern Maturity*. American Association of Retired Persons (AARP), 32-37.

Croce, B., & Ainslie, D. (1921). *The essence of the aesthetic.* London: W. Heinemann.

Damasio, A. (2010). *Self comes to mind: Constructing the conscious brain.* New York: Pantheon.

DeOrnellas, K. L., Kottman, T., & Millican, V. (1997). Drawing a family: Family art assessment in Adlerian therapy. *The Journal of Individual Psychology, 53(4),* 451-600.

Dewey, J. (1934). *Art as experience.* New York: Minton, Balch & Company.

Dinkmeyer, D., & McKay, G. (1976). *The parent's handbook (STEP) Systematic training for effective parenting.* Circle Pines, MN: American Guidance Service.

Dinkmeyer, D., & Sperry, L. (1987). *Adlerian counseling and psychotherapy.* Columbus, OH: Merrill Publishing.

Dinkmeyer, D., McKay, G. & McKay, J.1987. *New beginnings: skills for single parents and stepfamily parents.* Champaign, IL: Research Press.

Doherty, W. (2004). The citizen therapist: Finding the right lever. *Psychotherapy Networker, 28(6)* 44-47.

Dosamantes-Beaudry, I. (2000). Creative arts therapy and medicine. *Arts in Psychotherapy, 27(1),* 1-85.

Dreikurs, R. (1950). *Fundamentals of Adlerian psychology.* New York: Greenberg.

Dreikurs, R. (1954). The psychological interview in medicine. *American Journal of Individual Psychology. 10,* 99-122.

Dreikurs, R. (1957). The courage to be imperfect. Speech, University of Oregon, July 25, 1957.

Dreikurs, R. (1967). *Psychodynamics, psychotherapy, and counseling.* Chicago, IL: Alfred Adler Institute.

Dreikurs, R. (1971). *Social equality: the challenge of today.* Chicago, IL: Alfred Adler Institute.

Dreikurs, R. (1976). Why and how people become artists. Unpublished manuscript.

Dreikurs, R., & Mosak, H. (1967). The tasks of life II: The fourth life task. *Individual Psychologist 4(2),* 51-56.

Dreikurs, R. & Stoltz, V. (1990). *Children: The challenge.* New York: Hawthorn, New York: Plume.

Dreikurs, S. (1976). Art therapy: An Adlerian group approach. *The Journal of Individual Psychology, 32(1)* 69-80.

Dreikurs, S. (1984). Personal communication.

Dreikurs, S. (1986). *Cows can be purple: My life and art therapy.* Chicago, IL: Alfred Adler Institute.

Dushman, R. D., & Bressler, M. J., (1991). Psychodrama in an adolescent chemical dependency treatment program. *Individual Psychology, 47,* 515-520).

Dushman, R. D., & Sutherland, J. (1997). An Adlerian perspective on dreamwork and creative arts therapies. *Individual Psychology, 53*(4), 461-475.

Dweck, C. (2006). *Mindset: The new psychology of success.* New York: Random House.

Eleniak, D. (2014, June). Images of ethics: A Conversation with Vancouver Art Therapy Director, Duanita Eleniak, Ph.D. Gemeinschaftsgefühl. Chicago: Adler School of Professional Psychology, 11. Retrieved from http://www.adler.edu/page/news-events/features/features-sample-article-3

Ellenberger, H. F. (1970). *The discovery of the unconscious; The history and evolution of dynamic psychiatry.* New York: Basic Books.

Erikson, E., & Erikson, J. (1997) *The life cycle completed (extended version).* New York: W. W. Norton.

Farrell, Mary. Personal communication in the Couple and family course.

Fenton, J. (2000). Cystic fibrosis and art therapy. *The Arts in Psychotherapy, 27*(1), 15-25. doi:10.1016/s0197-4556(99)00015-5

Feehan, M., McGee, R., & Williams, S.M. (1993). Mental health disorders from age 15 to age 18 years. *Journal of the American Academy of Child and Adolescent Psychiatry. 32*(6), 1118-1126. doi:10.1097/00004583-199311000-00003

Ferguson, E.D. (1995). *Adlerian theory: An introduction.* Chicago, IL: Adler School of Professional Psychology.

Ferguson, E. D. (2010). Adler's innovative contribution regarding the need to belong. *The Journal of Individual Psychology 66*(1), 2-7.

Ferguson, E. D. (1999). Individual Psychology and organizational effectiveness. *The Journal of Individual Psychology 55*(1), 109-115.

Fletcher, J. (1966). *Situation ethics: The new morality.* Louisville, KY: Westminster John Knox Press.

Forgus, R. H., & Shulman, B. H. (1979). *Personality A cognitive view.* Englewood Cliffs, NJ: Prentice-Hall.

Frank, J. D. (1961). *Persuasion and healing: A comparative study of psychotherapy.* Baltimore: Johns Hopkins.

Frankenstein, E., & Brady, L. (1998). *Carved from the heart.* Hohokus, NJ: New Day Films.

Freud, S. (1932). *The interpretation of dreams.* London: George Allen & Unwin.

Froeschle, J. G., & Riney, M., (2008). Using Adlerian techniques to prevent social aggression among middle school children. *Journal of Individual Psychology, 64*(3), 416-431.

Gantt, L. M., & Anderson, F. (2009). The formal elements art therapy scale: A measurement system for global variables in art. Art *Therapy: Journal of the American Art Therapy Association, 26(3),* 124-129. do i:10.1080/07421656.2001.10129453

Fromm, E. (1947). *Man for himself, an inquiry into the psychology of ethics.* New York: Rinehart.

Garland, L., &, Garland, S., Koehnline Museum of Art. (2013). *The Art of Leon and Sadie Garland.* Des Plaines, IL: Oakton Community College.

Gendlin, E., (1981). *Focusing.* New York, Bantam Books.

Glasser, W. (1998). *Choice theory: A new psychology of personal freedom.* New York: HarperCollins Publishers.

Gold, L. (1981). Life style and dreams. In Leroy G. Baruth & Daniel G. Eckstein (Eds.), *Life style: Theory, practice, and research* (pp. 24-30). Dubuque, IA: Kendall/Hunt.

Gold, L. (2013). *Perchance to dream: Dream work in four movements: Language, symbolism, interpretation, therapy.* UK: Adlerian Society.

Goldstein, K. (1939). *The organism: A holistic approach to biology derived from pathological data in man.* New York: American Book Company.

Gorman-Smith, D. (2013, December 4). To sever violent crime, support families. *The Chicago Tribune.* Retrieved from http://www.chicagotribune.com/ct-violence-support-families-safe-children-plan-of-20131204-story.html

Grant, R. (1981). *The psychodrama handbook.* Santa Monica, CA. Private Printing.

Greenspan, S., & Wieder, S. (2009). *Engaging autism: Using the floortime approach to help children relate, communicate, and think.* Cambridge, MA: Da Capo Press.

Hanes, M. J. (1995). Utilizing road drawings as a therapeutic metaphor in art therapy. *American Journal of Art Therapy, 34*(1), 19-23.

Hawkins, J.D., Catalano, R.F., & Miller, J.Y. (1992). Risk and protection factors for alcohol and other drug problems in adolescence and early adulthood: Implications for substance abuse prevention. *Psychological Bulletin, 112*(1), 64-105.

Hays, R. (1981). The bridge drawing: A projective technique for assessment in art therapy. *The Arts in Psychotherapy, 8*(3), 207-217. doi:10.1016/0197-4556(81)90033-2.

Hegel, G. W. F., & Dyde, S. W. (2005). *Philosophy of right: The philosophy of history*. Mineola, NY: Dover Philosophical Classics.

Henri, R. (1923). *The art spirit*. New York: J.B. Lippincott.

Herman, J. (1997). *Trauma and recovery: The aftermath of violence – from domestic abuse to political terror.* New York: Basic Books.

Hocoy, D., (2005). Art therapy and social action: A transpersonal framework. *Art Therapy: Journal of the American Art Therapy Association, 22*(1), 7-16. doi:10.1080/07421656.2005.10129466

Hocoy, Dan. (2007). Cross-cultural issues in art therapy. *Art Therapy: Journal of the American Art Therapy Association, 24*(2), 141-145. do i:10.1080/07421656.2002.10129683

Horney, K. (1951). *Neurosis and human growth.* London: Routledge & Kegan Paul.

Houston, J. (1994). Entelechy: The dynamic unfolding of what we are. *Noetic Sciences Review, 32,* 6.

Hutchinson, R. (2011). *The silent weaver: The extraordinary life and work of Angus MacPhee.* Edinburgh: Birlinn.

John Howard Association. (2008). Retrieved from http://lightsfrominside. blogspot.com/

Jung, C. G., & Campbell, J. (1971). *The portable Jung.* New York: The Viking Press.

Jung, C.G., & Shamdasani, S. (2009). *The red book = Liber novus.* New York; London: W.W. Norton.

Kaiser, D. H., & Deaver, S. (2009). Assessing attachment with the bird's nest drawing: A review of the research. *Art Therapy: Journal of the American Art Therapy Association, 26*(1) 26-33. doi:10.1080/074216 56.2009.10129312

Kane, R., Lewis-Kane, M., & Richards, M. C. (2003). *M.C. Richards: The fire within.* [Sedgewick, Me.]: Kane-Lewis Productions.

Kapitan, L. (2003). *Re-enchanting art therapy: transformational practices for restoring creative vitality.* Springfield, IL: Charles C. Thomas.

Kapitan, L. (2010). *An introduction to art therapy research.* New York: Taylor & Francis, Routledge.

Kerr, C., Hoshino, J., Sutherland, J., Parashak, S. T., & McCarley, L. L. (2007). *Family Art Therapy: Foundations of theory and practice.* New York: Routledge.

Kohn, A. (1999). *Punished by rewards: The trouble with gold stars, incentive plans, A's, praise, and other bribes.* Boston: Houghton Mifflin Company.

Kohut, H. (2009). *The Restoration of the self.* Chicago: University of Chicago Press.

Kopp, R.R. (1989). Holistic-metaphorical therapy and Adlerian brief psychotherapy. *Journal of Individual Psychology, 45*(1-2), 57-61.

Kopp, R.R. (1995). *Metaphor therapy: Using client generated metaphors in psychotherapy.* New York: Brunner/Mazel.

Kolata, G. (2013, April 7). 5 disorders share genetic risk factors, study finds. *The New York Times.* Retrieved from http://www.nytimes.com/2013/03/01/health/study-finds-genetic-risk-factors-shared-by-5-psychiatric-disorders.html?_r=0

Kotulak, R. (2006, August 27). The healing mind. *The Chicago Tribune.* Retrieved from http://articles.chicagotribune.com/2006-08-27/features/0608270362_1_mind-body-placebo-effect-psychologists

Kramer, E. (1977). *Art therapy in a children's community: A study of the function of art therapy in the treatment program of Wiltwyck School for Boys.* Springfield, IL: Thomas.

Kramer, E. (1993). *Art as therapy with children.* Chicago: Magnolia Street Publishers.

Kris, E. (1952). *Psychoanalytic explorations in art.* New York: Schocken Books.

Kwiatkowska, H. (1978). *Family therapy and evaluation through art.* Springfield, IL: Charles C. Thomas.

Lachman-Chapin, M. (1993). From clinician to artist; from artist to clinician, part II: Another perspective. *American Journal of Art Therapy, 31*(3), 76-80.

Langer, S. K., (1953). *Feelings and form: A theory of art.* London: Charles Scribner's. Sons.

La Voy, S. K., Brand, M. L., & McFadden, C. R. (2013). An Important lesson from our past with significance for our future: Alfred Adler's *Gemeinschaftsgefühl. Journal of Individual Psychology, 69*(4), 280-293.

Lefèvre, A. (1879). *Philosophy Historical and Critical.* London, Chapman and Hall; Philadelphia, J.B. Lippincott and Co.

Lehrer, J. (2010, December). The truth wears off: Is there something wrong with the scientific method? *The New Yorker,* December 13, 2010, 52-57.

Lopez, B. (1989). *Crossing open ground.* New York: Vintage Books.

Lowenfeld, V. (1954). *Your child and his art: A guide for parents.* New York: Macmillan.

Lowenfeld, V., & Brittain, W. (1987). *Creative and mental growth.* New York: Macmillan.

Lydiatt. E. (1972). *Spontaneous painting and modelling: A practical approach in therapy.* London: Constable.

MacFarquhar, L. (2013, June). Last Call. *The New Yorker,* June 24, 2013), 56-63.

Malchiodi, C. (1997) *Breaking the silence: Art therapy with children from violent homes.* New York: Brunner/Mazel.

Manaster, G., & Corsini, R. (1982). *Individual psychology: Theory and practice.* Chicago, IL: Adler School of Professional Psychology.

Manning, T.M., (1987). Aggression depicted in abused children's drawings. *The Arts in Psychotherapy: An International Journal, 14,* 15-24. doi:10.1016/0197-4556(87)90031-1

Mansager, E. (2008). Affirming Lesbian, Gay, Bisexual, and Transgender Individuals. *Journal of Individual Psychology, 64*(2), 123-136.

Maslow, A. (1954). *Motivation and personality.* New York: Harper & Row.

Maslow, A. (1976). *Religions, values, and peak-experiences.* New York: Penguin Books.

May, R. (1975). *The courage to create.* New York: W.W. Norton and Company.

McAbee, H., & McAbee, N.L. (1979). Draw an early recollection. In H. Olson. (Ed.), *Early recollections: Their use in diagnosis and psychotherapy.* Springfield, IL: Charles C Thomas.

McAbee, N.L. (1992). (personal communication).

McNeil, E. (1986). *Art therapy with hospitalized children.* Unpublished manuscript.

McNeil, E. (1991). (personal communication).

McNiff, S. (1988). *Fundamentals of art therapy.* Springfield, IL: C.C. Thomas.

McNiff, S. (1992). *Art as medicine: Creating a therapy of the imagination.* Boston: Shambhala.

McNiff, S. (1998). *Art-based research.* London: Jessica Kingsley.

McNiff, S. (2011) The Red book [Liber Novus], *Art Therapy: Journal of the American Art Therapy Association, 28*(3), 145-146. doi: 10.1080/07421656.2011.600218

Meyer, F. (1961) *Marc Chagall: Life and work.* New York: Harry N. Abrams.

Mishlove, J. (1994). Intuition: The source of true knowing. *Noetic Sciences Review, 29,* 31-36. Sausalito, CA: Institute of Noetic Sciences.

Moon, B. (1990). *Existential art therapy: The canvas mirror.* Springfield, IL: Charles C Thomas.

Moore, T. (1992). *Care of the soul. A guide for cultivating depth and sacredness in everyday life.* New York: HarperCollins.

Moreno, J.L. (1953). *Who shall survive? Foundations of sociometry, group psychotherapy and sociodrama.* New York: Beacon House.

Moreno, J. L., & Fox, J. (1987). *The essential Moreno: Writings on psychodrama, group method, and spontaneity.* New York: Springer Publishing.

Mosak, H. (1958). Early recollections as a projective technique. *Journal of Projective Techniques, 22*(3), 302-311. doi:10.1080/08853126.195 8.10380855

Mosak, H. (1977). *On purpose.* Chicago, IL: Alfred Adler Institute.

Moustakas, C. E. (1990). *Heuristic research: Design, methodology, and applications.* Newbury Park, CA: Sage Publications.

Naumburg, M. (1966). *Dynamically oriented art therapy: Its principles and practice.* New York: Grune & Stratton.

Nussbaum, A. M. (2013). *The pocket guide to the DSM-5 ™ diagnostic exam.* Washington, DC: American Psychiatric Publishing.

Oaklander, V. (1988). *Windows to our children: A gestalt therapy approach to children and adolescents.* Highland, NY: Center for Gestalt Development,

Goodman, G. (2008, June 18). "Light from Inside: Art from Illinois Prisons," Retrieved from http://lightsfrominside.blogspot.com/2008/06/tom-odle-falling-apart.html

Ornstein, R. (1991). *The evolution of consciousness.* New York: Prentice Hall Press.

Ornstein, R., & Sobel, D. (1987). *The healing brain: Breakthrough discoveries about how the brain keeps us healthy.* New York: Simon & Schuster.

Papp, P. (1982). Staging reciprocal metaphors in a couples group. *Family Process, 21*(4), 453-167. doi:10.1111/j.1545-5300.1982.00453.x

Patton, G. (2002). *Qualitative research and evaluation methods.* Thousand Oaks, CA: Sage Publications, Inc.

Peck, M.S. (1978). *The road less traveled.* New York: Random House.

Perry, B.D. (2000). Traumatized children: How childhood trauma influences brain development. *The Journal of the California Alliance for the Mentally Ill, 11*(1), 48-51.

Piaget, J. (1999). *The construction of reality in the child.* New York: Routledge.

Piliavin, J., & Charng, H. (1990). Altruism: A review of recent theory and research. *Annual Review of Sociology, 16*, 27-65. doi:10.1146/annurev.soc.16.1.27

Polyani, M. (1967). *The tacit dimension.* Garden City, NY: Doubleday.

Quammen, D. (Dec. 2008). The man who wasn't Darwin. *National Geographic*, 106-133.

Rader, M. (1961). *The enduring questions: Main problems of philosophy.* New York, Holt, Rinehart & Winston.

Read, H. (1949). *Education through art.* New York: Pantheon Books.

Read, H. (1931). *The meaning of art.* London: Faber & Faber.

Regier, D. A., Kuhl, E. A., & Kupfer, D. J. (2013). The DSM-5: Classification and criteria changes. *World Psychiatry, 12*(2): 92–98. doi: 10.1002/wps.20050

Reik, T. (1948). *Listening with the third ear: The inner experience of a psychoanalyst.* New York: Farrar Strauss.

Rhyne, J. (1984). *The gestalt art experience.* Chicago: Magnolia Street Publishing.

Robbins, A. (1994). *A multi-modal approach to creative art therapy.* London: Jessica Kingsley.

Robbins, A., & Sibley, L. (1976). Creative *art therapy*. New York: Brunner/ Mazel.

Rodin, A., & Gsell, P. (1984). *Art: Conversations with P. Gsell*. Berkeley, CA: University of California Press.

Rogers, C. R. (1957). The necessary and sufficient conditions of therapeutic personality change. *Journal of Consulting Psychology, 21*(2), 95-103. doi: 10.1037/h0045357

Rogers, N. (1993). *The creative connection: Expressive arts as healing*. Palo Alto, CA: Science & Behavior Books.

Rotter, J. (1966). Generalized expectancies for internal versus external locus of control of reinforcement. *Psychological monographs, 80*(1), 1-28. doi:10.1037/h0092976

Rubin, J. (1987). *Approaches to art therapy: Theory and technique*. New York: Brunner/Mazel.

Rubin, J. (2010). *Introduction to art therapy: Sources & resources*. New York, Routledge.

Sacks, O., (2008). *Musicophilia: Tales of music and the brain*. NY: Alfred A. Knopf.

Samuels, M., & Samuels, N. (1975). *Seeing with the mind's eye: The history, techniques and uses of visualization*. New York: Random House.

Scott, C. N., Kelly, F. D., & Tolbert, B. L. (1995). Realism, constructivism, and the Individual Psychology of Alfred Adler. *Individual Psychology, 51*(1), 4-20.

Sebelius, K. (2013, February). Bring mental illness out of the shadows. *USA Today*, February 4, 2013. Retrieved from http://www.usatoday.com/story/opinion/2013/02/04/kathleen-sebelius-on-mental-health-care/1890859/

Sharfstein, S., & Stoline, A. (1992). Reform issues for insuring mental health care. *Health Affairs, 11,* 384-397. doi: 10.1377/hlthaff.11.3.84 84-97.

Shulman, B. (1973). *Contributions to Individual Psychology.* Chicago, IL: Alfred Adler Institute.

Shulman, B. (1980). Personal communication.

Shulman, B., & Mosak, H. (1988). Manual *for life style assessment.* Muncie, IN: Accelerated Development.

Siroka, R. (1982). Spontaneity-creativity. Unpublished manuscript.

Slavik, S., Carlson, J., & Sperry, L. (1995). Extreme life-styles of adults who have experienced sexual abuse. *Individual Psychology: The Journal of Adlerian Research, Theory and Practice, 51(4),* 358-374

Smuts, J. (1926). *Holism and evolution.* New York: Macmillan Co.

Specter. M. (2014, May) Partial recall. *The New Yorker.* May 19, 2014, 38-48.

Sperry, L. (1992). Aging: A developmental perspective. *Individual Psychology: Journal of Adlerian Theory, Research & Practice, 48(4),* 387-401

Sperry, L. (1992a). Psychotherapy systems: An Adlerian implication for older adults. *Individual Psychology: Journal of Adlerian Theory, Research & Practice, 48*(4), 451-461.

Sperry, L., & Carlson, J. (1996). *Psychopathology & psychotherapy: From DSM IV diagnosis to treatment.* Washington, DC: Accelerated Development.

Sperry, L., Carlson, J., & Maniacci, M. (1993). *Psychopathology and psychotherapy from diagnosis to treatment.* Muncie, IN: Accelerated Development.

Starr, A. (1977). *Rehearsal for living: Psychodrama: Illustrated therapeutic techniques.* Chicago, IL: Nelson-Hall.

Stone, M. (1997). Ibsen's life-lie and Adler's life-style. *Individual Psychology: Journal of Adlerian Theory, Research & Practice, 53*(3), 322-330.

Sutherland, J., Waldman, G., & Collins, C. (2010). Art therapy connection: Encouraging troubled youth to stay in school and succeed. *Art Therapy: Journal of the American Art Therapy Association, 27*(2), 69-74. doi:10. 1080/07421656.2010.10129720

Sutherland, J. (2011). Family art therapy. *The Journal of Individual Psychology, 67*(3), 292-304.

Sweitzer, E. (2005). The relationship between social interest and self-concept in conduct-disordered adolescents. *The Journal of Individual Psychology, 61*(1), 55-79.

Szalavitz, M. & Perry, B. D. (2010). *Born for love: Why empathy is essential – and endangered.* New York: William Morrow.

Terner, J., & Pew, W. (1978). *The courage to be imperfect: The life and work of Rudolf Dreikurs.* New York: Hawthorn Books, Inc.

Tierney, J. (2013, July 8). What Is nostalgia good for? Quite a bit, research shows. *The New York Times.* Retrieved from http://www.nytimes.com/2013/07/09/science/what-is-nostalgia-good-for-quite-a-bit-research-shows.html?pagewanted=all&_r=0.

Ulman, E., & Dachinger, P. (1975). *Art therapy in theory and practice.* New York: Schocken Books.

VanDeVelde, C. (2007). Carol Dweck: Praising intelligence: Costs to children's self-esteem and motivation. The Bing Times *33*(1). Stanford, CA: Bing Nursery School.

Vorus, S. (2013). *Suicide and dementia: Philosophical and psychological perspectives.* Unpublished manuscript.

Voss, J. (February 2014). Your memory is no video camera: It edits the past with present experiences. *ScienceDaily.* Retrieved from www.sciencedaily.com/releases/2014/02/140204185651.htm.

Wadeson, H. (1980). *Art psychotherapy.* New York: Wiley and Sons.

Wadeson, H., Durkin, J., Perach, D. (1989). *Advances in art therapy.* New York: Wiley.

Wallace, E. (1990). *A queen's quest: Pilgrimage for individuation.* Santa Fe, NM: Moon Bear Press.

Walters, A. (1989). *The spirit of native America: Beauty and mysticism in American Indian art.* San Francisco: Chronicle Books.

Watters, E. (2006, November). DNA is not destiny: The new science of epigenetics. *Discover Magazine, 27*(11). Retrieved from http://discovermagazine.com/2006/nov/cover

Weiner, J. (1994). *The beak of the finch: A story of evolution in our time.* New York: Knopf.

Wilson, L. (1997). Theory and practice of art therapy with the mentally retarded. *Art Therapy: Journal of the American Art Therapy Association, 16*(3), 87-97. doi:10.1016/0090-9092(78)90002-9

Winnicott, D.W. (1953). Transitional objects and transitional phenomena, *International Journal of Psycho-Analysis, 34,* 89-97.

Winnicott, D.W. (1971). *Therapeutic consultations in child psychiatry.* New York: Basic Books.

Wolpe, J. (1990). *The practice of behavior therapy.* New York: Pergamon Press.

Yablonsky, (1976). *Psychodrama: Resolving emotional problems through role-playing.* New York: Basic Books.

Yalom, I. & Leszcz, M. (2005). *Theory and practice of group psychotherapy.* New York: Basic Books.

Index

Abandonment, 85, 90, 91, 161-162, 198
Ables, A., 101
Acting "as if", 124, 144, 172, 203
Active imagination, 41-42, 60, 186
Addams, J., 3-4, 210
Adaptation, 207-208, 215
Addiction, 37, 45-46, 105, 112-113, 132, 139, 156-157, 159-169, 190
  purpose of, 168,
  role of denial in, 109, 164
Adjustment, 162, 164, 196
Adler, A., ix, x, xii, xiii, xiv, xvii, 1-2, 4-7, 11-13, 15, 17-18, 33, 49, 52, 54, 66, 68-70, 75, 81-82, 84, 97, 111, 128, 133, 135-136, 138, 140, 142-143, 145, 160, 162, 171, 175-176, 180, 186, 189, 198, 201, 204, 206-208, 211, 214, 215, 216
Adler, K., xiv, 142,
Adler, M., xiv
Adlerian theory, 1, 4-5, 14, 21, 35, 57, 70-71, 138, 176, 193
  and the DSM-V, 138

effectivess of, 203
Adolescence, 45, 70, 92, 95-98, 102
Advocacy, 64, 130, 185
Alcoholics Anonymous (AA), 160, 164-165
Allen, P., 193
Allport, G., 67
Altruism, 77-78
Alzheimer's disease, 116, 118, 132, 157, 190
American Art Therapy Association, (AATA) 12-13
Ansbacher, H. & R., 52, 143, 145, 185, 203, 208, 212
Anxiety, 37, 46, 49, 71, 79, 88, 92, 94-95, 98, 115, 118, 128, 143, 145, 156-157, 164, 177, 182, 190, 200, 203
Arguelles, J. & M., 60
Arnheim, R., 23, 54, 56-57, 124, 127, 129-130
Art Therapy Connection (ATC), xvii, 68, 99, 102
Archetypes, 42

Aristotle, 113, 170, 209
entelechy, 133, 135
Arrangement, neurotic, 160, 203
Art Directives
Bird's Nest Drawing, (Kaiser, 2009) 100-101
Bridge Drawing, The, (Hays, 1981) 197-198
Carousel (Dreikurs, 1986), 21-23
Chasm Drawing (McNeil, 1987), 51-52
Come to an Agreement (Dreikurs, 1986), 80-81
Create a Self-Portrait with Found Objects, 18
Create a Simple Symbol to Represent Yourself, 123-134
Create Form and "Something Beautiful" Using Colored Shapes, 47
Creative Process, 122
Draw a Garden or Create a Collage, 120
Draw a Person Picking an Apple from a Tree (Gantt, 1990; Lowenfeld, 1939), 147-148
Draw a Picture of Your Family doing Something Together (Burns, 1982), 39, 112
Draw a Road (Hanes, 1995), 101
Draw an Image of what Old Age Looks like to You, 120

Draw or Create an Early Recollection of a Spiritual Experience, 166
Draw How You See Yourself and How Others See You, 18
Draw Yourself Based on Expectations from Mother and Father, 18
Draw Yourself at Work, With Friends, With a Significant Other, 19
Draw the Family as You Would Like it to Be, 112
Draw the Family Atmosphere in Your Family of Origin, 111
Draw the Image that Comes to You when Listening to Music, 120
Draw the Memory of Your First Encounter with an Older Person, 120
Draw the Way Your Life is Now, Then Draw the Way You Want it to Be, 101
Draw Three Wishes (Ables, B. 1872), 101
Draw What Addiction Looks Like to You, 159
Draw What Family Means to You, 111
Draw What "Loss" Looks Like to You, 149-150

Draw Where You Are Right Now, 42

Draw Your Favorite Kind of Day (AFKD) (Manning, 1987), 100

Draw Your Response to the Work You are Doing in the Community, 71

Draw Your Space (Chickerneo, 1993), 163

Draw Your "Wall of Denial" (Chickerneo, 1993), 164-165

Draw Yourself as an Animal in Relation to a Conflict in your Family (Papp, 1982), 112

Draw Yourself as an Older Adult, 120

Draw Yourself Reaching Out to Your Child Self (Chickerneo,1993), 161-162

Drawing Another's Experience of Loss (McAbee, 1992), 151

Drawing the Dream, 172

Family Clay Ring (Farrell, 1999), 112

Family Crest, 61

Family Scribble (Kwiatkowska, 1967), 107-110

Fetish or Animal, 62-64

Free Drawing, 40

Frustration/Fulfillment Drawings (Dreikurs, 1986), 25-26

Hand Painting (Dreikurs, 1986), 24-25

House-Tree-Person (Buck, 1948), 39-40

Image of Ethics (Eleniak, 2014), 81-82

Listen to the Guided Meditation, 154-155

Magic Wand Painting (Dreikurs, 1986), 26-27

Make a Puppet, 101

Making a Mask, 55-56, 101

Mandala Drawing (McAbee, 1998), 60

Nine Square, The, 112

On the Sea of Life, 168

Open Door, The, 135

Painting Blind (Dreikurs, 1986), 27-28

Paint on the Same Piece of Paper (Dreikurs, 1986), 23-24

Paint as if you are a Young Child (Dreikurs, 1986), 29

Paint an Early Recollection (Dreikurs, 1986), 29

Portrait Drawings, 40-41

Puzzle Piece Circle, 120

Responsibility and Freedom, 73

Sand Painting, 62

Sand Tray (Oaklander, 1988), 62, 101, 122

Self Box, 38-39

Self-Symbol and Torn Away Paper, 166-167

Silence, 122

Stone Painting, 56
Tissue Paper Collage (Wallace, 1990), 43
Torn Paper Collage (Dreikurs, 1986), 50
Willow Branch, 167
Yin-Yang Symbol, 58-59
Art Therapy Connection (ATC), xvii, 68, 99, 102
"As if", 124, 144, 172, 203-204
Assessment, 35-36, 38-39, 100,136, 146, 181, 187, 197
Associations
    Alcoholics Anonymous (AA), 160, 164-165
    American Art Therapy Association (AATA), 12-13
    Art Therapy Connection (ATC), xvii, 68, 99, 102
    Compassion in Dying, 142
    Final Exit Network, 142
    International Committee for Adlerian Summer Schools and Institutes (ICASSI), 13-14
    Illinois Art Therapy Association (IATA), 11, 13
    Illinois Association for Music (IAMT), 11
    International Classification of Disease (ICD), 136
    John Howard Association, 69-70
    Loving Outreach to Survivors of Suicide (LOSS), 155
    North American Society of Adlerian Psychology (NASAP), 13
    SMART Recovery, 165-166
Attachment, 42, 76, 91, 100, 106, 129,142, 213
    symbiotic, 42
Attention seeking behavior, 28, 85, 98, 117, 144, 163, 165
Attitude, 11, 16, 26, 30-32, 69, 76, 86, 104, 106, 110, 115, 124,137, 146, 148, 160, 162, 166, 171, 173, 176, 192, 208, 211
Authority, 31, 75,103
Authoritarian behavior, 58, 110
Autism, 89, 132, 190
Autonomy, 16, 45, 67, 80, 94, 96-97, 103, 105
Bagemihl, B., 70
Baker, B., 36
Baker, H. & M., 44, 45
Balance, 58, 105, 127-128, 158
Basic mistakes in perception, 31, 143, 204
    exaggeration of the personal ideal or fictive goal, 143
    fictive goal, 55, 143, 209
    faulty values, 143
    impossible goals of security, 143
    meeting the demands of life, 143
    minimizing self-worth, 143
    overgeneralizations, 143
Behavior, 2, 10, 31-33, 35-36, 38-40, 44-49, 54-57, 59, 65, 66, 69,

76-82, 84-87, 94-98, 102, 104,
106-107, 190-110, 112, 115-117,
124, 128, 133-136, 140-148, 159-
169, 171-172, 176, 182, 186-187,
190-192, 195, 200, 203-216
attention-seeking, 28, 85, 98, 117,
    144, 163, 165
authoritarian, 58, 110
dysfunctional, 6, 190
motives for, 142-146
passive aggressive, 212
social purpose of, 55, 85, 96
socially useful, 31, 55, 96, 99, 198,
    215
socially useless, 96, 99, 134, 143,
    198
Behavior theory, 46-47
Belangee, S., 161
Belonging, feeling of, xiii, 2, 8, 22, 35,
    50, 68, 71, 79, 84, 95, 99, 106,
    162, 175, 209, 215
Bennett, H., 62
Biased apperception, 19, 204
Bipolar, 190
Birth order, 104, 108, 139, 204
Blatner, A., 174-175
Blos, P., 96, 120
Bohm, D., 77
Bowlby, J., 100
Brain, 157
    injury, traumatic, 156, 158
    disorders, 132, 190
Buck, J., 38, 39, 58
Burns, R & Kaufman, S., 39, 112

Byrne, D., 132
Campbell, J., 54, 126
Cane, F., 39
Cash, R. & Snow, M., 94
Categorical Imperative, 73-75
Chagall, M., 125-126
Challenge
    social challenge, 26, 31
    social action, 64-66, 68, 71, 78-79,
        82, 118, 201, 215
Chemical imbalance, 136
Chickerneo, N., xvii, 164, 187
Children
    abused, 92-95
    affiliation with primary
        caregiver, 84
    development of, 84-85
    foster, 91
    socially disadvantaged, 89-90
Circle, 57
Cognitive dissonance, 191, 205
Cohen, G., 116
Collective consciousness, xiv, 188
Color, 128, 194
Common lifestyle themes, 143
Common sense, 18, 52, 77, 144, 205
Community, xii, 9, 13, 64-71, 78-82,
    115-117, 122, 138, 149, 153, 156,
    160, 164, 180, 196, 205, 210
Compassion in Dying, 142
Compensation, 7, 117, 127-128, 133,
    165, 170, 205
Law of 128, 170
Competition, 74, 86, 134, 168

Completion, 33, 49, 64, 133, 134, 213

Conditioning, 46-47

Conduct disorder, 97-98

Conflict, 36, 37, 79, 112, 140, 163

   inner, 49, 200

Conformity, 47, 58, 103

Consciousness, xiii, xiv, 18, 28-29,

   31, 48, 54, 59,188-189, 192,

   201, 206

   collective, xiv, 188-189, 192, 201,

   206

Consequences, 24, 46, 74, 79, 98,

   107, 124, 160, 206

Continuum, 25, 27, 162

Control, 112, 173, 206

Cooperation, xiii, 2, 8, 22-23, 33, 35,

   50, 55, 68, 78-79, 82, 85, 95, 99,

   107, 109-110, 113, 134, 137-138,

   141, 144, 168, 173, 205, 206, 207,

   215

Coping behavior, 56

Core beliefs, 140

Counseling, 206

Courage, xiii, 5, 8, 12, 26, 28, 41, 55,

   70, 128, 171, 179, 186, 206

Creative power, 26, 116, 198

Creative process, 25-26, 122

Crisis situation, 137, 137, 141, 145,

   163

Croce, B., 187

Daimon, 175

Damasio, A., 78

Darwin, C., 74, 189, 210

Death, 45, 92, 141, 142

Deductive reasoning, 185

Defiance, 97-98

Delinquency, 40, 64

Dementia, 11, 116, 118-119, 132, 146,

   201

Democritus, 51

DeOrnellas, T. & Millican, V., 110

Depth in Plastic Illusion, 123-124

Depth psychology, 42, 49

Depression, 64, 94-95, 97, 105, 116,

   132, 137-138, 141, 143-147, 156,

   161, 190, 206, 212

   as temper tantrum, 141

   major, 132, 146-147, 190

Determinism, 37, 44, 50, 133-136, 167

Developmental stages in art, 86-87

Dewey, J., 76

Diagnostic labels, 133, 136, 192

Dialectic thought, 184, 188

Differentiation, Law of, 130

Dinkmeyer, D. & Dinkmeyer, D. &

   Sperry, L., 85, 100, 117

Discouragement, xiii, 2, 6, 28, 32, 57,

   66, 85, 91, 138, 141-144, 168,

   178-179, 182, 198, 207

Disease, 61, 88-90

Dissociation, 93-94

Distance, creation of, 55, 75, 112,

   133, 160, 164, 171, 179, 190,

   192, 213

Distortions of the truth,140

Diversity, 79, 82, 130, 207

Divorce, 16, 86, 90, 112-113, 141

DNA, xii, 133, 188

Doherty, W., 67

Dosamantes-Beaudry, I., 89

Dreams, 36, 42, 47, 119, 124, 170-172, 175, 176-179

    basic assumptions about 170-171

    and health 170, 178

    and projection 18, 41, 130, 174, 181, 187

Dreikurs, R., xiii, xiv-xv, 4-6, 8, 13-14, 18, 20-21, 27, 40, 49, 66, 75, 85, 98, 124, 137-138, 140, 144, 159, 162, 171

Dreikurs, R. & Stoltz. V., 85, 98

Dreikurs, S., ix, xi, xii, 1-6, 10, 12, 14, 20, 23-27, 31, 33, 35, 40, 50-51, 79-80, 84, 99, 108, 113, 115, 117, 121, 131, 137, 148, 166-170, 176, 186, 201

DSM-V, 133, 136, 138-139, 148, 156, 191,

    diagnostic labels 133, 136, 192

Dushman, R., xvii

Dushman, R. & Bressler, M., 174

Dushman, R. & Sutherland, J., 176

Dweck, C., 121

Early Recollections, 14, 21, 30-32, 63, 104, 124, 139-140, 166-167, 170, 189, 190, 208

Eating disorders, 91, 159-161

Ecology, 77

Eleniak, D., 81, 201

Ellenberger, H., 1, 33, 176

Emotion, 57

Empiricism, 185

Encouragement, 25, 44, 85, 91, 107, 110, 167, 203, 208

Endocrine balance, 133

Environment, 33, 44-45, 74, 77-79,

Entelechy, 133-135

Epictetus, 137

Erikson, E., 43, 119

Erikson, J., 119

Evolution, xii-xiii, 33, 53, 74, 188-189

Evolutionary psychology, 208

Existentialism, 41, 48-49, 74, 193

Expectancy Theory, 48

Expressive, 11, 41, 49, 56, 65, 186

Failure, 7, 17, 20, 22, 25, 33, 37, 44-45, 51, 85, 97, 108, 121, 127, 141, 142, 144, 153, 159, 161, 170, 172, 198, 205, 214

Family

    atmosphere, 109-111, 139, 208

    constellation, 21, 24, 80, 104, 109, 139-140, 209

    lifestyle pattern, 111

    values, 92, 209

Farrell, M., xvii, 112

Fear, 57, 95

Feehan, M., McGee, R. & Williams, S., 97

"Felt sense", 17, 19

Fenton, J., 89

Ferguson, E., xvii, 14, 137, 206

Fetish, animal, 62-63
Final Exit Network, 142
Forgiveness, 54, 77, 167
Forgus, R. & Shulman, B., 129, 142
Formal Elements Art therapy Scale, 146-147, 193
Fox, J., 173, 177, 213
Frankenstein, E. & Brady, L., 153
Free association, 186
Free will, 1, 37, 134, 191
Freedom, 58, 73, 142, 150, 193, 211
Freud, S., 35-38, 140, 170, 186, 203, 208
    id, ego, superego, 36-37
    dream images, 172, 178
Fromm, E., 43, 77
Froeschle, J. & Riney, M., 98
Frustration, 25-26, 85, 162, 170
Fulfillment, 25-26
Gamson, B., 15
Gantt, L & Anderson, F., 146-147, 193
Garland, L., 3-5
Gemeinschaftsgefühl, xiv, 2, 75, 79, 215
Gender, 70-71
Gendlin, E., 17
Genetic disease, 88-89
Genetic vulnerability, 132
Genius, 144, 205
Gestalt, 41, 48-49, 59, 129, 209
Goal, fictional or final fictive, 55, 143, 209, 211, 216

Gold, L., 175-176
"Gold mine", 40, 210
Goldstein, K., 33
Gorman-Smith, D., 113
Grant, R., 175
Greenspan, S. & Wieder, S., 90
Grief, 149-158
Group therapy, 131
Guiding self ideal, 28, 142, 175, 177
Guilt, 37, 66, 78, 142, 162, 165
Habit, 160
Haiku, 14, 122, 210
Hanes, M., 101
Happiness, 210
Hays, R., 197
Healing, 8, 21, 26, 36, 43, 49, 61, 62, 65, 79, 135-136, 138, 142, 149, 153, 156, 191, 195-196, 216
Hegel, G., 74, 184, 188
Heidegger, M., 48
Henri, R., 119
Herman, J., 94-95
Heuristic research, 186-187, 210
Hidden intention, 32, 210
Hocoy, D., 65-66
Holism, 13, 33, 47
Homeostasis, 127, 210
Homosexuality, 70, 113
Horney, K., 33, 43, 162
Hospitalized children, 87, 88
Houston, J., 134
Hull House, ix, 3-4, 201

Humanistic theory, xii-xiii, 35-35, 41, 46-50, 133-136, 185

Hutchinson, R., 197

Illinois Art Therapy Association (IATA), 11, 13

Illinois Association for Music (IAMT), 11

Imagination, 26, 41-42, 46, 60, 155, 186-187, 196

Immune system, 141, 211

Imperfection, 28, 107, 113, 122

Inadequacy, 7, 22, 28, 86, 95-966, 141, 144, 159, 162-163, 167, 198

Individual, uniqueness of, 8, 12, 25, 57, 79, 121, 130, 145

Individuation, 59, 96

Inferiority
    complex, 7
    feelings, xiii, 2, 6-7, 10, 27, 49, 55, 79, 95-98, 109, 140, 158, 161-162, 165, 167, 170, 203, 207, 209, 211

Innate potential ,2, 75, 162, 215

Inner world, 62, 148, 176

Insecurity, 21, 107, 162, 211

Integrity, 21, 81, 119, 135, 152, 182

Intelligence, 188

International Classification of Disease (ICD), 136

International Committee for Adlerian Summer Schools and Institutes (ICASSI), 13-14

Interpersonal, 44, 48, 94, 131, 140,

Intrapersonal, 140

Intuition, 23, 36, 59, 125-126, 174-175, 185-188, 212

John Howard Association, 69-70

Jung, C., 35, 41-43, 59-60, 129, 186

Kaiser, D & Deaver, S., 100

Kant, I., 73-74

Kapitan, L., 155, 188, 192, 198

Kerr, C., Hoshino, J., Sutherland, J., Parashak, S., & McCarley, L., 110

Knowledge
    implicit ,185
    tacit, 175

Kohler, W., 48

Kohn, A., 86

Kolata, G. 190

Kottman, T., 110

Kotulak, R., 64

Kramer, E., 40, 135, 183, 187

Kris, E., 37, 214

Kwiatkowska, H., 40, 109

Lachman-Chapin, M., 41

Langer, S., 35, 47, 162

Law of Compensation, 128, 170

Law of Differentiation, 130

Lehrer, J., 187

L'Hote, A., 3

Life force, 43, 133, 135

Life plan, 124, 203, 211

Life Style Inventory, 139-140, 182

Lifestyle, 2, 6, 17, 21, 23-24, 31, 51, 54, 66, 104-105, 109, 111,

138-139, 143, 171-172, 181, 189, 207,209, 211, 213
common themes, 143
family lifestyle pattern, 111
Light, 57-58, 124, 128-129
Locus of control, 47
Lopez, B., 52
Loving Outreach to Survivors of Suicide (LOSS), 155
Lowenfeld, V., 87, 92, 101, 147
Lowenfeld,V & Brittain, W., 87, 92
Lydiatt, E., 148
Magritte, R., 125
Maladaptive behaviors, 133
Malchiodi, C., 95
Manaster, G & Corsini, R., 94
Manning, T., 100
Mansager, E., 70
Maslow, A., 33, 47, 56
Mastery, 49
Materialism, 36
May, R., 126
McAbee, H & McAbee, N., 21
McAbee, N., 60, 151
McNeil, E., 51, 88, 103, 183
McNiff, S., 16, 19, 26, 49, 193, 195, 215, 216
Medication, 36, 89, 116, 136, 144, 200, 206, 211
Memorializing the Loss, 153-155
Memory, 7, 10, 32, 63, 78, 116, 119-120, 124, 143, 153, 157, 190, 208

Mental disorders, 55, 67, 132-133, 136-141-143,190-191, 194, 198, 209, 211
genetic vulnerability, 132
major depression, 132, 146-147, 190
schizophrenia, 132, 145-147, 190
Alzheimer's disease, 116, 118, 132, 157, 190
autism, 89, 132, 190
Mental health, 6, 11, 64, 69, 70, 77, 84, 98-99, 105, 191, 194, 206, 209
Metaphor,15, 35-36, 40, 42, 50, 56-58, 101, 119, 124-128, 155, 170, 173, 176-177, 194, 203, 207, 211, 212, 213
Meyer, F., 125
Millican, V., 110
Mishlove, J., 186
Mistaken goals, 85, 214, 216
Moon, B., 49, 117
Moore, T., 63
Moral responsibility, 134
Moreno, J,, 173, 175, 176-177, 213
Mosak, H., viii, xvii, 5, 29, 139, 141, 143, 145, 163, 171, 212
Motives for behavior, 142-146
Moustakas, C., 185
Movement
"frozen", 18
"letting go", 50, 56, 59, 96, 127, 164, 167, 201
passive or active, 139

Music, 10-11, 17, 20-21, 25-26, 115, 120, 194

Myth, xiv, 42, 54, 63, 126, 128, 130, 194

Nature, drawing from, 126-127

Nature-nurture question, 133

Naumburg, M., 38

Niebuhr, R., 76

Neurosis, 37, 77, 128, 143-144, 160, 212

Neurotic symptoms, 37, 143, 212

Neuroscience, 90, 136, 156-157

Nietzsche, F., 75, 213

North American Society of Adlerian Psychology (NASAP), 13

Nussbaum, A., 136

Oaklander, V., 101

Object Relations, 41, 44-46

Open Studio, 196-197

Optimism, xiii, 13, 21, 47, 58, 91, 140, 120, 145, 168,181, 208

Organs of the body, 140

Ornstein, R., xiii, 158

Ornstein, R. & Sobel, D., 158

Overcompensation, 7

Overgeneralizations, 143

Pain, 16, 85, 88, 90-91, 93, 103, 119, 122, 137, 139, 141, 153, 155, 161-162, 178, 198

Papp, P., 112

Paradox, 135

Parenting, 85-86, 106-107

Passive aggressive behavior, 212

Patton, G., 190

Patterson, K., xvii, 73

Peck, M., 201

Perception, 56, 94-95, 127, 143-146, 187, 203, 208, 212

problems in, 143-146

visual, 127

Perfection, xiii, 2, 7, 19, 21, 25, 27-28, 33, 45, 49, 51, 58, 72, 97, 121-122, 134-135, 144, 213, 215

Perry, B., 94, 102

Personality, 17, 22, 36, 38, 41, 45, 54-55, 77, 94, 96, 111, 117, 119, 130, 134, 137, 139, 143-144, 176, 190, 192, 199, 204, 207, 208, 209, 211, 212, 213

dsorders, 45-46, 94, 144

narcissistic, 45-46

unity of, 17, 45, 111, 130

Personality types, 45, 143

Pessimism, 58, 143, 212

Phenomenology, 48, 94

Philosophy, teaching, 8-9, 151

Piaget, J., 43

Piliavin, J. & Charng, H., 78

Plato, 10, 133, 184

Polyani, M., 175, 185

Portraits

of self, 14,16-19, 120

of self as older adult, 120

of self with found objects, 14

of each other, 40-41

Positive reinforcement, 46-47

Postmodernism, 35, 50-51, 78, 187
Post-traumatic stress disorder (PTSD), 94-95,156-157, 192
Power, 28, 75, 85
Praise, 85, 206
Prejudice, 25, 66, 70-71, 75, 82, 113
Prison, 11, 67-71, 90, 191
Private logic, xiv, 1, 2, 11, 18, 57, 63-64, 110, 124, 136, 138, 140-141, 143-144, 164, 176, 190, 195, 213, 214
Projective tests, 38, 58,194,197
Protest, 27, 129, 141, 143, 211
Psyche, 21, 42, 135, 175, 200
Psychodrama, 149, 151, 153, 155, 170, 173-179, 213
  action, 151, 173-175
  role play, 177
  rehearsal for living, 175
  role repertoire, 177
  role reversal, 174
  sharing, 175
  social exploration, 174
  spontaneity-creativity, 177
  symbolism, 175
  warm-up, 122, 172-174, 213
Psychological integration, 213
Psychosis, 143-144
Qualitative approach, 187
Quammen, D., 189
Ouestion, the, 137
Rader, M., 130
Rationalization, 185, 203
Read, H., 121, 130

Reality, 1, 46, 48, 51, 56, 130, 144, 146, 148, 164, 172, 177, 184, 192, 196, 203, 204, 211, 212
  inner, 48, 56, 130, 144, 177
  other, 125
  outer, 46, 56, 144, 152, 196
Reasoning, 1, 76, 85, 184-186, 188
  deductive, 184-186
  inductive, 184-186
Reflection, 18-19, 50, 53, 56-57, 59, 80-81, 127, 171, 197
  Portraits in, 15-19
Reik, T., 40
Religion, 54, 72, 94, 130, 186, 200
  in art, 54
Repression, 93
Resistance, 48, 67, 85111, 127, 200
Responsibility, x, xiii, 2, 8, 21-22, 27, 31, 33, 35, 46, 48, 49, 58, 65, 67, 71, 73, 75-77, 81, 85, 96, 99, 105, 107-108, 111, 113, 117, 129, 134, 138, 141, 163, 167, 172, 179, 182, 185, 187, 191, 205, 206, 210, 211, 214
  social, 48, 65, 67, 185
Revenge, 28, 75, 85, 98, 117, 142, 144
Rhyne, J., 41
Richards, M.C., 196
Robbins, A., 6
Robbins, A. & Sibley, L., 46, 180
Rodin, A., 9
Rogers, C., 48-49, 100
Rogers, N., 49
Rothko, M., 194
Rubin, J., 37, 193

Sacks, O., 11

Safeguarding, 28, 145

Samuels, M. & Samuels, N., 56, 63

Sand tray, 62, 101, 122, 214

Schizophrenia, 132, 144-147, 150

Science, 152, 177, 189-190, 192, 201

Segregation, 130, 189

Selective listening, 21

Self-deception, 124, 171, 214

Self-fulfilling prophecy, 48

Self-ideal, 28, 142, 175, 177, 213, 214

Sexual abuse, 92-95, 145, 151

Shulman, B., xvii, 5, 31, 129, 133, 135, 139, 142, 144, 171, 175, 204

Siblings, 24, 80, 109, 117, 209

Significance, striving for, 11, 49, 55, 84, 134, 189, 211, 214

Silence, 95, 122

Simplicity, 123-124, 126, 129

Sirotka, R., 177

Skinner, B., 35, 46

Slavik, S., Carlson, J., Sperry, L., 92, 93, 95

Sleep, 102, 170, 192

Sloan, J., 15

SMART Recovery, 165-166

Smuts, J., 33, 48

Social Darwinism, 74

Social equality, xiv, 2, 12-13, 29, 33, 66, 70, 82, 146

Social experience, 1, 133-134

Social feeling, 2, 94, 215

Social interest, x, xiii, 2, 6, 8, 13, 22, 29, 34, 52, 67, 69-71, 75-77, 79,

84, 94-95, 99-100, 111, 134, 146, 160, 162, 165, 199, 201, 209, 215

 contribution and, 204, 215

Social isolation, 66, 71, 98, 179

Social problems, xiii, 2, 28, 76, 82, 188

Social responsibility, 46, 65, 67, 185

Socrates, 175

Sokol, D., 5

Specter, M., 157

Sperry, L., 116

Sperry, L. & Carlson, J., 35, 66, 92, 139, 141, 143-145, 160, 212

Spirit, xiv, 2, 8, 10, 12, 29, 61, 63, 70, 112, 117-119, 135, 175-176, 200

Spiritual, 17, 36, 42, 54, 61-63, 120, 130, 154, 165-166

Spirituality, 54, 60-61, 165, 196, 200

Squiggle Drawings, 44

Starr, A., 175

Stone, M., xvii

Stream of consciousness, 48

Stress, 8, 28, 60, 93, 102, 128, 137, 143, 160, 163, 167, 189, 205, 207

"Striving from a felt minus to a felt plus", 135

Subjective condition, 138-139

Sublimation, 39-40, 215

Success, 10, 22, 55, 66, 85, 87, 134, 145, 209, 212

Suffering, 28, 66, 79, 88, 93, 113, 130, 138, 149, 163, 179, 212

Suicide, 119, 141-142, 152-153, 155-156, 194

Superiority, 7, 55, 96, 134, 171, 199, 209, 211, 215

Survival, xii, 25, 29, 53, 55-56, 65, 72, 74-75, 85, 160, 189

Sutherland, J., Waldman, G., & Collins, C., 100

Sweitzer, E., 97

Symbolic speech, 38

Symbols, 21, 26, 36, 39, 42, 47, 53-55, 57-64, 119, 125, 173, 175-176, ⌐178, 213,

Symptoms, 27, 37, 45, 64, 77, 97, 109, 111, 113, 136-141,168, 191-192, 143-144, 161, 205, 212, 214

of neurotic behavior, 37, 143, 212

or organic malfunction, 143

Taoism, 58, 123, 152

Tasks of living, xiii, 7, 70, 145, 206, 207, 209

Teleology, 216

Terner, J. & Pew, W,. 6-7

Therapeutic alliance, 138, 182, 195-196

Transference, 40-41, 44

Transforming the Pain of Loss, 158

Transition, 59

Trauma, 64, 92-95, 156-157, 189, 201

Traumatic memories, 156-157

"Trust only movement", 176

"Trust the process", xviii

Truth, 7, 9, 23, 43, 47, 51-52, 63, 66, 74, 96, 101, 124, 129-130, 140,

164, 166, 177, 179, 183-186, 188-189, 195-197, 217

Ulman, E. & Dachinger, P., 41

Unconscious, 11, 16-17, 28, 35-38, 40, 42, 47, 55-57, 59-60, 63, 95-96, 103-104, 116, 124, 126, 128-129, 134-135, 140-143, 148, 157, 159, 166, 170-173, 190, 192, 207, 208, 210, 214, 216

Unity, 12, 17, 23, 33, 40, 45, 58, 61, 64, 78, 105, 111, 125, 130

Useless behavior, 98, 134, 214, 215

Vaihinger, H., 124, 213

Veterans, 156-157

Victim, 138

Violence, 58, 67-68, 78, 93-94, 97-98, 109, 113, 132

Vorus, S., 142

Voss, J., 190

"Yes, but", 144

Yin-yang, 58-59

Wadeson, H., 173, 193-194

Wallace, E., 43

Walters, E., 61

Weiner, J., xii

Will power, 132

"Will to power", 75

Wilson, L., 91

Winnicott, D., 43-46, 196, 216

Wolpe, J., 46

Yablonsky, L., 174

Yalom, I., 131

Made in the USA
San Bernardino, CA
29 May 2016